Considering Cultural Difference

Other readers featured in the Longman Topics series include:

Issues of Gender
Ellen Friedman and Jennifer Marshall

Language and Prejudice
Tamara Valentine

Translating Tradition
Karen E. Beardslee

The Counterculture Reader
E. A. Swingrover

Citizenship Now
Jon Ford and Marjorie Ford

A Longman Topics Reader

Considering Cultural Difference

PAULINE UCHMANOWICZ
State University of New York, New Paltz

PEARSON
Longman

New York   San Francisco   Boston
London   Toronto   Sydney   Tokyo   Singapore   Madrid
Mexico City   Munich   Paris   Cape Town   Hong Kong   Montreal

Senior Vice President and Publisher: Joseph Opiela
Senior Acquisitions Editor: Lynn M. Huddon
Marketing Manager: Deborah Murphy
Managing Editor: Bob Ginsberg
Project Coordination, Text Design, and Electronic Page Makeup:
    Sunflower Publishing Services
Cover Design Manager: Nancy Danahy
Cover Image: © Corbis
Manufacturing Buyer: Alfred C. Dorsey
Printer and Binder: RR Donnelley & Sons Company
Cover Printer: Lehigh Press, Inc.

For permission to use copyrighted material, grateful acknowledgment is made to the copyright holders on pp. 235–236, which are hereby made part of this copyright page.

Library of Congress Cataloging-in-Publication Data

Considering cultural difference / [edited by] Pauline Uchmanowicz.
    p. cm. — (longman topics)
    ISBN 0-321-11581-3
    1. Pluralism (Social sciences)—United States. 2. Pluralism
(Social Sciences)—United States—Literary collections. 3. Group
identity—United States. 4. Culture conflict—United States.
5. Minorities—United States—Social conditions. 6. United
States—Ethnic relations. 7. United States—Race relations.
8. Authorship—Social aspects—United States. 9. Authors,
American—Biography. 10. United States—Biography.
I. Uchmanowicz, Pauline. II. Series.

E184.A1C595 2004
305′0973—dc22   2003062346

Please visit our website at http://www.ablongman.com

ISBN 0-321-11581-3

    45678910—DOH—0605

CONTENTS

Rhetorical Contents   *x*

Related Readings   *xv*

Preface   *xvii*

PART 1   Ritual   1

Introduction   1

CHAPTER 1   Schooling   3

Anna Quindlen, How Reading Changed My Life   3

"Reading makes immigrants of us all," Anna Quindlen
quotes from one of her literary idols. "It takes us away
from home, but, most important, it finds homes for us
everywhere."

Nathan McCall, Alford J. Mapp   9

"My harshest introduction to the world of white folks
came in September 1966, when my parents sent me to
Alford J. Mapp, a white school across town."

Lois-Ann Yamanaka, Pidgin Politics   14

"Well, *dear,* we need to speak to each other in standard
English for the duration of this conference. I find the
pidgin you children speak to be so limited in its ability to
express fully what we need to cover today," says a
schoolteacher in Hawaii.

Francisco Jiménez, The Circuit   20

"It was Monday, the first week of November. The grape
season was over and I could now go to school."

Naomi Shihab Nye, Biography of an Armenian
Schoolgirl   28

"What is the history of Europe to us if we cannot / choose
our own husbands?"

David Brooks, The Next Ruling Class: Meet the
Organization Kid   31

"I went to Princeton University to see what the young
people who are going to be running our country in a few
decades are like."

CHAPTER 2 Sports   **38**

Hunki Yun, Trail Blazer

> "'My son teaches me English,' says the 32-year-old Choi, whose language isn't as polished as his game, which was good enough to win twice last year, making him the first Korean winner on the PGA Tour."

Darcy Frey, The Last Shot   42

> The neighborhood's best players practice at an O'Dwyer projects court dubbed the Garden. "Even the hoodlums decline to vandalize the Garden, because in Coney Island the possibility of transcendence through basketball is an article of faith."

Timothy Harper, The Best Pickup-Basketball Player in America   49

> Allan Dalton, the best pickup-basketball player in America, "may be the only white person on the court, and he will almost certainly be the oldest, by twenty or thirty years."

Colette Dowling, Throwing Like a Guy: The Mystique of Innate Ability   55

> "The much ballyhooed skill of throwing a baseball is *learned.* Boys aren't born with it."

Ruth Conniff, Title IX: Political Football   60

> "Despite all the good feeling Title IX has engendered among girls and their parents, the law is currently under attack."

Jack Newfield, The Shame of Boxing   67

> "The fighters are powerless workers of color. . . . They need representation, rights and a collective voice."

Responding in Writing   76

PART II Representation   **79**

Introduction   79

CHAPTER 3 Media   **83**

Ward Churchill, Smoke Signals in Context   83

> "In 1911, James Young Deer, a Winnebago Indian, directed the film *Yacqui Girl.* . . . For the next 70 years, with the exception of a brief flurry of self-produced releases by Cherokee comedian/radio commentator/actor Will Rogers, no American Indian was allowed to direct a major motion picture."

Julia Alvarez, I Want to Be Miss América   91

"There they stood, fifty puzzle pieces forming the pretty
face of America, so we thought, though most of the color
had been left out, except for one, or possibly two, light-
skinned black girls."

Michael Massing, Press Watch   98

"A few minutes into ABC's *World News Tonight* on
September 21 [2001]—the night after George W. Bush's
speech to Congress—Peter Jennings somberly noted that
it was 'time for all Americans to begin learning more
about Afghanistan.'"

John Nichols, Huey Freeman: American Hero *and
Aaron McGruder, The Boondocks* Illustration   102

"The creation of 27-year-old cartoonist Aaron McGruder,
Huey Freeman appears daily in *The Boondocks*, a comic
strip featured in 250 of America's largest newspapers. . . .
Bitingly blunt in its examination of race and class issues,
The Boondocks has made more waves more often than
any nationally syndicated comic strip since Garry
Trudeau's *Doonesbury. . . .*"

Tim Wise, Blinded by the White: Crime, Race,
and Denial at Columbine High   109

"Of course, that the school killers have all been white
lately has gone without mention in the media."

CHAPTER 4   Visibility   **117**

Michael Bronski, Queering the Vast Wasteland   117

"Gay TV—clearly, this is an idea whose time has come. . . .
Critics of liberation-through-visibility politics also note
that increased media exposure does not ensure that the
actual lives of gay men and lesbians are better."

Peggy McIntosh, White Privilege: Unpacking
the Invisible Knapsack   123

"I remembered the frequent charges from women of color
that white women whom they encounter are oppressive.
. . . I began to count the ways in which I enjoy unearned
skin privilege and have been conditioned into oblivion
about its existence."

Robert S. Boynton, The New Intellectuals   130

An impressive group of African-American public
intellectuals "have been sought out by the electronic
media, and shows like *Nightline, Today,* and *The Oprah
Winfrey Show* give them extraordinary visibility."

Ali Hossaini, A "Hyphenated Perspective"   141

"No one takes me for Middle Eastern—I was born in West
Virginia, and I'm only a quarter Arab. But thanks to the
peculiarities of history, and naming, I have an Arab-
American identity."

Rudolph Chelminski, Turning Point   144

According to a blurb appearing in the *New York Times* on
September 13, 2001, French high-wire artist Philippe
Petit "turned the tide of public regard" for the World
Trade Center in 1974 when he crossed between the Twin
Towers on a tightrope.

Arno Peters, The Peters Projection World Map   154

Although not a trained cartographer, Arno Peters created
one of the first world maps to show all land areas on the
same scale.

Responding in Writing   156

PART III   Rights   **159**
    Introduction   159

CHAPTER 5   Language   **161**
    Judith Ortiz Cofer, The Paterson Public Library   161

"It was a Greek Temple in the ruins of an American city.
To get to it I had to walk through neighborhoods where
not even the carcasses of rusted cars on blocks nor the
death traps of discarded appliances were parted with. . . ."

Committee on CCCC Language Statement,
    Students' Right to Their Own Language   167

"Differences in language have always existed, and the
schools have always wrestled with them, but . . . the
insistence of submerged minorities on a greater share in
America society [has] posed the question more insistently,
and [has] suggested the need for a shift in emphasis in
providing answers."

Amy Tan, Mother Tongue   176

"Lately, I've been giving more thought to the kind of
English my mother speaks. Like others, I have described
it to people as 'broken' or 'fractured' English. But I wince
when I say that."

Luc Sante, Living in Tongues   184

"My three languages revolve around and inform one another. I live in an English-speaking world, of course, and for months on end I may speak nothing else."

Robert King, Should English Be the Law?   192

"Traditionally, the American way has been to make English the national language—but to do so quietly, locally, without fuss. . . . That tradition began to change in the wake of the anything goes attitudes and the celebration of cultural differences arising in the 1960s."

CHAPTER 6   Workplace   199

Ellis Cose, Affirmative Action and the Dilemma of the "Qualified"   199

"Not surprisingly, people who see blacks as lazier than whites tend to be among those most strongly opposed to affirmative action."

Bob Muldoon, White-Collar Man in a Blue-Collar World   209

"Like thousands last year, I was downsized from one of those sizzling dot-coms, now dot-gone. Faced with a shrinking job market, I turned to manual labor."

Martín Espada, The Foreman's Wallet   213

"The conspiracy to shrink-wrap / the foreman's head, turning red / in a wrestling hold, was a failure."

Barbara Ehrenreich, Serving in Florida   215

"So begins my career at the Hearthside, where for two weeks I work from 2:00 till 10:00 P.M. for $2.43 an hour plus tips."

Marc Peyser, The Insiders   225

"The stock scandal involving Martha Stewart has pulled back the curtain on a world where the rich pass around business gossip the way the help passes out canapés."

Responding in Writing   233

Credits   235

RHETORICAL CONTENTS

Narration: Telling a Story

Anna Quindlen, How Reading Changed My Life 3
Nathan McCall, Alford J. Mapp 9
Lois-Ann Yamanaka, Pidgin Politics 14
Francisco Jiménez, The Circuit 20
Naomi Shihab Nye, Biography of an Armenian
    Schoolgirl 28
Ward Churchill, Smoke Signals in Context 83
Julia Alvarez, I Want to Be Miss América 91
Rudolph Chelminski, Turning Point 144
Judith Ortiz Cofer, The Paterson Public Library 161
Luc Sante, Living in Tongues 184
Martín Espada, The Foreman's Wallet 213
Barbara Ehrenreich, Serving in Florida 215

Description: Using the Senses

Nathan McCall, Alford J. Mapp 9
Hunki Yun, Trail Blazer 38
Darcy Frey, The Last Shot 42
Timothy Harper, The Best Pickup-Basketball
    Player in America 49
Jack Newfield, The Shame of Boxing 67
Julia Alvarez, I Want to Be Miss América 91
Tim Wise, Blinded by the White: Crime, Race,
    and Denial at Columbine High 109
Rudolph Chelminski, Turning Point 144
Judith Ortiz Cofer, The Paterson Public Library 161
Luc Sante, Living in Tongues 184
Bob Muldoon, White-Collar Man in a
    Blue-Collar World 209
Martín Espada, The Foreman's Wallet 213
Barbara Ehrenreich, Serving in Florida 215
Marc Peyser, The Insiders 225

Illustration: Explaining with Examples

Anna Quindlen, How Reading Changed My Life 3
Francisco Jiménez, The Circuit 20
David Brooks, The Next Ruling Class: Meet
    the Organization Kid 31
Darcy Frey, The Last Shot 42
Timothy Harper, The Best Pickup-Basketball
    Player in America 49

Ruth Conniff, Title IX: Political Football 60
Jack Newfield, The Shame of Boxing 67
Ward Churchill, Smoke Signals in Context 83
Julia Alvarez, I Want to Be Miss América 91
Michael Massing, Press Watch 98
John Nichols, Huey Freeman: American Hero 102
Michael Bronski, Queering the Vast Wasteland 117
Peggy McIntosh, White Privilege: Unpacking
    the Invisible Knapsack 123
Robert S. Boynton, The New Intellectuals 130
Rudolph Chelminski, Turning Point 144
Arno Peters, The Peters Projection World Map 154
Committee on CCCC Language Statement,
    Students' Right to Their Own Language 167
Amy Tan, Mother Tongue 176
Luc Sante, Living in Tongues 184
Robert King, Should English Be the Law? 192
Ellis Cose, Affirmative Action and the Dilemma
    of the "Qualified" 199
Barbara Ehrenreich, Serving in Florida 215
Marc Peyser, The Insiders 225

Process Analysis: Explaining Step-by-Step How Something Operates

Naomi Shihab Nye, Biography of an Armenian
    Schoolgirl 28
Darcy Frey, The Last Shot 42
Timothy Harper, The Best Pickup-Basketball Player
    in America 49
Colette Dowling, Throwing Like a Guy: The
    Mystique of Innate Ability 55
Peggy McIntosh, White Privilege: Unpacking
    the Invisible Knapsack 123
Rudolph Chelminski, Turning Point 144
Robert King, Should English Be the Law? 192
Bob Muldoon, White-Collar Man in a
    Blue-Collar World 209
Martín Espada, The Foreman's Wallet 213
Barbara Ehrenreich, Serving in Florida 215

Comparison and Contrast: Finding Similarities and Differences

David Brooks, The Next Ruling Class:
    Meet the Organization Kid 31
Hunki Yun, Trail Blazer 38
Colette Dowling, Throwing Like a Guy:
    The Mystique of Innate Ability 55
Ruth Conniff, Title IX: Political Football 60
Jack Newfield, The Shame of Boxing 67
Julia Alvarez, I Want to Be Miss América 91
John Nichols, Huey Freeman: American Hero 102

Tim Wise, Blinded by the White: Crime, Race,
  and Denial at Columbine High 109
Peggy McIntosh, White Privilege: Unpacking
  the Invisible Knapsack 123
Robert S. Boynton, The New Intellectuals 130
Arno Peters, The Peters Projection World Map 154
Judith Ortiz Cofer, The Paterson Public Library 161
Committee on CCCC Language Statement,
  Students' Right to Their Own Language 167
Amy Tan, Mother Tongue 176
Robert King, Should English Be the Law? 192
Ellis Cose, Affirmative Action and the Dilemma of the "Qualified" 199
Bob Muldoon, White-Collar Man in a
  Blue-Collar World 209

Classification: Arranging by Category

David Brooks, The Next Ruling Class: Meet
  the Organization Kid 31
Darcy Frey, The Last Shot 42
Colette Dowling, Throwing Like a Guy:
  The Mystique of Innate Ability 55
Jack Newfield, The Shame of Boxing 67
Ward Churchill, Smoke Signals in Context 83
Michael Massing, Press Watch 98
John Nichols, Huey Freeman: American Hero 102
Tim Wise, Blinded by the White: Crime, Race,
  and Denial at Columbine High 109
Michael Bronski, Queering the Vast Wasteland 117
Peggy McIntosh, White Privilege: Unpacking
  the Invisible Knapsack 123
Robert S. Boynton, The New Intellectuals 130
Arno Peters, The Peters Projection World Map 154
Committee on CCCC Language Statement,
  Students' Right to Their Own Language 167
Amy Tan, Mother Tongue 176
Ellis Cose, Affirmative Action and the Dilemma
  of the "Qualified" 199
Bob Muldoon, White-Collar Man in a
  Blue-Collar World 209

Definition: Expressing the Nature of Something

David Brooks, The Next Ruling Class: Meet
  the Organization Kid 31
Colette Dowling, Throwing Like a Guy:
  The Mystique of Innate Ability 55
Ruth Conniff, Title IX: Political Football 60
Ward Churchill, Smoke Signals in Context 83
Julia Alvarez, I Want to Be Miss América 91
Michael Bronski, Queering the Vast Wasteland 117

Peggy McIntosh, White Privilege: Unpacking
    the Invisible Knapsack   123
Robert S. Boynton, The New Intellectuals   130
Ali Hossaini, A "Hyphenated Perspective"   141
Committee on CCCC Language Statement,
    Students' Right to Their Own Language   167
Amy Tan, Mother Tongue   176
Ellis Cose, Affirmative Action and the Dilemma
    of the "Qualified"   199
Bob Muldoon, White-Collar Man in a
    Blue-Collar World   209
Barbara Ehrenreich, Serving in Florida   215

Cause and Effect: Determining Relationships

Francisco Jiménez, The Circuit   20
Colette Dowling, Throwing Like a Guy:
    The Mystique of Innate Ability   55
Ruth Conniff, Title IX: Political Football   60
Jack Newfield, The Shame of Boxing   67
Julia Alvarez, I Want to Be Miss América   91
Tim Wise, Blinded by the White: Crime, Race,
    and Denial at Columbine High   109
Michael Bronski, Queering the Vast Wasteland   117
Peggy McIntosh, White Privilege: Unpacking
    the Invisible Knapsack   123
Robert S. Boynton, The New Intellectuals   130
Ali Hossaini, A "Hyphenated Perspective"   141
Committee on CCCC Language Statement,
    Students' Right to Their Own Language   167
Amy Tan, Mother Tongue   176
Luc Sante, Living in Tongues   184
Ellis Cose, Affirmative Action and the Dilemma
    of the "Qualified"   199
Bob Muldoon, White-Collar Man in a
    Blue-Collar World   209
Martín Espada, The Foreman's Wallet   213
Barbara Ehrenreich, Serving in Florida   215

Profile: Closely Observing People

Naomi Shihab Nye, Biography of an
    Armenian Schoolgirl   28
David Brooks, The Next Ruling Class:
    Meet the Organization Kid   31
Hunki Yun, Trail Blazer   38
Darcy Frey, The Last Shot   42
John Nichols, Huey Freeman: American Hero   102
Robert S. Boynton, The New Intellectuals   130
Rudolph Chelminski, Turning Point   144
Amy Tan, Mother Tongue   176

Bob Muldoon, White-Collar Man in a
    Blue-Collar World 209
Barbara Ehrenreich, Serving in Florida 215
Marc Peyser, The Insiders 225

Argument: Making Logical Appeals

Anna Quindlen, How Reading Changed My Life 3
Timothy Harper, The Best Pickup-Basketball
    Player in America 49
Colette Dowling, Throwing Like a Guy:
    The Mystique of Innate Ability 55
Ruth Conniff, Title IX: Political Football 60
Jack Newfield, The Shame of Boxing 67
Ward Churchill, Smoke Signals in Context 83
Michael Massing, Press Watch 98
John Nichols, Huey Freeman: American Hero 102
Tim Wise, Blinded by the White: Crime, Race,
    and Denial at Columbine High 109
Michael Bronski, Queering the Vast Wasteland 117
Peggy McIntosh, White Privilege: Unpacking
    the Invisible Knapsack 123
Robert S. Boynton, The New Intellectuals 130
Committee on CCCC Language Statement,
    Students' Right to Their Own Language 167
Robert King, Should English Be the Law? 192
Ellis Cose, Affirmative Action and the Dilemma
    of the "Qualified" 199

Exposé: Revealing Controversy

Nathan McCall, Alford J. Mapp 9
Francisco Jiménez, The Circuit 20
Jack Newfield, The Shame of Boxing 67
Ward Churchill, Smoke Signals in Context 83
Tim Wise, Blinded by the White: Crime, Race,
    and Denial at Columbine High 109
Peggy McIntosh, White Privilege: Unpacking
    the Invisible Knapsack 123
Arno Peters, The Peters Projection World Map 154
Ellis Cose, Affirmative Action and the Dilemma
    of the "Qualified" 199
Barbara Ehrenreich, Serving in Florida 215
Marc Peyser, The Insiders 225

Humor and Satire: Making Ironic Appeals

John Nichols, Huey Freeman: American Hero 102
Tim Wise, Blinded by the White: Crime, Race,
    and Denial at Columbine High 109
Amy Tan, Mother Tongue 176
Barbara Ehrenreich, Serving in Florida 215
Marc Peyser, The Insiders 225

Related Readings

Literacy

Anna Quindlen, How Reading Changed My Life — 3
Francisco Jiménez, The Circuit — 20
Judith Ortiz Cofer, The Paterson Public Library — 161

Bilingualism

Francisco Jiménez, The Circuit — 20
Amy Tan, Mother Tongue — 176
Luc Sante, Living in Tongues — 184

English-Only Debate

Lois-Ann Yamanaka, Pidgin Politics — 14
Committee on CCCC Language Statement,
 Students' Right to Their Own Language — 167
Robert King, Should English Be the Law? — 192

Schooling and Status

Naomi Shihab Nye, Biography of an
 Armenian Schoolgirl — 28
David Brooks, The Next Ruling Class: Meet
 the Organization Kid — 31
Robert S. Boynton, The New Intellectuals — 130
Bob Muldoon, White-Collar Man in a
 Blue-Collar World — 209

Basketball

Darcy Frey, The Last Shot — 42
Timothy Harper, The Best Pickup-Basketball
 Player in America — 49

Gender and Sports

Colette Dowling, Throwing Like a Guy:
 The Mystique of Innate Ability — 55
Ruth Conniff, Title IX: Political Football — 60

Television and Film

Ward Churchill, Smoke Signals in Context — 83
Julia Alvarez, I Want to Be Miss América — 91
Michael Massing, Press Watch — 98
Michael Bronski, Queering the Vast Wasteland — 117

Affirmative Action

Ellis Cose, Affirmative Action and the Dilemma
of the "Qualified"   199
Barbara Ehrenreich, Serving in Florida   215

Triumphing over Adversity

Lois-Ann Yamanaka, Pidgin Politics   14
Francisco Jiménez, The Circuit   20
Hunki Yun, Trail Blazer   38
Julia Alvarez, I Want to Be Miss América   91
Robert S. Boynton, The New Intellectuals   130
Rudolph Chelminski, Turning Point   144
Amy Tan, Mother Tongue   176
Bob Muldoon, White-Collar Man in a
Blue-Collar World   209

Geography and Destiny

Naomi Shihab Nye, Biography of an
Armenian Schoolgirl   28
Ali Hossaini, A "Hyphenated Perspective"   141
Rudolph Chelminski, Turning Point   144
Arno Peters, The Peters Projection World Map   154

September 11, 2001

Michael Massing, Press Watch   98
John Nichols, Huey Freeman: American Hero   102
Ali Hossaini, A "Hyphenated Perspective"   141
Rudolph Chelminski, Turning Point   144

PREFACE

Considering Cultural Difference is a concise thematic reader featuring multiethnic writing by contemporary American authors. Showcasing diverse subjects and genres, the selections illustrate how categories of race, class, gender, and nationality intersect and diverge in common places, both in society and in writing. These sites of "cultural difference" are represented in three main parts, each further subdivided into two chapters. A glance at the titles of the parts and of the corresponding chapters suggests the book's overall theme.

Ritual: "Schooling" and "Sports"
Representation: "Media" and "Visibility"
Rights: "Language" and "Workplace"

Each chapter contains five to six reading selections, averaging ten per part.

Authored by writers of multiethnic descent and representing the lives, voices, and experiences of people of Arab, Asian, African, European, Latino, and Native American heritages, the mix of excerpts and full-length selections comes from scholarly books and journals, memoirs, general-interest magazines, news reporting, fiction, and poetry. Though the majority of readings originally were published between the mid-1990s and the present, a small number—such as "Students' Right to Their Own Language," a special edition of *College Composition and Communication* (1974), and "White Privilege: Unpacking the Invisible Knapsack" (1988) by Peggy McIntosh—are included to provide historical context for issues raised in *Considering Cultural Difference* as well as to illustrate their enduring appeal.

The thirty-three selections in *Considering Cultural Difference* illustrate a range of composing strategies similar to those required in a variety of first-year writing courses. Readers will find memoir, new journalism, and examples of creative nonfiction reflective of works published in *Harper's*, the *Atlantic Monthly*, and other literary magazines frequently anthologized in collections, such as *The Best American Essays* (Houghton Mifflin) series. In addition to samples of expressive writing, students also will find informative writing, excerpted from such periodicals as *Newsweek*, the *Nation*, and *Z Magazine*. Examples of critical and academic writing likewise appear, culled from scholarly studies published by both mainstream and independent trade presses. Finally, two fiction and two poetry selections, as well as one visual (serving as an illustration), and a suggested interaction with one web site are included. These six selections encapsulate the fact that thematic concerns and stylistic devices originating in creative writing, visual culture, and electronic media have merged with other forms of writing in the United States in recent years.

Thematically, the sections and subdivisions of this reader aim to render sites of U.S. culture commonly perceived as "shared" from the viewpoint and complexity of difference. For example, in Part I dealing with rituals, issues surrounding schooling (such as integration) and sports (including basketball and boxing) are examined through the lenses of ethnicity, class, and gender. Designed overall to broaden interest in the challenges and triumphs one encounters living in and representing a multicultural, multilingual society, *Considering Cultural Difference* aims to stimulate students to think critically, engage in classroom discussion, and write about issues of cultural identity and difference.

Considering Cultural Difference includes a brief introduction to each main part; this introduction offers a synopsis of the interrelationships among its respective chapters and individual selections. The selections within the chapters each begin with a head note, providing pertinent background on the text or visual and its author or creator. Intended to encourage students to embrace the reader's prevailing themes, the prefatory materials also emphasize historical contexts. To further stimulate critical thinking as well as in-class conversations, five discussion questions called "Engaging the Text" follow each selection. Finally, at the end of each part students will find a list of prompts called "Responding in Writing," which ask for synthesis between two or more readings or offer suggestions for further research.

ACKNOWLEDGMENTS

I would like to thank the reviewers who read earlier versions of *Considering Cultural Difference* and supplied me with helpful comments and suggestions for revision. They are Lilia Benenson, De Vry University; Marcus C. Lopez, Solano Community College;

and Ken Smith, Indiana University-South Bend. I am grateful for your feedback.

I also am indebted to the people of Pearson Longman, especially my editor, Lynn Huddon. Many thanks for your insight, encouragement, and patience at all stages of this project, from development to preparation of the final manuscript. For providing me with additional support and guidance, I am grateful to Esther Hollander, editorial assistant. Thank you for your invaluable help. Additional credit goes to Paula Grant, my copyeditor, as well as to Kevin Bradley, the production editor, for all of their hard work.

PAULINE UCHMANOWICZ

PART I

Ritual

Schooling and Sports

A bell rings and another school year commences. A coin is tossed and players position themselves for the start of a game. Both schooling and sports abound with ritual and routine familiar to many people who grow up in the United States. Think of how rules, regulations, and protocols commonly influence classroom and playground behavior or structure ceremonial observances, such as graduations and annual sporting events. But within our multicultural nation, largely populated by immigrants and their offspring, how individuals experience education or athletics may differ as a consequence of race, ethnicity, gender, class, or language ability. Divided into a chapter on schooling and another on sports, the twelve selections in Part I aim to show how rituals found in both cultural locations mutually relate, crisscrossing like competitors on a playing field. They also profile how cultural differences collide in the same two arenas.

The first essay in Part I, Anna Quindlen's "How Reading Changed My Life," provides an impressionistic look at how reading, often a private and ritualistic act, shapes human character from childhood on. The essay that follows, Nathan McCall's "Alford J. Mapp," adopts as a narrative-framing device the ritual of back-to-school in September (a technique likewise employed by sports essayist Darcy Frey in "The Last Shot"). Lois-Ann Yamanaka's "Pidgin Politics" considers the challenges of speaking in dialect at a school where standard English is the norm, while Francisco Jiménez's "The Circuit" provides perspective on the experience of entering an English-only school without fully knowing the language. Out of the classroom and onto the golf links, Hunki Yun's "Trail Blazer" likewise addresses the issue of entering an English-speaking culture as a foreigner.

Among paired readings in this part, Frey's "The Last Shot" and Timothy Harper's "The Best Pickup-Basketball Player in America" examine basketball culture through the lens of race. Two other companion essays, "Throwing Like a Guy: The Mystique of Innate Ability" by Colette Dowling and "Title IX: Political Football" by Ruth Conniff, use quantitative research and statistical data to challenge differing views surrounding gender and sports. Additionally, Naomi Shihab Nye's poem, "Biography of an Armenian Schoolgirl," considers gender and destiny within the context of schooling.

Themes and motifs migrate between the two chapters of Part I, such as when references to educational testing and instruction turn up in the writings about sports. For instance, Frey explores the relationship between the SATs and the NCAA (National Collegiate Athletic Association), while Conniff explains why the National Wrestling Coaches Association recently filed a lawsuit against the U.S. Department of Education. Language and rhetorical devices used to discuss schooling and sports similarly overlap in the twelve readings. For example, Dowling characterizes athletic ability or "physical intelligence" as analogous to "IQ," while McCall embraces a sports analogy to liken a racially motivated scuffle in a school corridor to a prizefight, the combatants ritualistically separating at the sound of a bell. Meanwhile, in "The Shame of Boxing," Jack Newfield determines that actual prizefighters by and large are undereducated "workers of color" who frequently end up destitute. In contrast, in "The Next Ruling Class: Meet the Organization Kid," David Brooks describes "elite" students who attend Princeton University as "cooperative team players" assured of "ascent in the social hierarchy." As these writers consistently illustrate, education and athletics are intricately entwined in our culture.

The rituals of schooling and sports also influence how we speak and interact with others. Not surprisingly, linguists in the United States point to competing metaphors generated in the discourses of schooling and sports to account for differences between how women and men communicate. Women supposedly adopt the root metaphor of life as a traditional schoolroom, where people follow rules and tell the truth. On the other hand, men typically view life as a football game, where it's okay to break rules, lie, and even take out players on your own team as long as a touchdown is scored.

What rituals do you equate with schooling or sports? How does your cultural identity influence your perspectives about their meaning and purpose? Do you find yourself using the language of schooling or sports in conversation or in writing? As you read the selections that follow, try providing answers to these questions.

CHAPTER 1

Schooling

How Reading Changed My Life
ANNA QUINDLEN

Learning to read is a rite of passage familiar to schoolchildren from all walks of life. The building blocks of literacy—sound reading skills and habits—may improve an individual's educational opportunities, as Anna Quindlen argues in this retrospective narrative. According to the author, books likewise offer readers portraits of cultures different from their own. Yet historically, literary "pundits and professionals," as well as the general public, have questioned what and why people read. Did particular books or authors that you read during childhood make an impact on you? If so, what makes them stand out in your memory? Can you recall a time when your reading ability either influenced your advancement in school or was called into question by those around you?

The author of three best-selling novels—including *Object Lessons*, a story of coming-of-age in an Irish-Italian American family—Quindlen frequently writes about women's issues. The winner of a 1992 Pulitzer Prize in commentary for her *New York Times* column "Public and Private," she is currently a biweekly columnist at *Newsweek*.

◆

The neighborhood where I grew up was the sort of place in which people dream of raising children—pretty, privileged but not rich, a small but satisfying spread of center-hall colonials, old roses, rhododendrons, and quiet roads. We walked to school, wandered wild in the summer, knew everyone and all their brothers and sisters, too. Some of the people I went to school with, who I sat next to in sixth and seventh grade, still live there, one or two in the houses that their parents once owned.

Not long ago, when I was in town on business, I determined to test my memories against the reality and drove to my old block, my old school, the homes of my closest friends, sure that I had inflated it all in my mind. But the houses were no smaller, the flowers no less bright. It was as fine as I had remembered—maybe more so, now when so much of the rest of the world has come to seem dingy and diminished.

Yet there was always in me, even when I was very small, the sense that I ought to be somewhere else. And wander I did, although, in my everyday life, I had nowhere to go and no imaginable reason on earth why I should want to leave. The buses took to the interstate without me; the trains sped by. So I wandered the world through books. I went to Victorian England in the pages of *Middlemarch* and *A Little Princess*, and to Saint Petersburg before the fall of the tsar with *Anna Karenina*. I went to Tara, and Manderley, and Thornfield Hall, all those great houses, with their high-ceilings and high drama, as I read *Gone with the Wind*, *Rebecca*, and *Jane Eyre*.

When I was in eighth grade I took a scholarship test for a convent school, and the essay question began with a quotation: "It is a far, far better thing that I do, than I have ever done; it is a far, far better rest that I go to, than I have ever known." Later, over a stiff and awkward lunch of tuna-fish salad, some of the other girls at my table were perplexed by the source of the quotation and what it meant, and I was certain, at that moment, weeks before my parents got the letter from the nuns, that the scholarship was mine. How many times had I gone up the steps to the guillotine with Sydney Carton as he went to that far, far better rest at the end of *A Tale of Two Cities*?

Perhaps only a truly discontented child can become as se-   5
duced by books as I was. Perhaps restlessness is a necessary
corollary of devoted literacy. There was a club chair in our
house, a big one, with curled arms and a square ottoman; it
sat in one corner of the living room, catty-corner to the fire-
place, with a barrel table next to it. In my mind I am always
sprawled in it, reading with my skinny, scabby legs slung over
one of its arms. "It's a beautiful day," my mother is saying; she
said that always, often, autumn, spring, even when there was a
fresh snowfall. "All your friends are outside." It was true; they
always were. Sometimes I went out with them, coaxed into the
street, out into the fields, down by the creek, by the lure of
what I knew intuitively was normal childhood, by the promise
of being what I knew instinctively was a normal child, one
who lived, raucous, in the world.

But at base it was never any good. The best part of me was
always at home, within some book that had been laid flat on
the table to mark my place, its imaginary people waiting for
me to return and bring them to life. That was where the real
people were, the trees that moved in the wind, the still, dark
waters. I won a bookmark in a spelling bee during that time
with these words of Montaigne[1] upon it in gold: "When I am
reading a book, whether wise or silly, it seems to me to be alive
and talking to me." I found that bookmark not long ago, at the
bottom of a box, when my father was moving.

Years later I would come to discover (through reading,
naturally) that while I was sprawled, legs akimbo, in that chair
with a book, Jamaica Kincaid was sitting in the glare of the
Caribbean sun in Antigua reading in that same way that I did,
as though she was starving and the book was bread. When she
was grown-up, writing books herself, winning awards for her
work, she talked in one of her memoirs of ignoring her little
brother when she was supposed to be looking after him: "I
liked reading a book much more than I liked looking after him

---

[1]Sixteenth-century French Renaissance thinker credited with originating
the nonfiction essay as a literary genre.

(and even now I like reading a book more than I like looking after my own children . . .)."

While I was in that club chair with a book, Hazel Rochman and her husband were in South Africa, burying an old tin trunk heavy with hardcovers in the backyard, because the police might raid their house and search it for banned books. Rochman, who left Johannesburg for Chicago and became an editor for the American Library Association's *Booklist,* summed up the lessons learned from that night, about the power of reading, in a way I would have recognized even as a girl. "Reading makes immigrants of us all," she wrote years later. "It takes us away from home, but, most important, it finds homes for us everywhere."

While I was in that club chair with a book, Oprah Winfrey was dividing her childhood between her mother in Milwaukee and her father in Nashville, but finding her most consistent home between the covers of her books. Even decades later, when she had become the host of her eponymous talk show, one of the world's highest-paid entertainers, and the founder of an on-air book club that resulted in the sale of millions of copies of serious literary novels, Winfrey still felt the sting as she talked to a reporter from *Life* magazine: "I remember being in the back hallway when I was about nine—I'm going to try to say this without crying—and my mother threw the door open and grabbed a book out of my hand and said, 'You're nothing but a something-something bookworm. Get your butt outside! You think you're better than the other kids.' I was treated as though something was wrong with me because I wanted to read all the time."

10   There is something in the American character that is . . . secretly hostile to the act of aimless reading, a certain hale and heartiness that is suspicious of reading as anything more than a tool for advancement. This is a country that likes confidence but despises hubris, that associates the "nose in the book" with the same sense of covert superiority that Ms. Winfrey's mother did. America is also a nation that prizes sociability and community, that accepts a kind of psychological domino effect: alone leads to loner, loner to loser. Any sort of turning away from human contact is suspect, especially one that inter-

feres with the go-out-and-get-going ethos that seems to be at the heart of our national character. The image of American presidents that stick are those that portray them as men of action: Theodore Roosevelt on safari, John Kennedy throwing a football around with his brothers. There is only Lincoln as solace to the inveterate reader, a solitary figure sitting by the fire, saying, "My best friend is a person who will give me a book I have not read."

There also arose, as I was growing up, a kind of careerism in the United States that sanctioned reading only if there was some point to it. Students at the nation's best liberal arts colleges who majored in philosophy or English were constantly asked what they were "going to do with it," as though intellectual pursuits for their own sake had had their day, and lost it in the press of business. Reading for pleasure was replaced by reading for purpose, and a kind of dogged self-improvement period.

Reading has always been used as a way to divide a country and a culture into the literati and everyone else, the intellectually worthy and the hoi polloi. But in the fifteenth century Gutenberg invented the printing press, and so began the process of turning the book from a work of art for the few into a source of information for the many. After that, it became more difficult for one small group of people to lay an exclusive claim to books, to seize and hold reading as their own. But it was not impossible, and it continued to be done by critics and scholars. When I began to read their work, in college, I was disheartened to discover that many of them felt that the quality of poetry and prose, novels and history and biography, was plummeting into some intellectual bargain basement. But reading saved me from despair, as it always had, for the more I read the more I realized it had always been thus, and that apparently an essential part of studying literature, whether in 1840, 1930, or 1975, was to conclude that there had once been a golden age, and it was gone. "The movies consume so large a part of the leisure of the country that little time is left for other things," the trade magazine of the industry, *Publishers Weekly*, lamented in 1923. "The novel can't compete with cars, the movies, television, and liquor," the French writer Louis-Ferdinand Céline said in 1960.

Reading is like so much else in our culture, in all cultures: the truth of it is found in its people and not in its pundits and its professionals. If I believed what I read about reading I would despair. But instead there are letters from readers to attend to, like the one from a girl who had been given one of my books by her mother and began her letter, "I guess I am what some people would call a bookworm."

"So am I," I wrote back.

Engaging the Text

1. What is the relationship between the town in which Quindlen grew up and the places that she encountered in the pages of books? Do her recollections resemble your own memories of reading during childhood? Explain why or why not.

2. Quindlen considers herself a "bookworm." Highlight passages in the essay supporting this conclusion. According to the author, what are some advantages and disadvantages associated with being an avid reader? What does the inclusion of information about Oprah Winfrey's reading habits contribute to this line of reasoning?

3. More than once in the essay Quindlen mentions reading to herself in a club chair in the living room of her childhood home. What does this repetition accomplish in the narrative? How might you devise a similar rhetorical strategy for your own writing?

4. "Reading makes immigrants of us all," Quindlen writes in paragraph 8, quoting Hazel Rochman, a former editor at the American Library Association. Discuss the meaning of this statement. When possible, cite examples from works of literature you have read to illustrate your interpretation.

5. In the latter section of the essay, Quindlen sets up a series of comparisons, for example, between "reading for pleasure" and "reading for purpose." What do these opposing ideas say about what we value as a culture? How do they serve the author's closing argument? What does she ultimately conclude about the importance of reading in her life?

Alford J. Mapp

NATHAN MCCALL

In the 1954 landmark decision *Brown v. Board of Education,* the U.S. Supreme Court unanimously declared school segregation unconstitutional, citing Thomas Jefferson's words "all men are created equal." In the aftermath, television cameras rolled as white mobs threatened physical harm to African-American students who attempted to enter previously all-white schools. Indeed, the results of the Supreme Court ruling were not fully enacted until several years later. Nor were racial hatred and violence fully eradicated, as Nathan McCall documents in this essay about attending school in Portsmouth, Virginia, in 1966. Based on your own experiences and observations, would you claim that schools today are successfully integrated? What evidence would you cite that the United States has made progress in recent years in support of racial equality?

McCall attended Norfolk State University after serving three years in prison. He has been a reporter for the *Virginian Pilot-Ledger Star,* the *Atlanta Journal-Constitution,* and the *Washington Post,* and has taught journalism at Emory University. Author of the 1994 best-selling memoir *Makes Me Wanna Holler,* in which "Alford J. Mapp" first appeared, McCall's essay collection *What's Going On* was published in 2000.

————————— ✦ —————————

My harshest introduction to the world of white folks came in September 1966, when my parents sent me to Alford J. Mapp, a white school across town. It was the beginning of my sixth-grade school year, and I was walking down the hall, searching for my new class, when a white boy timed my steps, extended his foot, and tripped me. The boy and his friends nudged each other and laughed as I stumbled into a locker, spilling books and papers everywhere. "Hey, nigger," the boy said. "You dropped something."

The word sounded vile coming from his white mouth. When I regained my footing, I tore into that cat and tried to take his head off. Pinning him against a locker, I punched him in the face and kept on punching him until his two buddies jumped in to help him out. While other white students crowded around and cheered them on, we scuffled there in the hall until the bell rang, signaling the start of the next class period. Like combatants in a prizefight, we automatically stopped throwing punches and separated at the sound of the bell. The white boys went their way down the hall, calling me names along the way and threatening to retaliate. I gathered my papers, straightened my clothes, and reeled toward my next class, dazed, trying to figure out what had just happened to me.

My parents sent me to Mapp in 1966 because that was the first year that blacks in Portsmouth were able to attend school wherever they wanted. The U.S. Supreme Court had long before ruled against the notion of separate but equal schools; still, Virginia, one of the states that had resisted desegregation, was slow in putting together a busing plan. Without a plan to ship black students to schools across town, over the years blacks and whites in Portsmouth had simply remained in separate schools. I could have gone to W. E. Waters, a junior high school that had just been built in our neighborhood, but, like many blacks then, my parents figured I could get a better education at the white school across town.

I was proud of their decision and held it out teasingly to my brothers as proof that I was the smart one in the family, that I held more academic promise than them. Billy had flunked the second grade, and Dwight and Junnie never showed much interest in books. My less studious brothers would attend their regular, all-black high school, but I was going to a *white* school, which made me feel special.

5   My parents didn't talk with me beforehand about the challenge I would face as one in the first wave of blacks to integrate Mapp. We had all seen TV news footage of police in riot gear escorting black students through hostile, jeering crowds to enroll in all-white high schools and colleges across the country, but for various reasons my parents saw no cause for alarm at Mapp. It was only a junior high school, which seemed far less menacing than the racially torn high schools

and college campuses we heard about. Besides, there were no warning signals in Portsmouth to tip off my parents, no public protests by white citizens or high-profile white supremacist politicians like Alabama governor George Wallace threatening to buck the school integration plan.

At Mapp, I was the only African American in most of my classes. When I walked into one room and sat down, the students near me would get up and move away, as if my dark skin were dirty and hideous to them. Nobody talked directly to me. Instead, they shot daggers to each other that were intended for me. "You know, I hate niggers," they would say. "I don't understand why they're always following white people everywhere. We can't seem to get away from them. Why don't they just stay in their own schools?"

It wasn't much better dealing with white teachers. They avoided eye contact with me as much as possible and pretended not to see or hear white student hecklers. It was too much for an eleven-year-old to challenge, and I didn't try. Instead, I tried to become invisible. I kept to myself, remained quiet during class discussions, and never asked questions in or after class. I kept my eyes glued to my desk or looked straight ahead to avoid drawing attention to myself. I staggered, numb and withdrawn, through each school day and hurried from my last class, gym, without showering so that I wouldn't miss the only bus headed home. Students who missed the first school bus had to walk through the white neighborhood to the main street to catch the city bus. Mapp was located in a middle-class section of town called Craddock, where the whites were as hateful as the poor whites in Academy Park.

The daily bus ride home brought its own set of fears. A group of white boys got on our bus regularly for the sole purpose, it seemed, of picking fights. I was scared to death of them. With older brothers to fight at home, I was confident I could whip any white boy my age and size, but many of the white guys who got on that bus were eighth graders, and they looked like giants to me. Others were older, white, leather-jacket-wearing hoods who I was certain were high school dropouts.

When we boarded the bus, blacks automatically moved to the rear, as if Jim Crow laws[1] were still in effect. The white boys would board last, crowd into the aisles, and start making racial slurs when the bus pulled away from school. "I hate the smell of niggers. They sure do stink. Don't you think niggers stink, Larry?"

"They sure do, man. They smell bad."

Before long, fists flew, girls screamed, and people tussled in the aisles. Few of the black guys on the bus were big and bad enough to beat the tough white boys, who outnumbered us seven to one. I never joined in to help the black guys out. I huddled in the far corner at the rear of the bus, tense, scared as hell, hoping the fighting wouldn't reach that far before the driver broke it up.

Children have an enormous capacity to adapt to insanity. I took my lumps in school and tried as much as possible to shrug it off when I went home. Billy, Dwight, and Junnie came home most days full of stories about the fun they were having at pep rallies and football games at their all-black high school. I envied them because I couldn't match their stories with tales of my own about fun times at Mapp. I savored every minute of my weeknights at home and used weekends to gather the heart to face Mapp again. Monday mornings, I rose and dutifully caught the school bus back to hell.

The harassment never let up. Once, when my English teacher left the room, a girl sitting near me drew a picture of a stickman on a piece of paper, colored it black, scribbled my name below it, and passed it around the classroom for others to see. I lost my temper, snatched it from her, and ripped it up. She hit me. I hit her back, then the whole class jumped in. When the teacher returned, I was standing up, punching one guy while another one was riding my back and hitting me in the head. The teacher demanded, "What's going on here?"

---

[1]Ethnic discrimination especially against blacks by legal enforcement or traditional sanctions.

The white kids cried out in unison, "That *black* boy started a fight with us!"

Without another word, the teacher sent me to the principal's office and I was dismissed from school. The weeklong suspension alerted my parents that something was wrong. Mama sat me down and tried to talk to me about it. "Why were you fighting in school?"

"It wasn't my fault, Mama. That girl drew a picture of me and colored it black."

"That's no reason to fight. What's the matter with you? Your grades are falling and now you get into a fight. Don't you like your school?"

I tried to explain, then choked up and broke down in tears. Seeing that, my parents sought and got approval to transfer me to the neighborhood school, W. E. Waters.

But it wasn't over yet. One day, before the transfer went through, I was sitting on the gym floor with the rest of the student body, watching a school assembly program, when a group of rowdy white upperclassmen began plucking my head and ridiculing me. I got confused. *What should I do?* To turn around and say something to them would start another fight. To get up and leave would require me to wade through a sea of hostile white students to reach the nearest exit. With nowhere to go, I sat there and took the humiliation until I broke. Tears welled in my eyes and started running, uncontrollably, down my face. I sat silently through the remainder of the assembly program with my vision blurred and my spirit broken. That was the only time, then or since, that I've been crushed so completely. When it was over, I collected myself, went to the boys' bathroom, and boohooed some more.

There was no greater joy than that last bus ride home from Mapp. I sat near a window and stared out, trying to make sense of those past few months. Everything that had happened to me was so contrary to all I'd been taught about right and wrong. Before Mapp, every grudge I had ever held against a person could be traced to some specific deed. I couldn't understand someone hating me simply for being black and alive. I wondered, *Where did those white people learn*

15

20

to hate so deeply at such a young age? I didn't know. But, over time, I learned to hate as blindly and viciously as any of them.

Engaging the Text

1. Analyze the story McCall tells in the first two paragraphs of the essay. What purpose does it serve? How does the language that McCall employs in the opening call attention to cultural differences between himself and other characters? Do you find his word choice controversial? If so, does the author's ethos (ethical appeal) influence your reaction? Explain your answer.

2. What historical event inspired McCall's parents to send him to Alford J. Mapp and why does he agree to attend? How does the narrator's use of the words "white" and "black" in paragraphs 3–5 reflect his attitude toward that decision today?

3. Why does McCall emphasize the bus ride home from school? Why does he fear both missing and riding the bus? How familiar to you are the circumstances that McCall describes in this section? Do you find anything surprising about this development in the plot? Explain your answer.

4. McCall writes, "Children have an enormous capacity to adapt to insanity" (paragraph 12). What does he mean by this statement? Do you agree or disagree with his assessment? Explain your answer.

5. In the final paragraph of the essay, McCall expresses bewilderment at having been the target of unaccounted-for hatred at Mapp. According to the author, where does the capacity to hate come from? Is there implicit cause for hope in identifying its source? Discuss your view.

Pidgin Politics
Lois-Ann Yamanaka

Children of immigrant families who arrived to the Hawaiian Islands from Europe and Asia during the nineteenth century learned their parents' languages put picked up English at school. But the kind of English they spoke included words, phrases, and sounds created by blending features of their own first languages. What emerged is a dialect that linguists call Hawaiian Creole English, sometimes referred to as "pidgin." Though school-aged children in Hawaii continue to speak pidgin, they are admonished against using it the classroom. Poet and novelist Lois-Ann Yamanaka, a third-generation descendent of Japanese immigrant sugar and pineapple plantation workers who settled on the Hawaiian island of Moloka'i, frequently writes in pidgin. In this portrait of schooling excerpted from Yamanaka's novel *Blu's Hanging* (1997), the story of three Japanese-American children (Ivah, Blu, and Maisie Ogata) growing up impoverished and motherless on Moloka'i, the author illustrates how the pidgin they speak conflicts with the standard English they are told should be their academic goal.

Yamanaka has earned many grants and awards for her writing, including a Pushcart Prize, a National Endowment for the Arts grant, and an Asian American Studies National Book Award. She is the author of six books, including the poetry collection *Saturday Night at Pahala Theatre* (1993) and the novels *Heads by Harry* (1999) and *Father of the Four Passages* (2001).

———————————— ◆ ————————————

The phone rings.

"Yes, yes, yes. I will be there." Poppy talks in perfect English. "I'm very sorry. Yes, Yes."

When he hangs up, he says, "Ivah, you go talk confrence with Maisie's teacha tomorrow. I no can get off work jes like that. Sheez, I lose pay, I take off. Plus I gotta work with Furtado tomorrow night. I neva tell her this, but I send you in my place. You the one look over the kid's work anyways." And then my Poppy looks me in the eye. He's mad at himself for kowtowing: Ve-lee so-lee, ve-lee so-lee, Missy Owens.

"I no can handle haoles.[1] Think they so holier-than-thou with their fast-talking mouth and everybody mo' brown than

———————————————————————————

[1]A Hawaiian Creole English term describing people who are considered "white." The word "haole" may be used either in jest or as a derogatory term.

them is dirt under their feet. All the lunas all haole before on the sugar plantation—they mean sunnavabitches with bull-whips for hit the kids and all. And they live in the biggest, most nicest house made special for the plantation bosses. Then they made some of the Portagees lunas. The damn Portagees was workers like us, but they was the closest to white."

5   "Poppy, Mama said not all haoles *haoles* to her," I tell my father softly. He's madder after thinking back to his days in Hilo. "She said some of um like reg-la people. They was born here and no act like they hot. And some, she said, help the sick. She said she knew some real good haoles. Only the real haolified haoles you gotta watch out for."

"Sick"—Poppy pauses—"and dying. Yeah, them haoles your Mama was talking about was damn good haoles."

"Hah? Who was sick?"

"Nobody." He catches himself. "A haole is a haole to me." *Tell me, Poppy, tell me.*

10   "One in a hundred you can trust as one friend. I told you all this before. The rest of um see your Jap face and you be sitting at the worse table in the place. Talk circles around you till you know you the stupidest jerk in the room. Think they so goddamned betta than the rest of us. I ain't talking to Maisie's teacha. You go, Ivah, but be like your Mama. No talk wise, bumbye we get mo' trouble."

I guess Miss Tammy Owens didn't tell Poppy how I swore at her that day in the hall. *Thank you, Jesus.* For that, I know I would've been sent headfirst into the kitchen counter. Why didn't she tell? She's saving it to make the effect greater when she meets with Poppy in person. But *what a shame*, Poppy's not going to be there.

Mrs. Nishimoto says Miss Owens hates it here on Moloka'i. "That's why we have so much in common," she says. "You know, when you're from the Midwest, Hawaii sounds like a paradise. But once you're here, oh for heaven's sake, the heat and the children are just so, so, oh never mind."

The next day after school, I walk with Blu to Maisie's classroom. She's sitting at her desk, so I send Blu in to gather up all of her books, papers, and wet panties into her straw school bag. Maisie wraps her wet panties in drawing paper.

They go to sit on the steps of the kindergarten wing. When I look out the door, Blu turns to look at me. My brother puts his arm around Maisie and she curls into him.

"Will your father be here soon?" Miss Owens asks without even looking at me.

"No. Just me."

"And why is that? Should we reschedule the conference for another day?"

"No need. I mean, no can. My fadda no can come ever 'cause he gotta work. So he wen' send me for take his place. I here to talk with you about Maisie, then I gotta tell him."

"Can we set a few ground rules—what's your name again? It seems to have *slipped* my mind."

"Ivah."

"Ivah, that's right. *Unusual* name. Well, *dear*, we need to speak to each other in standard English for the duration of this conference. I find the pidgin English you children speak to be so limited in its ability to express fully what we need to cover today. Am I clear?" Miss Owens turns her back to me and erases the chalkboard. She mutters something about "the darn lyin' recruiter" and a "lousy teacher's cottage in paradise."

I nod my head.

"Well, first of all, as you probably well know at home, Maisie's rather uncommunicative. Has her hearing ever been tested?"

"She not deaf." Miss Owens gives me a sneering smile for my pidgin. I don't even care.

"Has she ever been tested for Special Ed?"

"She not stupid. She understand everything you say."

"She can't even tell me she wants to use the bathroom. We're talking an accident every day. Nobody wants to sit near

15

20

25

Maisie and my room smells like a *janitor's* nightmare." She talks mean. That's how she must talk to my sister.

She catches herself. She *knows* about Poppy's jobs. Miss Tammy Owens and Mrs. Susie Nishimoto are best buddies. You see the two haole teachers all over town and on picnics and at church. That's how Miss Owens knows about us. I should've put two and two together when Mrs. Nishimoto told me to be ready for a parent conference.

"And she's been exposing her vagina and buttocks to the boys in the schoolyard."

30 "How you know?" She's never there. She's smoking cigarettes and drinking coffee in the Teachers' Lounge.

"Word gets around and I have seen it myself."

Word gets around. Mrs. Nishimoto's exact words. Two rotten haoles. Go home to the Midwest. Who told you to come here?

"Maisie has on a number of occasions been forced to stay in school without underwear because of her constant wetting. It was on those days that Maisie exposed herself to several of the boys in our wing."

Why, why, why didn't you call me from the intermediate campus? Or Blu in the next building? You wanted to humiliate her, that's why. Make the boys fall on the broken sidewalk outside of Room 3 and see my sister, her thighs squeezed together, the wind lifting the gathered skirt of her plaid dress, and take turns around her.

35 "Well, Ivah? What have you got to say? These are incredibly sociopathic behaviors we're seeing exhibited in a very young child. Do you have a mother?"

How come Mrs. Nishimoto never told her that my Mama died? Or is she playing with my head? "No, Miss Owens."

"No, what?"

"No. Mother. Dead. Just. Us."

"*Oh?*"

40 "Dead and my sista no talk."

"*Oh.*"

She wanted me to say the word. *Dead.*

"In any case, I'm glad we met to talk things over. I'll be putting in a request for Special Ed testing. Maisie has social, emotional, psychological, and academic problems that need addressing. Thank you for coming, Ivah." Miss Owens gets up and starts shuffling papers on her desk. Then she starts to close the windows. "By the way, Ivah. I've informed the VP of your profane, racial remarks in the hall the other day. He will be calling your father any day now. Am I clear? You will inform your father, won't you?"

I look at Miss Owens, and think: *She's show. All show.* Acting like she's in control. With fists clenched and teeth gritted, I nod my head once. Tammy Owens smells scared, she can smell it herself, so she turns. I stare hard at her. Red eyes, right inside her.

Read my mind, haole: *I don't care. I answer all the phone* 45 *calls anyway. My Poppy's never home. My mother's dead.*

I walk out the door of Room 3 into afternoon sunlight that might burn the skin right off a freckled haole. Blu and Maisie scuffle after me. There's dust in the beams of sunlight that cut across the wooden hallways. It looks like pixie dust. But it's red dirt from the pineapple fields. That's all.

Engaging the Text

1. Throughout the selection, Yamanaka makes use of "code switching," a rhetorical strategy in which a piece of writing shifts from its primary language to foreign words or dialects without offering translations. How does Yamanaka's use of code switching between pidgin and standard English relay differences among characters in the story? What effect does code switching have on how you read the excerpt? How might you adopt code switching in your own writing and for what purpose?

2. Describe your reaction to the raw, sometimes vulgar, language Yamanaka uses throughout the narrative. What do you think the author intends to show by using this language? Do you find this rhetorical strategy effective? Explain why or why not.

3. Why does Poppy refuse to talk to Maisie's teacher? What does his resistance suggest about cultural differences among the characters in the selection? Use specific examples to support your point of view.

4. Describe the encounter between Ivah and her sister's teacher Miss Owens. How does Ivah react when Miss

Owens insists that they "speak to each other in standard English for the duration of [their] conference" (paragraph 21)? What does her reaction suggest about the writer's attitude toward the teacher? How does this episode relate to the overall tone of the story? Does Yamanaka indicate whether or not the Ogata characters *can* speak in standard English? Use specific examples from the text to discuss your answers.

5. Locate references in the selection that describe different perspectives about Hawaii. What do these conflicting images suggest about the cultural themes explored in Yamanaka's narrative?

The Circuit
FRANCISCO JIMÉNEZ

The legacy of migrant workers who cross our southern border into the United States may be traced to the Bracero Program of 1943–1964. A "wartime emergency" initiative sponsored by the U.S. government to supply seasonal agricultural labor to the American Southwest, it allowed short-term workers to enter the country from Mexico. The migratory patterns of undocumented immigrant Chicanos (Mexican Americans) who arrive to harvest crops continues in the present day. Though many come seeking the American Dream, they move from town to town, one step ahead of *la migra* (immigration officers). Children from these migrant-worker families may attend school sporadically or encounter learning difficulties when shifting between English and their native language, situations described by Francisco Jiménez in the following award-winning short story.

Born in San Pedro, Mexico, Jiménez immigrated to the United States in 1947, becoming a naturalized citizen in 1965. He has taught at colleges throughout the United States and Mexico and in 2002 was named one of four U.S. Professors of the Year by the Council for Advancement and Support of Education (CASE) and the Carnegie Foundation for the Advancement of Teaching. A widely published author who writes in both English and Spanish, Jiménez has earned many awards, including the *Boston Globe* Horn Book Award, the 1998 California Library Association John and Patricia Beatty Award, and the 1997 Américas Award for Children's and Young Adult Literature, all for *The Circuit: Stories from the Life of a Migrant Child*, in which "The Circuit" appeared. Jiménez continues his saga of migrant worker camps and schooling in the sequel *Breaking Through* (2001).

———————— ◆ ————————

It was that time of year again. Ito, the strawberry sharecropper, did not smile. It was natural. The peak of the strawberry season was over and the last few days the workers, most of them braceros,[1] were not picking as many boxes as they had during the months of June and July.

As the last days of August disappeared, so did the number of braceros. Sunday, only one—the best picker—came to work. I liked him. Sometimes we talked during our half-hour lunch break. That is how I found out he was from Jalisco, the same state in Mexico my family was from. That Sunday was the last time I saw him.

When the sun had tired and sunk behind the mountains, Ito signaled us that it was time to go home. "Ya esora,"[2] he yelled in his broken Spanish. Those were the words I waited for twelve hours a day, every day, seven days a week, week after week. And the thought of not hearing them again saddened me.

As we drove home Papá did not say a word. With both hands on the wheel, he stared at the dirt road. My older brother, Roberto, was also silent. He leaned his head back and closed his eyes. Once in a while he cleared from his throat the dust that blew in from outside.

---

[1]Mexican laborers admitted to the United States for seasonal work in agriculture.

[2]"It's time," or "Time's up."

5   Yes, it was that time of year. When I opened the front door
to the shack, I stopped. Everything we owned was neatly
packed in cardboard boxes. Suddenly I felt even more the
weight of hours, days, weeks, and months of work. I sat down
on a box. The thought of having to move to Fresno and knowing what was in store for me there brought tears to my eyes.

   That night I could not sleep. I lay in bed thinking about
how much I hated this move.

   A little before five o'clock in the morning, Papá woke
everyone up. A few minutes later, the yelling and screaming of
my little brothers and sisters, for whom the move was a great
adventure, broke the silence of dawn. Shortly, the barking of
the dogs accompanied them.

   While we packed the breakfast dishes, Papá went outside
to start the "Carcanchita." That was the name Papá gave his
old '38 black Plymouth. He bought it in a used-car lot in Santa
Rosa in the winter of 1949. Papá was very proud of his little
jalopy. He had a right to be proud of it. He spent a lot of time
looking at other cars before buying this one. When he finally
chose the "Carcanchita," he checked it thoroughly before driving it out of the car lot. He examined every inch of the car. He
listened to the motor, tilting his head from side to side like a
parrot, trying to detect any noises that spelled car trouble. After being satisfied with the looks and sounds of the car, Papá
then insisted on knowing who the original owner was. He
never did find out from the car salesman, but he bought the
car anyway. Papá figured the original owner must have been
an important man because behind the rear seat of the car he
found a blue necktie.

   Papá parked the car out in front and left the motor running. "Listo,"[3] he yelled. Without saying a word, Roberto and I
began to carry the boxes out to the car. Roberto carried the
two big boxes and I carried the two smaller ones. Papá then
threw the mattress on top of the car roof and tied it with ropes
to the front and rear bumpers.

---

[3]"Ready."

Everything was packed except Mamá's pot. It was an old   10
large galvanized pot she had picked up at an army surplus
store in Santa María the year I was born. The pot had many
dents and nicks, and the more dents and nicks it acquired the
more Mamá liked it. "Mi olla,"⁴ she used to say proudly.

I held the front door open as Mamá carefully carried out
her pot by both handles, making sure not to spill the cooked
beans. When she got to the car, Papá reached out to help her
with it. Roberto opened the rear car door and Papá gently
placed it on the floor behind the front seat. All of us then
climbed in. Papá sighed, wiped the sweat off his forehead with
his sleeve, and said wearily: "Es todo."⁵

As we drove away, I felt a lump in my throat. I turned
around and looked at our little shack for the last time.

At sunset we drove into a labor camp near Fresno. Since
Papá did not speak English, Mamá asked the camp foreman if
he needed any more workers. "We don't need no more," said
the foreman, scratching his head. "Check with Sullivan down
the road. Can't miss him. He lives in a big white house with a
fence around it."

When we got there, Mamá walked up to the house. She
went through a white gate, past a row of rose bushes, up the
stairs to the front door. She rang the doorbell. The porch light
went on and a tall husky man came out. They exchanged a few
words. After the man went in, Mamá clasped her hands and
hurried back to the car. "We have work! Mr. Sullivan said we
can stay there the whole season," she said, gasping and pointing to an old garage near the stables.

The garage was worn out by the years. It had no windows.   15
The walls, eaten by termites, strained to support the roof full
of holes. The dirt floor, populated by earth worms, looked like
a gray road map.

That night, by the light of a kerosene lamp, we unpacked
and cleaned our new home. Roberto swept away the loose

---

⁴"My pot."
⁵"That's all."

dirt, leaving the hard ground. Papá plugged the holes in the walls with old newspapers and tin can tops. Mamá fed my little brothers and sisters. Papá and Roberto then brought in the mattress and placed it on the far corner of the garage. "Mamá, you and the little ones sleep on the mattress. Roberto, Panchito, and I will sleep outside under the trees," Papá said.

Early next morning Mr. Sullivan showed us where his crop was, and after breakfast, Papá, Roberto, and I headed for the vineyard to pick.

Around nine o'clock the temperature had risen to almost one hundred degrees. I was completely soaked in sweat and my mouth felt as if I had been chewing on a handkerchief. I walked over to the end of the row, picked up the jug of water we had brought, and began drinking. "Don't drink too much; you'll get sick," Roberto shouted. No sooner had he said that then I felt sick to my stomach. I dropped to my knees and let the jug roll off my hands. I remained motionless with my eyes glued on the hot sandy ground. All I could hear was the drone of insects. Slowly I began to recover. I poured water over my face and neck and watched the dirty water run down my arms to the ground.

I still felt a little dizzy when we took a break to eat lunch. It was past two o'clock and we sat underneath a large walnut tree that was on the side of the road. While we ate, Papá jotted down the number of boxes we had picked. Roberto drew designs on the ground with a stick. Suddenly I noticed Papá's face turn pale as he looked down the road. "Here comes the school bus," he whispered loudly in alarm. Instinctively, Roberto and I ran and hid in the vineyards. We did not want to get in trouble for not going to school. The neatly dressed boys about my age got off. They carried books under their arms. After they crossed the street, the bus drove away. Roberto and I came out from hiding and joined Papá. "Tienen que tener cuidado,"[6] he warned us.

20   After lunch we went back to work. The sun kept beating down. The buzzing insects, the wet sweat, and the hot dry dust

---

[6]"You have to be careful," or "You have to watch out."

made the afternoon seem to last forever. Finally the mountains around the valley reached out and swallowed the sun. Within an hour it was too dark to continue picking. The vines blanketed the grapes, making it difficult to see the bunches. "Vámonos,"[7] said Papá, signaling to us that it was time to quit work. Papá then took out a pencil and began to figure out how much we had earned our first day. He wrote down numbers, crossed some out, wrote down some more. "Quince,"[8] he murmured.

When we arrived home, we took a cold shower underneath a waterhose. We then sat down to eat dinner around some wooden crates that served as a table. Mamá had cooked a special meal for us. We had rice and tortillas with "carne con chile,"[9] my favorite dish.

The next morning I could hardly move. My body ached all over. I felt little control over my arms and legs.

This feeling went on every morning for days until my muscles finally got used to the work.

It was Monday, the first week of November. The grape season was over and I could now go to school. I woke up early that morning and lay in bed, looking at the stars and savoring the thought of not going to work and of starting sixth grade for the first time that year. Since I could not sleep, I decided to get up and join Papá and Roberto at breakfast. I sat at the table across from Roberto, but I kept my head down. I did not want to look up and face him. I knew he was sad. He was not going to school today. He was not going tomorrow, or next week, or next month. He would not go until the cotton season was over, and that was sometime in February. I rubbed my hands together and watched the dry, acid-stained skin fall to the floor in little rolls.

When Papá and Roberto left for work, I felt relief. I walked to the top of a small grade next to the shack and watched the "Carcanchita" disappear in the distance in a cloud of dust.

25

---

[7]"Let's go."
[8]"Fifteen."
[9]A spicy bean and meat stew.

Two hours later, around eight o'clock, I stood by the side of the road waiting for school bus number twenty. When it arrived I climbed in. Everyone was busy either talking or yelling. I sat in an empty seat in the back.

When the bus stopped in front of the school, I felt very nervous. I looked out the bus window and saw boys and girls carrying books under their arms. I put my hands in my pant pockets and walked to the principal's office. When I entered I heard a woman's voice say: "May I help you?" I was startled. I had not heard English for months. For a few seconds I remained speechless. I looked at the lady who waited for an answer. My first instinct was to answer her in Spanish, but I held back. Finally, after struggling for English words, I managed to tell her that I wanted to enroll in the sixth grade. After answering many questions, I was led to the classroom.

Mr. Lema, the sixth grade teacher, greeted me and assigned me a desk. He then introduced me to the class. I was so nervous and scared at that moment when everyone's eyes were on me that I wished I were with Papá and Roberto picking cotton. After taking roll, Mr. Lema gave the class the assignment for the first hour. "The first thing we have to do this morning is finish reading the story we began yesterday," he said enthusiastically. He walked up to me, handed me an English book, and asked me to read. "We are on page 125," he said politely. When I heard this, I felt my blood rush to my head; I felt dizzy. "Would you like to read?" he asked hesitantly. I opened the book to page 125. My mouth was dry. My eyes began to water. I could not begin. "You can read later," Mr. Lema said understandingly.

For the rest of the reading period I kept getting angrier and angrier with myself. I should have read, I thought to myself.

30   During recess I went into the restroom and opened my English book to page 125. I began to read in a low voice, pretending I was in class. There were many words I did not know. I closed the book and headed back to the classroom.

Mr. Lema was sitting at his desk correcting papers. When I entered he looked up at me and smiled. I felt better. I walked up to him and asked if he could help me with the new words. "Gladly," he said.

The rest of the month I spent my lunch hours working on English with Mr. Lema, my best friend at school.

One Friday during lunch hour Mr. Lema asked me to take a walk with him to the music room. "Do you like music?" he asked me as we entered the building.

"Yes, I like corridos,"[10] I answered. He then picked up a trumpet, blew on it, and handed it to me. The sound gave me goose bumps. I knew that sound. I had heard it in many corridos. "How would you like to learn how to play it?" he asked. He must have read my face because before I could answer, he added, "I'll teach you how to play it during our lunch hours."

That day I could hardly wait to get home to tell Papá and   35
Mamá the great news. As I got off the bus, my little brothers and sisters ran up to meet me. They were yelling and screaming. I thought they were happy to see me, but when I opened the door to our shack, I saw that everything we owned was neatly packed in cardboard boxes.

Engaging the Text

1. How does the title relate to the general theme of the story? In formulating your response, consider the author's references to time and travel throughout. How might you use time or travel as a motif in your own writing and for what purpose?

2. How would you describe the narrator's, Panchito's, outlook in terms of age, class, gender, and nationality? Why does Jiménez present the story through this character's point of view? Do you find it an effective rhetorical strategy? Use examples from the text to support your ideas.

3. Identify passages in the story that portray seasonal rituals affecting Panchito's family. What do these depictions suggest about the migrant labor circuit? How does this circuit correlate to the cycle of the traditional school year?

---

[10]Traditional Mexican folk ballads.

4. Explain why Panchito and his brother Roberto hide from the school bus (paragraph 19). Next, summarize how Panchito later experiences the first day of sixth grade. Then locate points of comparison between his account and that of the first day of school chronicled by Nathan McCall in "Alford J. Mapp," another reading in this chapter. What do similarities and differences between these details suggest about the educational experiences and needs of students from diverse cultural backgrounds?

5. Discuss the significance of Spanish versus English in "The Circuit," including the author's use of code switching (writing that shifts between more than one language or dialect). What do these references to language suggest about Panchito's ability to succeed in school? Refer to the text to explain your answer.

Biography of an Armenian Schoolgirl
Naomi Shihab Nye

A lifelong chronicler of Arab-American experience, Naomi Shihab Nye was born in the United States to a Palestinian father and an American mother. During her childhood she moved with her family to Jerusalem (then a part of Jordan), where she attended a year of high school before returning to America. The author of ten books of poetry, she frequently confronts her dual heritage and geographic destiny in her verses. In *19 Varieties of Gazelle: Poems of the Middle East* (2002), Nye celebrates the beauty and inhabitants of her ancestral homeland while commenting on the region's cultural struggles and war-torn plight, often implicated in the identity politics of our own country. The same poetry collection also explores issues of gender, including arranged marriages, as in the poem included here, "Biography of an Armenian Schoolgirl."

Among her many literary honors, Nye has received a Guggenheim fellowship, four Pushcart Prizes, and awards from the Academy of American Poets as well as the Library of

Congress. Her *19 Varieties of Gazelle* was a finalist for the National Book Award.

─────────── ✦ ───────────

I have lived in the room of stone
where voices become bones
buried under us long ago.
You could dig for years
uncovering the same sweet dust.   5

My hands dream crescent-shaped cakes,
trapped moons on a narrow veined earth.
All day I am studying my hands—giving them
    new things to hold.

Travel, I say. They become boats.   10
Go—the bird squirms to detach from the arm.
Across the courtyards, a radio rises up and explodes.

What is the history of Europe to us if we cannot
    choose our own husbands?
Yesterday my father met with the widower,   15
    the man with no hair.
How will I sleep with him, I who have never slept
    away from my mother?

Once I bought bread from the vendor with the
    humped back.   20
I carried it home singing,
the days had doors in them
that would swing open in front of me.

Now I copy the alphabets of three languages,
imagining the loops in my Arabic letters are eyes.   25
What you do when you are tired of what you see,

what happens to the gray body
when it is laid in the earth,
these are the subjects which concern me.
But they teach algebra.   30
They pull our hair back and examine our nails.

Every afternoon, predictable passage of sun
    across a wall.

I would fly out of here. Travel, I say.
I would go so far away my life would be   35
   a small thing behind me.

They teach physics, chemistry.
I throw my book out the window,
watch the pages scatter like wings.
I stitch the professor's[1] jacket   40
to the back of his chair.

There is something else we were born for.
I almost remember it. While I write,
a ghost writes on the same tablet,
achieves a different sum.   45

Engaging the Text

1. Provide a brief gloss (a summary of actions, events, or ideas) of the poem as well as a description of its narrator, including her approximate grade level in school. How would you characterize the narrator's reaction to her "biography"? Hopeful? Accepting? Resigned? Refer to specific words and images to support your answers.

2. Discuss the theme of travel in the poem. What does it symbolize for the Armenian schoolgirl and why?

3. What subjects does the narrator study in school? How would you characterize the method of instruction under which she pursues them? Which subjects "concern" her (line 29) and why? Using your own experiences as a high school student as a source of comparison, discuss similarities or differences between your education and that of the Armenian schoolgirl.

4. The narrator of the poem states, "What is the history of Europe to us if we cannot / choose our own husbands?" (lines 13–14). Explain what she means in posing this question. Is it merely rhetorical? How do other characters named in the poem figure into this source of tension?

---

[1]A term sometimes used to refer to a secondary school teacher.

5. How does figurative language and inventive imagery used throughout the poem establish parallels between the narrator's ordinary awareness and flights of imagination? How does the movement between these two states of consciousness inform the alternative biography she speculates about in the final stanza of the poem?

The Next Ruling Class: Meet the Organization Kid

DAVID BROOKS

What does it take to get into an elite college or university? For some individuals, the process begins in the womb, listening to Mozart. From "play dates" (an oxymoron of sorts) and soccer camp to an endless succession of extracurricular activities, children's free time more and more mirrors the organizational structures of formal schooling. Curious about college students from privileged backgrounds raised in such a manner, David Brooks visited some at Princeton University. The title of his essay gives you an idea about what he found. What kinds of people do you think will be running the country in the near future? Do they resemble those profiled by Brooks in this essay?

A senior editor at the *Weekly Standard* and the author of a book about bourgeois-bohemian culture titled *Bobos in Paradise* (2000), Brooks is a frequent contributor to the *Atlantic Monthly*, in which this essay first appeared.

───────────── ◆ ─────────────

A few months ago I went to Princeton University to see what the young people who are going to be running our country in a few decades are like. Faculty members gave me the names of a few dozen articulate students, and I sent them e-mails, inviting them out to lunch or dinner in small groups. I would go to sleep in my hotel room at around midnight each night, and when I awoke, my mailbox would be full of replies—sent at 1:15 A.M., 2:59 A.M., 3:23 A.M.

In our conversations I would ask the students when they got around to sleeping. One senior told me that she went to bed around two and woke up each morning at seven; she could afford that much rest because she had learned to supplement her full day of work by studying in her sleep. As she was falling asleep she would recite a math problem or a paper topic to herself; she would then sometimes dream about it, and when she woke up, the problem might be solved. I asked several students to describe their daily schedules, and their replies sounded like a session of Future Workaholics of America: crew practice at dawn, classes in the morning, resident-adviser duty, lunch, study groups, classes in the afternoon, tutoring disadvantaged kids in Trenton, a cappella practice, dinner, study, science lab, prayer session, hit the StairMaster, study a few hours more. One young man told me that he had to schedule appointment times for chatting with his friends. I mentioned this to other groups, and usually one or two people would volunteer that they did the same thing. "I just had an appointment with my best friend at seven this morning," one woman said. "Or else you lose touch."

There are a lot of things these future leaders no longer have time for. I was on campus at the height of the election season, and I saw not even one Bush or Gore poster. I asked around about this and was told that most students have no time to read newspapers, follow national politics, or get involved in crusades. One senior told me she had subscribed to the *New York Times* once, but the papers had just piled up unread in her dorm room. "It's a basic question of hours in the day," a student journalist told me. "People are too busy to get involved in larger issues. When I think of all that I have to keep up with, I'm relieved there are no bigger compelling causes." Even the biological necessities get squeezed out. I was amazed to learn how little dating goes on. Students go out in groups, and there is certainly a fair bit of partying on campus, but as one told me, "People don't have time or energy to put into real relationships." Sometimes they'll have close friendships and "friendships with privileges" (meaning with sex), but often they don't get serious until they are a few years out of college and meet again at a reunion—after their careers are on track and they can begin to spare the time.

Not just Princetonians lead a frenetic, tightly packed existence. Kids of all stripes lead lives that are structured, supervised, and stuffed with enrichment. Time-analysis studies done at the University of Michigan's Institute for Social Research provide the best picture of the trend: From 1981 to 1997 the amount of time that children aged three to twelve spent playing indoors declined by 16 percent. The amount of time spent watching TV declined by 23 percent. Meanwhile, the amount of time spent studying increased by 20 percent and the amount of time spent doing organized sports increased by 27 percent. Drive around your neighborhood. Remember all those parks that used to have open fields? They have been carved up into neatly trimmed soccer and baseball fields crowded with parents in folding chairs who are watching their kids perform. In 1981 the association U.S. Youth Soccer had 811,000 registered players. By 1998 it had nearly three million.

Today's elite kids are likely to spend their afternoons and weekends shuttling from one skill-enhancing activity to the next. By the time they reach college, they take this sort of pace for granted, sometimes at a cost. In 1985 only 18 percent of college freshmen told the annual University of California at Los Angeles freshman norms survey that they felt "overwhelmed." Now 28 percent of college freshmen say they feel that way. 5

But in general they are happy with their lot. Neil Howe and William Strauss surveyed young people for their book *Millennials Rising* (2000); they found America's young to be generally a hardworking, cheerful, earnest, and deferential group. Howe and Strauss listed their respondents' traits, which accord pretty well with what I found at Princeton: "They're optimists . . . They're cooperative team players . . . They accept authority . . . They're rule followers." The authors paint a picture of incredibly wholesome youths who will correct the narcissism and nihilism of their Boomer parents.

In short, at the top of the meritocratic ladder we have in
America a generation of students who are extraordinarily
bright, morally earnest, and incredibly industrious. They like
to study and socialize in groups. They create and join organizations with great enthusiasm. They are responsible, safety-
conscious, and mature. They feel no compelling need to
rebel—not even a hint of one. They not only defer to authority;
they admire it. "Alienation" is a word one almost never hears
from them. They regard the universe as beneficent, orderly,
and meaningful. At the schools and colleges where the next
leadership class is being bred, one finds not angry revolution-
aries, despondent slackers, or dark cynics but the Organization
Kid.

They're so clean, inside and out. They seem like exactly the
sort of young people we older folks want them to be. Baby
Boomers may be tempted to utter a little prayer of gratitude:
Thank God our kids aren't the royal pains in the ass that we
were to our parents.

But the more I talked to them and observed them, the
more I realized that the difference between this and preceding generations is not just a matter of dress and comport-
ment. It's not just that these students work harder, are more
neatly groomed, and defer to their teachers more readily.
There are more fundamental differences: they have different
mental categories.

10   It takes a while to realize this, because unlike their prede-
cessors, they don't shout out their differences or declare them
in political or social movements. In fact, part of what makes
them novel is that they don't think they are new. They don't see
themselves as a lost generation or a radical generation or a
beatnik generation or even a Reaganite generation. They have
relatively little generational consciousness. That's because this
generation is for the most part not fighting to emancipate itself from the past. The most sophisticated people in preceding
generations were formed by their struggle to break free from
something. The most sophisticated people in this one aren't.

Today's elite college students don't live in that age of rebellion and alienation. They grew up in a world in which the

counterculture and the mainstream culture have merged with, and co-opted, each other. For them, it's natural that one of the top administrators at Princeton has a poster of the Beatles album *Revolver* framed on her office wall. It's natural that hippies work at ad agencies and found organic-ice-cream companies, and that hi-tech entrepreneurs quote Dylan and wear black jeans to work. For them, it's natural that parents should listen to Led Zeppelin, Jimi Hendrix, and the Doors—just like kids. They don't have the mental barriers that exist between, say, the establishment and rebels, between respectable society and the subversive underground. For them, all those categories are mushed together. "They work for Save the Children and Merrill Lynch and they don't see a contradiction," says Jeffrey Herbst, the politics professor. Moreover, nothing in their environment suggests that the world is ill constructed or that life is made meaningful only by revolt. There have been no senseless bloodbaths like World War I and Vietnam, no crushing economic depressions, no cycles of assassination and rioting to foment disillusionment. They've mostly known parental protection, prosperity, and peace.

During most of the twentieth century the basic ways of living were called into question, but now those fundamental debates are over, at least among the young elite. Democracy and dictatorship are no longer engaged in an epic struggle; victorious democracy is the beneficent and seemingly natural order. No more fundamental arguments pit capitalism against socialism; capitalism is so triumphant that we barely even contemplate an alternative. Radicals no longer assault the American family and the American home; we accept diverse family patterns but celebrate family and community togetherness. The militant feminists of the 1960s are mostly of a grandmotherly age now. Even theological conflicts have settled down; it's fashionable to be religious so long as one is not aggressively so.

Unlike their elders, in other words, these young people are not part of an insurrection against inherited order. They are not even part of the conservative reaction against the insurrection. The debates of the Reagan years are as distant as the trial of the

Chicago Seven,[1] which is as distant as the Sacco and Vanzetti[2] case. It's not that they reject one side of that culture war, or embrace the other. They've just moved on. As people in northern California would say, they're living in a different place.

The world they live in seems fundamentally just. If you work hard, behave pleasantly, explore your interests, volunteer your time, obey the codes of political correctness, and take the right pills to balance your brain chemistry, you will be rewarded with a wonderful ascent in the social hierarchy. You will get into Princeton and have all sorts of genuinely interesting experiences open to you. You will make a lot of money—but more important, you will be able to improve yourself. You will be a good friend and parent. You will be caring and conscientious. You will learn to value the really important things in life. There is a fundamental order to the universe, and it works. If you play by its rules and defer to its requirements, you will lead a pretty fantastic life.

Engaging the Text

1. What gets established in the opening paragraphs of the essay about the students whom Brooks interviewed at Princeton? How does the author reveal his attitude toward his subjects? Explain your answer.
2. Brooks argues that "kids of all stripes" lead hectic lives. Underline all the statistics in paragraphs 3–4 that support his position. Do you find the statistics more or less conclusive than the anecdotal evidence attributed to the Princeton students? How would you have replied to the survey Brooks cites? Make a list of your own daily campus routine. Does it in any way resemble those described in the es-

---

[1]Seven radicals accused of and put on trial for conspiring to incite a riot at the 1968 Democratic National Convention in Chicago.

[2]Political anarchists Nicola Sacco and Bartolomeo Vanzetti, tried, convicted and executed in 1927 for a Braintree, Massachusetts, robbery and murder. Many observers believed that they were innocent, charged not because of what they did but because of their beliefs.

say? What does all of this information suggest to you about college life in the twenty-first century?

3. Using information presented in the essay, provide a definition for "organization kid." Brooks seems to be both critical and accepting of such an individual. Summarize the grounds for his dual perspective as presented in paragraphs 8–11.

4. Brooks claims that fundamental debates about "the basic ways of living" familiar to twentieth-century thinkers no longer compel "the young elite" (paragraph 12). Make a list of the topics to which Brooks refers. Do you agree that young people no longer take interest in them? Explain your answer.

5. According to the last paragraph of the essay, how can one "lead a pretty fantastic life"? Does the essay suggest that a college education plays a role in this outcome? Why or why not?

CHAPTER 2

Sports

Trail Blazer

HUNKI YUN

Historically, golf has been considered an elite pastime, engaged in primarily by white, male players who can afford the game's expensive equipment and country club course fees. Yet the complexion and gender of the sport have changed in recent times. Chi Chi Rodriguez, who learned to play the game in his native Puerto Rico with clubs he fashioned out of guava tree limbs, is now an established figure in the United States on the PGA (Professional Golfers' Association) circuit. LPGA (Ladies Professional Golf Association) sensation Annika Sorenstam crossed the gender divide in 2003 as the only woman to qualify for the PGA Tour since Babe Didrikson Zaharias in 1945. But perhaps no player has electrified the sport as much as Tiger Woods, who identifies himself as "Cablinasian," encompassing his black, Indian, white, Chinese, and Thai ancestry. Though perplexed by being called upon as a spokesperson for ethnic and gender reform in the sport, Woods has continued to pave the way for golfers such as Kyung Ju (K. J.) Choi, himself characterized as a "trail blazer" in this profile by Hunki Yun.

Born in South Korea, Yun moved to the United States at age six and grew up on Long Island. As an Urban Studies major at Columbia University, he wrote his senior thesis on illegal Chinese immigration. A sports writer who has authored books as well as contributed to *Golf Digest* and the *Orlando Sentinel*, he is currently executive editor of *GOLF Magazine*.

———————— ✦ ————————

A bug is a bug, unless you're standing in a store 7,000 miles from home trying to decipher the hieroglyphics that indicate which of the millions of different types of insects a particular spray will kill. Luckily for Kyung Ju (K.J.) Choi, he had brought a trusty codebreaker, his 5-year-old son, with him. David read the labels and picked the right spray for the job.

"My son teaches me English," says the 32-year-old Choi, whose language isn't as polished as his game, which was good enough to win twice last year, making him the first Korean winner on the PGA Tour. But as Choi talks about himself in his native Korean, the feeling is that if he applied himself to learning English the same way he did to golf, he eventually could win a Pulitzer Prize.

Choi, the son of a rice farmer, grew up on Wando, a group of islands off the southwest coast of South Korea, and he didn't pick up his first golf club until he was 16, at the suggestion of a teacher who thought the aspiring powerlifter might have a talent for golf. "Both have a strong element of timing," Choi says.

Athleticism aside, there were a lot of obstacles for Choi before he could reach the PGA Tour—or even become a pro. Not only did he do so, but he arrived well ahead of schedule.

In addition to starting at a late age for a Tour player—only a handful of major winners, including Greg Norman and Larry Nelson, started later—Choi had another major disadvantage. Tiger Woods used to sit in a high chair and watch his father hit balls into a net in the garage. Growing up, Phil Mickelson and Ernie Els had practice greens in their yards. Sergio Garcia's father was a teaching pro, as was David Duval's. Their golf was accessible. Not so Choi's. 5

There was a driving range on Wando, but the nearest course was on the mainland, three hours away. Choi had to compensate for the lack of access with a tremendous will to practice, play, and improve. Several months after his first range visit, Choi began making the trip to the mainland a couple of times a week.

"I would leave the house at three in the morning," Choi says, "arrive at 6:30, have breakfast, and play all day—students had unlimited access. My record is 70 holes in one day. I got home at one in the morning."

Although not even close to being good, Choi was infatuated with golf and embarked on a career path even Walter Mitty[1] might have found delusional. "After about eight months, my dreams started forming," Choi says. "I thought I could have a career in golf, but my parents had no idea what being a golf pro was. I didn't listen to anyone; it was my decision alone."

After high school, Choi's progress stalled during his military service, compulsory for all South Korean males—the country is still technically at war with North Korea. His big breakthrough came after returning to civilian life. "Once those [military] responsibilities were lifted, my mind was cleared," he says. "It left me free to focus on golf. I was 21 when I first broke par. Once I went under it, I never went back."

10   Choi turned pro several years later, in 1994, and the dreams kept getting bigger, as did his determination. "At the time, Korea was the entire world for me," he says. "But if I could be ranked first in Korea, I would go to the World Cup. That was no easy task. I went to the World Cup in 1997 [at the Ocean Course at Kiawah Island], and after that my mind was made up. From then on, playing throughout Asia was no longer the goal. It was the U.S."

After seeing the first-class conditions and competition, Choi knew his place was the PGA Tour. "I gave myself five years to get ready for the U.S. Not only did I practice, I ate more Western food, like Burger King. Then, my ranking in Japan in 1999 [he won twice on the Japan PGA Tour] made me exempt to the finals of Q-School.[2] I received a chance earlier than planned. I didn't know if I was ready, but I grabbed it."

Choi qualified for the 2000 PGA Tour by tying for the final spot. As before, there was a plan: top 100 the first year, top 60

---

[1]Title character in James Thurber's 1942 short story "The Secret Life of Walter Mitty," he imagines himself the hero of his own extravagant fantasies.
[2]Annual three-stage PGA qualifying tournament known as the "Q-School."

the next, top 30, and so on. Despite having to return to Q-School after a difficult rookie year—"Before I knew it, eight months had passed. Just as I was getting comfortable, the season was over"—Choi is right on schedule. In 2002, his third year on Tour, Choi earned $2.2 million to finish 17th on the money list, along with the two wins.

He also has made the transition to living in the U.S., having settled in The Woodlands, Texas, outside Houston, with his wife, Hyunjung, and children, Amanda, who will be 1 in March, and David. "We never have any trouble communicating," says Chris DiMarco, whose son, Cristian, is a frequent playmate of David's on the road. "He gives you a little smile if he doesn't understand you, but he's too polite to tell you so. It's amazing how much you can communicate through more than talking."

Choi always had the will, but he didn't win until he developed a repeatable swing under the tutelage of *GOLF Magazine* Top 100 Teacher Phil Ritson. "He has a great work ethic; he is very strong mentally. But his worst enemy is speed—*polli, polli,*" says Ritson, using the Korean word for hurry.

Hurrying may be a detriment to his swing, but it hasn't hurt his career. After giving the Korean women—Se Ri Pak, Grace Park, Mi Hyun Kim—a head start in the U.S., Choi has caught up. Normally, his achievements would have made him an instant hero at home. But he couldn't have picked a worse year: In soccer-mad South Korea, Choi was overshadowed by a national team that cohosted the World Cup, won its first Cup game, then reached the quarterfinals, galvanizing the entire country.

Choi doesn't mind. He is a big soccer fan, and got up in the middle of the night to watch the telecasts. Plus, he knows if he wins a major, he will be as popular an athlete as Korea has ever seen.

That's no easy feat, but if he pulls it off, it might just be sooner rather than later. *Polli, polli.*

Engaging the Text

1. Notice the metaphors and figures of speech used in the first two paragraphs of the profile to describe Choi's struggles to master English. By writing the introduction in this way, what does Yun establish about Choi's character?

2. Summarize Choi's rise from "aspiring powerlifter" in South Korea (paragraph 3) to pro golfer in the United States. Discuss ways in which Choi's career path embodies the so-called American Dream. Can you relate to Choi's perseverance in any way? If so, provide examples to illustrate your answer.

3. What does Yun's essay suggest about how sports heroes in the United States are made? How does it reflect the importance and popularity of sports on a global scale?

4. What evidence does Yun provide to suggest that Choi and his family are making "the transition to living in the U.S." (paragraph 12)? Do you find it persuasive? Why or why not?

5. Throughout the essay, Yun makes use of direct quotations from Choi. What are the strengths of this rhetorical strategy? Do you find it effective in illustrating the theme of the essay? How does ending the essay with transliteration (to approximate a word written in the language of one alphabet into equivalent sounds in another) of a Korean phrase emphasize Yun's overall purpose for writing?

The Last Shot

Darcy Frey

This award-winning essay tells the story of teenage basketball stars from the projects of Coney Island. It became the basis for Darcy Frey's book *The Last Shot: City Streets, Basketball Dreams*, released the same year as the popular documentary film *Hoop Dreams*, which chronicles the lives of inner-city high school basketball sensations in Chicago. Both the book and the movie explore how faith in the game permits such players to dream of college scholarships and NBA glory, despite the pressures of academics, economics, and athletic competitiveness. To what extent does Frey call attention in his essay to the exploitation of teenage athletes? Is it unreasonable for them to believe that excelling at sports will lead to a potentially better life?

"The Last Shot" won the National Magazine Award and the Livingston Award and appeared in *The Best American Es-*

says 1994. A freelance writer since graduating from Oberlin College in 1984, Frey is a contributing editor at *Harper's* and the *New York Times Magazine.*

———————————— ◆ ————————————

Russell Thomas places his right sneaker one inch behind the three-point line, considers the basket with a level gaze, cocks his wrist to shoot, then suddenly looks around. Has he spotted me, watching from the corner of the playground? No, something else is up: he is lifting his nose to the wind like a spaniel, he is gauging air currents. He waits until the wind settles, bits of trash feathering lightly to the ground. Then he sends a twenty-five-foot jump shot arcing through the soft summer twilight. It drops without a sound through the dead center of the bare iron rim. So does the next one. So does the one after that. Alone in the gathering dusk, Russell works the perimeter against imaginary defenders, unspooling jump shots from all points. Few sights on Brooklyn playgrounds stir the hearts and minds of the coaches and scouts who recruit young men for college basketball teams quite like Russell's jumper; they have followed its graceful trajectory ever since he made varsity at Abraham Lincoln High School, in Coney Island, two years ago. But the shot is merely the final gesture, the public flourish of a private regimen that brings Russell to this court day and night. Avoiding pickup games, he gets down to work: an hour of three-point shooting, then wind sprints up the fourteen flights in his project stairwell, then back to the court, where (much to his friends' amusement) he shoots one-handers ten feet from the basket while sitting in a chair.

At this hour Russell usually has the court to himself; most of the other players won't come out until after dark, when the thick humid air begins to stir with night breezes and the court lights come on. But this evening is turning out to be a fine one—cool and foggy. The low, slanting sun sheds a feeble pink light over the silvery Atlantic a block away, and milky sheets of fog roll off the ocean and drift in tatters along the project walkways. The air smells of sewage and saltwater. At the far end of the court, where someone has torn a hole in the chicken-wire fence, other players climb through and begin warming up.

Like most of New York's impoverished and predominantly black neighborhoods, Coney Island does not exactly shower its youth with opportunity. In the early 1960s, urban renewal came to Coney Island in the form of a vast tract of housing projects, packed so densely along a twenty-block stretch that a new skyline rose suddenly behind the boardwalk and amusement park. The experiment of public housing, which has isolated the nation's urban poor from the hearts of their cities, may have failed here in even more spectacular fashion because of Coney Island's utter remoteness. In this neighborhood, on a peninsula at the southern tip of Brooklyn, there are almost no stores, no trees, no police; just block after block of gray cement projects—hulking, prisonlike, and jutting straight into the sea.

Yet even in Coney Island there are some uses to which a young man's talent, ambition, and desire to stay out of harm's way may be put: there is basketball. Hidden behind the projects are dozens of courts, and every night they fill with restless teenagers, there to remain for hours until exhaustion or the hoodlums take over. The high-school dropouts and the aging players who never made it to college usually show up for a physical game at a barren strip of courts by the water known as Chop Chop Land, where bruises and minutes played are accrued at a one-to-one ratio. The younger kids congregate for rowdy games at Run-and-Gun Land. The court there is short and the rims are low, so everyone can dunk, and the only pass ever made is the one inbounding the ball.

5   The neighborhood's best players—the ones, like Russell, with aspirations—practice a disciplined, team-driven style of basketball at this court by the O'Dwyer projects, which has been dubbed the Garden after the New York Knicks' arena. In a neighborhood ravaged by the commerce of drugs, the Garden offers a tenuous sanctuary. A few years ago, community activists petitioned the housing authority to install night lights. And the players themselves resurfaced the court and put up regulation-height rims that snap back after a player dunks. Russell may be the only kid at the Garden who practices his defensive footwork while holding a ten-pound brick

in each hand, but no one here treats the game as child's play. Even the hoodlums decline to vandalize the Garden, because in Coney Island the possibility of transcendence through basketball is an article of faith.

Corey is Russell's best friend and one of Lincoln High's other star seniors. He, too, expects to play college ball. But he specializes in ironic detachment and normally shows up courtside with his Walkman merely to watch for girls beneath his handsome, hooded eyes. Tonight he is wearing a fresh white T-shirt, expertly ripped along the back and sleeves to reveal glimpses of his sculpted physique; denim shorts that reach to his knees; and a pair of orange sneakers that go splendidly with his lid—a tan baseball cap with orange piping, which he wears with the bill pointing skyward.

Last spring the Lincoln team, with Russell leading the way, won the New York City public-school championship in a rout at Madison Square Garden that was broadcast citywide on cable TV. But one can never predict what may happen to Russell, because, as Corey observes, "Russell is Russell." I can guess what this means: Russell lives in one of the neighborhood's toughest projects, and misfortune often seems to shadow him. Last year a fight between Russell and his girlfriend turned violent. Terrified that his college scholarship had just been replaced by a stiff prison term, Russell climbed to the top of one of Coney Island's highest buildings. It took almost half an hour of reasoned talk by his high-school coach and members of the Sixtieth Precinct to bring him back from the edge.[1]

Russell may be tightly wound, but no Coney Island player can avoid for long the agonizing pressures that might bring a teenager with his whole life ahead of him to the edge of a roof. Basketball newsletters and scouting reports are constantly scrutinizing the players, and practically every day some coach

---

[1]Some New York City newspapers withheld Russell's name when reporting this incident. In keeping with the practice of withholding the names of minors involved in suicide threats or attempts, [Frey] changed Russell's name and the name of his mother in this article. No other names have been altered.

shows up—appraising, coaxing, negotiating, and, as often as not, making promises he never keeps. Getting that scholarship offer is every player's dream—in anticipation, no one steps outside in Coney Island without a Syracuse cap or a St. John's sweatshirt. But in reality only a handful of the neighborhood's players have ever made it to such top four-year programs; most have been turned back by one obstacle or another in high school. Others who have enrolled in college never saw their dream to completion.

SEPTEMBER

Abraham Lincoln High School is a massive yellow-brick building of ornate stonework and steel-gated windows a few blocks north of the boardwalk. As Coney Island has deteriorated, so has Lincoln High, though the school itself sits about a mile from the projects at the end of Ocean Parkway, a stately, tree-lined boulevard. Across the parkway are Brighton Beach and several other Jewish neighborhoods, but the kids from those areas are usually sent elsewhere for their education, as Lincoln has become, little by little, a ghetto school for the projects.

10   A malaise has set in at Lincoln, as it has at so many inner-city public schools. Students regularly walk in and out of class, sleep at their desks, throw projectiles through doorways at friends in the hall. In the teachers' cafeteria, conversation often reverts to pension plans and whether the 2,500 Lincoln kids are as bad as last year or worse.

     Into this chaos walk the college coaches—pinstriped and paisley-tied, bearing four-color photos of sold-out college arenas and statistics on how many games their teams play on national television. Usually they precede their visits by dropping the players brief notes, like the one from a Fordham coach to a Lincoln player describing how one of the college's basketball stars became rich beyond his wildest dreams. "This could be you someday," the coach wrote. "See how Fordham can change your life?" The coach signed off with the salutation, "Health, Happiness, and Hundreds."

Most of the coaches are leery of Corey right now; he spends too much time with girls, and despite his intelligence, his grades are among the worst on the team. Stephon[2] is, as far as the NCAA rules are concerned, off-limits for the next three years. So they come to see Russell. In the first week of school, Wichita State, St. Bonaventure, and the University of Delaware have paid him visits. After school today he sits down with Rod Baker, the head coach at the University of California at Irvine.

"My apologies for not coming to see you before, but the fact is one of our players just dropped out and suddenly we need another guard." Coach Baker is a trim, handsome black man wearing a natty blue suit, tasseled loafers, and a gleaming gold NCAA ring. "And the first person we thought of was Russell Thomas. I'm not bullshitting you. Frankly, I think you're an impact player, a franchise player. Five years from now, I wouldn't be surprised if people were saying, 'Remember when Russell Thomas came in and changed the fortunes of Cal-Irvine?' " Baker runs a finger down each side of his well-groomed mustache. Russell smiles uncertainly.

The recruiting circus has been a fact of life for Russell and his friends ever since they were in junior high. But today Russell seems agitated in the old way, restless with an emotion he can't identify. "You know, I used to say that I couldn't wait to be a senior," he says. "But I got to worry about classes, the season, recruiting, the SATs. That's *a lot* of pressure." According to NCAA rules, students who want to play sports at a four-year, Division I school, those with the nation's top athletic programs, must enter college having maintained at least a 70 average in high school and having received a combined score of 700 on the math and verbal sections of the SATs—the last an insurmountable obstacle to many black players with poor educations and little experience taking standardized tests. Failing that, a player must earn a two-year degree at a junior college

---

[2]The youngest of a Coney Island family basketball-player dynasty, Stephon Marbury graduated from Georgia Tech in 1996 and was drafted into the NBA. He currently plays for the Phoenix Suns.

before moving on to a four-year school. Many Division I coaches, however, refuse to recruit junior-college players, considering them damaged goods. So players who don't go directly to a four-year school often never get to play top college ball or earn their bachelor's degrees.

15   The first time Russell took the SATs, he received a combined score somewhere in the mid-500s. (You receive 400 points for signing your name.) This year he gave up his lunch period to study, and lately he's been carrying around a set of vocabulary flash cards, which he pulls out whenever there isn't a basketball in his hands. By dint of tremendous effort, Russell had also brought his average up to 78—the highest on the team. These are extraordinary developments for someone whose schooling over the years has been so bad that he had never, until recently, finished a book or learned the fundamentals of multiplication, even as he was being called upon to answer reading comprehension and algebra questions on the SATs. "I used to think there were smart people and dumb people, but that's not true," Russell says forcefully. "Everybody's got the same brain. They say a human mind can know a thousand words—it's like a little computer! But you got to practice." He pauses. "But how come it's always the guys who don't study who get their 700s? Seems like the guys who work hard always get screwed. But oh, well."

Engaging the Text

1. How does the title of the essay prepare readers for what comes next? What is the connection between its irony and Frey's observations that "in Coney Island the possibility of transcendence through basketball is an article of faith" (paragraph 5)?

2. Note how Frey establishes setting in the opening paragraphs of the essay by appealing to the senses. What do these introductory images convey about the socioeconomic circumstances of inner-city basketball players, such as Russell Thomas?

3. In describing activities at Abraham Lincoln High School, what does Frey suggest about the ability of "so many

inner-city public schools" (paragraph 10) to prepare students for higher education? Do you agree or disagree with the author's implications? Give specific reasons for your point of view.

4. What part does the entry of college coaches and recruiters play in the narrative? Do these characters appear as emblems of hope or exploitation? Explain your answer.

5. Frey characterizes the possibility of receiving "a combined score of 700 on the math and verbal sections of the SATs" as "an insurmountable obstacle to many black players" (paragraph 14). How does this observation relate to his argument overall? Why does Frey document in the final paragraph the fact that Russell, a high school senior, "had never, until recently, finished a book or learned the fundamentals of multiplication"?

The Best Pickup-Basketball Player in America
Timothy Harper

Urban basketball courts can become a stage where cultural differences play out in tough pickup games between players from diverse backgrounds. The 1992 film *White Men Can't Jump*, which stars Wesley Snipes as a black basketball hustler and Woody Harrelson as his white counterpart, humorously explores this asphalt phenomenon by preying on stereotypes surrounding the ability of individual players. In this essay, Timothy Harper continues the critique of inner-city playground competitions by dubbing a fifty-one-year-old white man "the best pickup-basketball player in America."

An award-winning freelance writer, editor, and consultant, Harper teaches at the Columbia University Graduate School of Journalism. His publishing credits include *Reader's Digest*, *Forbes*, *Time*, the *Washington Post*, the *Detroit News*, and many other magazines and journals. This essay first appeared in the April 2000 issue of the *Atlantic Monthly*.

——————— ✦ ———————

Late on a Saturday afternoon the best pickup-basketball player in America is ready to look for a game. He is wearing battered low-cut sneakers, sagging mismatched socks that may once have been white, a logo-free T-shirt that is fraying at the seams, plain cotton shorts that are unfashionably unbaggy and several inches above the knee, and a brace on his left leg. He is fifty-one years old, and his name is Allan Dalton.

Other husbands and fathers of his age in the leafy suburb of Franklin Lakes, New Jersey, are kicking back, stowing golf bags, putting away garden tools, firing up gas grills. Dalton climbs into his BMW and weaves along the winding lanes, past lawns tended by gardeners better dressed than he is, toward the spare, hard playgrounds of New York City: Harlem, Riverside Park, West Fourth Street, Chinatown, Battery Park, Brooklyn. He will keep driving until he finds a good pickup game. He may be the only white person on the court, and he will almost certainly be the oldest, by twenty or thirty years. The other players may argue over who has to play with this old guy. At first no one will pass Dalton the ball. Within an hour, however, the other players will be touching knuckles with Dalton and hoping to play on his team in the next game.

Dalton is living the hoop dreams of many aging pickup players who refuse to give up the game of basketball. "You still play?" they are asked, often skeptically, sometimes incredulously. At some point they were told, or they recognized on their own, that they were not good enough to play with a certain team, in a certain league, or at a certain level. But they keep playing, sometimes with old friends, sometimes with strangers—with whoever shows up on the court. They no longer dream of playing for the high school team, or for a major college, or in the NBA. They dream of doing what Dalton does: getting in pickup games anywhere and everywhere they can, playing good team basketball within their limitations, and winning not just games but also the respect of the other players.

Allan Dalton is not always the most skilled player on the court, although he was good enough to rate a mention in a 1995 *Boston Sunday Herald* article about Boston's best playground players ever (Dalton is a Bostonian born and raised). He can't dunk anymore, and every year he encounters more young guys he can't beat off the dribble. But he's the player—or at least the kind of player—that any true pickup-basketball devotee wants to play with or against. Physically he's not intimidating: six feet two, about 185 pounds, with a weakened left knee that probably should have surgery someday, if he ever quits playing. He has broken his foot, his arm, some ribs, and his nose playing basketball. He once had a herniated disk that kept him off the courts for six months, and he still gets occasional backaches. His vision is fading, and he is talking about getting contacts or having laser surgery on his eyes. He still plays any position, depending on what talent is on the court with him, but he usually takes over as point guard. He controls games.

He will play with anyone. At the end of a grueling two-hour session in August heat he'll put his shoes back on to go one-on-one against a sixty-seven-year-old who can't find anyone else to play. He will play with disabled guys and with young girls. "Dalton would shovel off a court at three a.m. in a snowstorm and then bang on the door of a convent till he got three nuns to come out and go two-on-two" is the admiring comment of a regular at the YMCA in Ridgewood, New Jersey, one of Dalton's frequent pickup haunts.

Teammates quickly learn that Dalton will make them look good. After his first couple of no-look passes bounce off a teammate's head, he'll stop throwing passes the player can't catch. When he sees that a teammate likes a certain spot on the low block for turnarounds, even against bigger guys, he'll wait for the player to get into position and then give him the ball where and when he wants it. Teammates know he trusts them, and they trust him. At game point he'll motion for a teammate who shoots well from the outside to set a pick for him at the top of the key. Both Dalton's man and the teammate's defender will go with Dalton, naturally. Double-teamed, Dalton will flip the ball back to the all-alone teammate, who has set his feet and is waiting to shoot the jumper that will win the game.

A Ridgewood Y regular describes having seen Dalton get into a trash-talking dunkfest on a tough playground in Miami. When Dalton finally touched the ball, several minutes into the game, he got his teammates' attention with his signature move, a behind-the-back feint. From the top of the key he faked left with a jab step and then drove past his defender down the right side of the lane. As the opposing center stepped up to cover him, Dalton cupped his right-handed dribble behind his hip and looked left, as if he was going to pass behind his back. The opposing center, and everyone else on the court, looked and leaned in the direction of the seemingly inevitable behind-the-back pass. But Dalton pulled the ball back in and swept past the center for an unmolested lay-up. The next time down the court his teammates gave him the ball. He brushed off his defender on a pick and went up for a three-pointer, but instead of shooting he zipped a bullet pass to a teammate alone beneath the basket for another lay-up. Within minutes the game was transformed. Dalton was at the point, and the play had gone from undisciplined one-on-one to what could have been a Princeton instructional video, complete with pick-and-rolls, screens off the ball, and back-door cuts and passes. Dalton's team won four straight games, and his teammates were certain he was a former NBA player. "What's your name, man?" they asked. "Who'd you play for?"

Allan Dalton was a schoolboy star at Hyde Park High School, in Boston, and averaged twenty-six points a game as a senior in 1970–1971 for Suffolk University, a Division II team in Boston. He was incredibly quick, and could drive past almost anyone back then. One of his teammates in club games during the 1970s was Jim O'Brien, a former Boston College star who played in the American Basketball Association and is now the head basketball coach at Ohio State. "Allan was your prototypical gym rat," O'Brien says. "I always called him the poor man's Pete Maravich.[1] Great shooter, great moves . . . an unerring ability to pass the ball."

---

[1]Known as "Pistol Pete," Maravich played for the NBA from 1970–1980, most notably as a star on the Utah Jazz. He died in 1988.

In the spring of 1971 Dalton was drafted by the Boston Celtics, but he didn't make the team that started Dave Cowens, John Havlicek, Don Nelson, Jo Jo White, and Don Chaney, and went 56–26 in 1971–1972. He played one season professionally in Greece, as Alexos Daltos, and another with a touring Lithuanian-American team, under the name Janus Ambrosius. He played club basketball for several years, and when Celtics officials told him he might still earn a spot with the NBA team, he spent a year as a player-coach for the Quincy Chiefs in the old Eastern League, the precursor of today's Continental Basketball Association.

Unlike many frustrated would-be pros, Dalton had little trouble putting his hoop dreams behind him. "I wanted to start a life, a family, a career," he says. By the late 1970s he was working in an office and was married, with three daughters. Basketball became a hobby that had to fit around family and career in evening, weekend, and occasional lunchtime pickup games. Over the past quarter of a century Dalton has played pickup basketball an average of three or four times a week, usually for at least two hours a session and sometimes for as long as six hours.

Dalton has played in all fifty states and in eight foreign countries. When his family wanted to vacation in Hawaii, Dalton would not book a resort until he found a nearby court. He reluctantly agreed to a vacation in the woods of Maine last summer, knowing he'd have difficulty finding a game. But he took a basketball along anyway, and one day walked and jogged twenty miles into the nearest town, dribbling all the way. "I wanted to work on my left hand," he told his wife.

Is he proud of his basketball ability? "No," Dalton says. "I'm proud that I've been the best man at eight weddings." In many ways, he says, his basketball career has been a failure, because he never made the NBA. Maybe, he muses, that's why he keeps playing—to prove himself. "I'm not impressed with myself as a basketball player," he says. "I'm more impressed with my good fortune in business." He is flattered to be called "the best" pickup-basketball player as long as the reference is to his love of the game rather than to his ability to play it. "I've yet to meet a person more dedicated to playing the game," he says. "I'm into basketball as much as anybody, but I'm not even the best over-fifty player around."

The end of his basketball career, or at least his career as a force on the playground, is looming. "It's not natural to be limping across the country seeking to play strenuous games with people thirty years younger," he concedes. "But basketball keeps me competitive. The day I stop playing basketball is probably the day I retire." He has vague thoughts of retiring to an inner-city coaching job. But he has also started contemplating the gloomy possibility that basketball, which he plays in part for health reasons, could end up killing him. Three times he has been on the court when a player has died, twice in the past year; one was a friend who passed away as Dalton administered CPR. Sometimes on Saturday evenings, back in his hotel room after a day proving himself yet again, on yet another playground, against yet another group of springy young legs, too tired to take off his sneakers, his head pounding from an exertion headache, he wonders whether he should have accepted one of those invitations to go out to dinner. But the next morning he's up early again, looking out the hotel window, hoping for sunshine so that he can play basketball, checking the breeze to see if he and his teammates can shoot from the outside.

Engaging the Text

1. Harper opens the essay by establishing Allan Dalton's age, race, socioeconomic class, and geographic residence. How do these cultural referents shape the extended profile that follows? Refer to explicit passages from the text to explain your answer.

2. More than once in the essay, Harper refers to Dalton's physical limitations as an aging athlete. What purpose does this descriptive strategy serve? Do you find it effective? Explain why or why not.

3. Using paragraphs 6 and 7 as models, discuss how process-analysis (the step-by-step explanation of a procedure, an activity, or a task) is used in this essay to lend credibility to Harper's thesis. How does this rhetorical device reflect the overall theme of the essay?

4. According to Harper, how difficult was Dalton's career move from "would-be pro" to office worker? Do you think that Dalton's cultural background contributed to his ability to make this transition? How does Dalton's situation compare to the career opportunities of the Coney Island basketball players, described in Darcy Frey's "The Last Shot," who don't earn college scholarships or turn pro? What do your findings suggest about the intersections between race, class, geography, and destiny in the United States?

5. Make a list of all the amateur basketball players introduced in Harper's essay as competing against Dalton. Next, summarize general details about their identities, such as race, age, and gender. What purpose does the presence of these characters serve? Can a playing field act as a location where cultural differences fade? Explain your answer, referring to the text for support.

Throwing Like a Guy: The Mystique of Innate Ability

COLETTE DOWLING

Historically, belief in female anatomical and physiological inferiority has prevented many women from realizing the joys and benefits of physical activity and competitive sports. But as the 1999 World Cup champion U.S. women's soccer team proved, new young athletes are shattering this previously held attitude. Colette Dowling investigates the premise of innate physical ability in her nationally acclaimed book *The Frailty Myth: Women Approaching Physical Equality* (2000), in which this essay appeared. The central argument of Dowling's book is that women succumb to societal pressures to appear weak in order to seem "feminine." Do you agree with this position? Can women be equal to men as long as men are physically stronger? Is strength biologically determined or only a matter of learning and training?

An internationally recognized writer and lecturer whose work has been translated into twenty languages, Dowling is the author of numerous magazine articles and books, including the 1981 bestseller *The Cinderella Complex*.

———————— ✦ ————————

An early notion about motor abilities—and one that's still widespread among people not familiar with the research—was that motor skills are the result of a single, all-encompassing ability—a kind of body IQ. "Athletic ability," "coordination," "motor ability"—whatever the term used, the implication was the same: If a person had a strong *general* motor ability, he would do well at almost any motor task. If Johnnie could throw, that is, it was a foregone conclusion that he could hit, catch, kick to a fare-thee-well, and punch out an opponent's lights if need be. If a boy did one thing well, he was assumed to have "the Power" and likely would be encouraged to try developing other skills. The reverse was how it was seen for girls. If Jenny *couldn't* throw (or hit or catch), it was assumed she was useless in every physical domain. Jenny wouldn't get the chance to try other sports—in part because teachers had written her off as hopeless and in part because she'd written herself off.

The idea that motor ability was "general" came out of the same research on cognitive abilities done in the 1930s that produced the concept of a "general" intelligence—the capacity to act purposefully, think rationally, and deal effectively with one's environment. This hypothesized "general" mental ability—which supposedly could be measured and was called "intelligence quotient," or "IQ"—was thought to be important for success in every mental arena. Ultimately, as we know, the theory of IQ didn't hold up, as researchers came to a more sophisticated understanding of how minds work. "Instead of a single dimension called intellect, on which individuals can be rank-ordered, there are vast differences among individuals in their intellectual strengths and weaknesses and also in their styles of attack in cognitive pursuit," writes Howard Gardner in *Multiple Intelligences*. Gardner, a cognitive psychologist at Harvard, was the first to identify the existence of what he called "body-kinesthetic intelligence"—I call it physical intelli-

950s through the 1990s, Dowling
ng like a guy" is a learned skill.
Dowling presents from this re-
position. How well does it con-
logos (logic)?
nvironmental causes possibly ac-
ifferences between girls and boys.
theory? If so, what environmental
in support of it?
ploys first-person plural "we" in a
in paragraph 9 of the essay. Make
opics for which the use of gender-
ld be appropriate, as for example
breast-feeding.

litical Football

TH CONNIFF

ghts Act of 1964 prohibiting race,
discrimination, Title IX was enacted
72 to promote gender equality in ed-
tutions that receive federal funding
discrimination in educational pro-
w "has become synonymous with the
ccording to commentator Ruth Con-
llege track star and one-time high
tistics show that Title IX has suc-
laying field between males and fe-
ly under attack by athletes, coaches,
rs, as Conniff reports in this essay
e *Nation*. Based on your experiences
, or critical observer, do you believe
ntinue to be equally divided between
programs?
or the *Progressive*, Conniff has con-
taries and articles to the *Washington*
es, the *Miami Herald*, and other na-

gence. It refers to the fact that our bodies learn, and we learn through them.

The rigid, unidimensional view of intelligence began unraveling in the 1950s and 1960s, when both general intellectual ability *and* general motor ability came to be seen as inaccurate and limiting. Franklin Henry, a psychologist at the University of California at Berkeley, discovered that different motor abilities are specific to particular tasks and function independently of one another. You could be great at throwing but lousy at sewing, for example. Or, like a brilliant neurosurgeon named Charlie Wilson (he was profiled in the *New Yorker* in 1999), you could have performed three thousand resections of pituitary tumors as small as 18 millimeters in diameter and still not be able to get off a good game of tennis. Wilson is good at other sports, but with tennis, for some reason, he has a problem with mental imaging. He just can't *see* the game in his mind.

Those who *can* see the game of tennis in their minds don't necessarily all see it in the same way. Partly it's a matter of the particular skills an individual has developed. Negotiating the wind, for example, is something one tennis player might have learned and another not. Martina Hingis was able to "recalibrate" inside "a virtual wind tunnel," as one onlooker put it, watching tennis balls behaving like stunt kites at the U.S. Open following Hurricane Dennis. Her opponent, Anke Huber, hadn't learned this skill. Hingis credits her wind-management finesse to her coach and mother, Melanie Molitor, who's been teaching her since she was an infant. It's a practiced skill that gives Martina the capacity to keep up with the erratic flight of a wind-driven ball. "You don't get born with that thing," she told a reporter. "You learn it."

In the 1980s those who were studying motor skills became interested in the gender differences in acquiring them. The distinction between the ability to *learn* a movement and the ability to *perform* it seemed relevant when making motor skill comparisons between males and females. Since it had been discovered that performance skills are actually learned, a salient question was now pressing: To what degree were scores on motor skills tests being affected by differences in what subjects had *learned*, and to what degree did they reflect "natural" differences in male and female abilities?

First, motor development researchers had to clarify what an ability actually is. They decided it's a relatively stable trait having to do with biological processes of growth and maturation, one that remains more or less unchanged by practice. A *skill*, by comparison, is modified by practice. Essentially it is learned. The much ballyhooed skill of throwing a baseball is *learned*. Boys aren't born with it.

There's a remarkable amount of literature comparing throwing in girls and boys. Only recently, though, have sports scientists attempted to investigate possible *environmental* causes for the performance differences. One fascinating 1996 study looked for a possible training effect to account for gender differences. Researchers wanted to know what the influence of *practice* might be. To find out, they made a comparison of dominant and nondominant arm throws. Videotapes were made of three age-groups of kids (seven to eight years, nine to ten years, and eleven to twelve years) performing forceful overarm throws with both their dominant and nondominant hands. The dominant-hand results were typical of those reported in earlier studies. One of these, for example, reported second-grade boys as throwing 72 percent faster than second-grade girls. But when the use of the nondominant hand was compared, what do you know? There were *no* differences in how fast boys and girls threw!

What could this mean? Simply, that *practice* is what gave boys superior throwing skills. If gender differences in performance were, in fact, "strongly related to biological factors," these researchers argued, "then gender differences should persist when children throw with their nondominant arm." In fact, performance differences between the use of boys' dominant and nondominant hands were so huge, it strengthened the authors' theory that practice, and practice only, is what gives boys the edge.

Until we [females] were allowed to develop our mental powers in the halls of higher academe, everyone thought our brains were weaker than men's. They still think our bodies are weaker. Sports sociologists interested in how gender differences in physical development are maintained have begun to talk about the political implications of "learned weakness" and

3. Citing studies from the
determines that "throwi
Summarize the evidenc
search that supports he
vince through appeals to

4. According to the text,
count for performance
Do you agree with this
factors would you name

5. Notice how Dowling en
gender-specific manner
a list of possible essay
specific pronouns wou
professional football or

Title IX: P

Modeled on the Civil Ri
color, and national origin
by the U.S. Congress in 19
ucation. Prohibiting insti
from practicing gender
grams or activities, the la
rise of women's sports,"
niff, herself a former c
school coach. While sta
ceeded in leveling the
males, the law is curren
politicians, and reform
originally published in t
as an athlete, sports fa
that funding should co
male and female sports

A political editor
tributed op-ed commer
Post, the *New York Ti*

tional publications. A regular political commentator on the Fox News Channel, she appears frequently on CNN, CSPAN, PBS, NPR, and other national television and radio broadcasts.

————————— ✦ —————————

Girls in ponytails and soccer jerseys packed the front of a room at the National Press Club in Washington, DC. They elbowed each other and giggled as kids from across the nation spoke lovingly of basketball, pole vaulting and field hockey, and in support of Title IX—the 1972 law that has become synonymous with the rise of women's sports. Since Title IX went into effect thirty-one years ago, girls' athletic participation has skyrocketed. The number of girls playing varsity sports has gone up from one in twenty-seven in 1972 to almost one in two today.

Despite all the good feeling Title IX has engendered among girls and their parents, the law is currently under attack. The National Wrestling Coaches Association filed a lawsuit against the Education Department claiming that Title IX is decimating men's college sports, forcing colleges to cut hundreds of wrestling programs—along with gymnastics, diving and other teams—in order to meet "quotas" for female athletes. The aggrieved jocks have found an ally in President Bush, who formed the Commission on Opportunity in Athletics last [2002] June to re-examine the law.

The high school girls descended on Washington for their press conference-cum-pep rally just as the commission convened its final meeting at the Hotel Washington. Outside the hotel, the Feminist Majority and the conservative Independent Women's Forum held dueling press conferences. Inside the grand ballroom, a wrestling coach wearing a "No Quotas" button cruised the perimeter, handing out literature calling on the commission to "reject the gender politics of the special interest groups."

That would be groups like the Women's Sports Foundation—which helps girls seek equal funding and facilities for their teams—and Dads and Daughters, whose executive director, Joe Kelly, emceed the high school girls' event.

Title IX, said Kelly, "is one of the best things that ever happened to fathers." 5

"Sports is a natural comfort zone for men, and Title IX makes it a bridge to our daughters," he said. He told the story of a friend, Dave, who coached his son and daughter in basketball, and was appalled by the inferior facilities provided to his daughter's team.

"Dads get angry when daughters play on old fields or gyms that are in disrepair," Kelly said. And that's what Title IX was designed to fix. "Guys like Dave are not radical feminists. They simply know sports are good for girls. They also know sports are good for boys. Don't tell me you're going to treat my daughter differently than my son."

High school girls still get about 1.1 million fewer opportunities than boys to play sports, according to the National Coalition for Women and Girls in Education. But Bush's commission finished its work by making a series of recommendations to weaken Title IX. Instead of making girls' sports proportional to the number of female students enrolled, the commission recommended that schools aim for approximately 50/50 boy-girl representation. Schools that don't reach parity would be allowed to use interest surveys to show that girls are getting as much opportunity as they desire. According to the Women's Sports Foundation, the changes could result in the loss of 300,000 participation opportunities and $100 million in scholarships for female athletes.

The deck was stacked at the commission from the beginning. High school athletes and coaches who support Title IX didn't get to testify. Title IX opponents like wrestlers' groups and the Independent Women's Forum had disproportionate input. The commission's two strongest Title IX advocates, Julie Foudy, captain of the U.S. National Women's Soccer Team, and Olympic gold medalist Donna de Varona, were treated to eye-rolling by fellow commissioners and outright hostility by wrestlers' groups. In late February, the two refused to sign the final report, charging that the commission failed to acknowledge continuing discrimination against female athletes.

10   Still, despite the battle-of-the-sexes tone in DC, some sincere anguish is driving the backlash against Title IX.

Doug Klein coaches high school wrestling at the Ida Crown Jewish Academy in Chicago. "I had such a good time when I walked on the team at William and Mary," he recalls. Today his old college team has been cut, and other teams no longer take walk-ons (as opposed to recruits) because, he says, they have to keep their rosters small in order to comply with Title IX gender-equity rules. His star wrestler recently visited Lehigh and Cornell, and couldn't even get a coach to talk to him.

"Boys who aren't superstars—nobody is interested in them. And that's really unfair," Klein says. "Somebody made the point on one of these [wrestling] websites: 'I'm 5'5'', 120 pounds, what sport am I going to do?' There are not many opportunities in sports for little boys and little men."

That may be the most painfully honest comment ever made by an opponent of Title IX. Instead of focusing on the big men's sports that suck up all the resources in college athletics, a lot of little guys who are getting crushed blame women. Klein, too, blames Title IX for "gutting wrestling"—though he concedes that Title IX may not be the main problem.

"When you read the wrestling magazines, they're reluctant to point the finger at football," Klein says. "But football is the 800-pound gorilla." Indeed, major teams award up to eighty-five scholarships a year and field rosters of 100 or more players, while top football coaches can earn more than $2 million a year. Schools could easily comply with Title IX by making small cuts in these big-budget programs, instead of cutting men's roster spots. Title IX advocates calculate that just by dropping scholarship spots for football bench-warmers—cutting back from the eighty-five players now allowed by the NCAA to the fifty-three used by the NFL, for example—and by dropping a few of the most ridiculous perks, such as hotel-room stays on home-game nights, schools could add back all those smaller programs they've been eliminating.

There is a myth that spending huge amounts of money on 15 football makes sense because the game will bring in even more. The reality is that in the race to field a winning team, jack up alumni giving and secure lucrative TV contracts, even big-time football schools are losing money. Take the University of Wisconsin. UW lost $286,700 on its Rose Bowl appearance in 1998. Until schools get off the football treadmill, athletic program budgets will feel the squeeze, with or without Title IX.

Donna Shalala, President Clinton's Secretary of Health and Human Services, is one of the nation's biggest boosters of Title IX—and of big-budget football. As UW chancellor, Shalala brought the university's football program into the big time. She hired coach Barry Alvarez and built a giant new sports facility the same year she presided over the elimination of UW's baseball, men's and women's gymnastics, and men's and women's fencing teams. Now president of another football powerhouse, the University of Miami, Shalala is an unabashed proponent of Title IX: "It's had a huge impact on providing opportunities for women's sports." Yet she is also an unabashed proponent of big-time football.

Shalala says it was a budget crisis, not Title IX, that forced the cuts at Wisconsin. "We cannot use Title IX as an excuse for our lack of disciplined management and our financial problems," she says. She argues that it's possible to pay for minor sports and be a football power: "People have to restrain their costs, and they have to be honest about what football costs, and go out and raise more money."

Shalala uses the populist language of Title IX, saying, "The whole point is to provide opportunities for men and women." But in practice, building an athletic department around big-time football has resulted in schools—including UW—killing sports programs that once provided opportunities for regular students. It has also meant that college sports, more and more, are not about promoting amateur participation, sportsmanship or character but rather about raising a school's profile and getting a piece of the sports entertainment action. "This is not," says Shalala, "intramural sports." While Title IX has protected many women from these trends, no structures are in place to save minor men's teams from the football monster.

According to Cheryl Marra, senior associate director of sports administration at UW, "We don't spend any more here than any where else. But who's gonna give first?" UW has to offer its football players chartered jets and posh facilities, says Marra; otherwise, "Ohio and Michigan will say to recruits, 'You know, at Wisconsin they don't treat you right.'" The only way out, according to Marra, is for the NCAA to crack down on excessive football spending. Then no school would be placed at a disadvantage.

The wrestlers' attack on Title IX is based on a gamble: that [20] if the government relaxes Title IX rules, athletic departments will shift money back to their teams. But that's hardly a sure thing. Athletic directors are no more interested in minor men's sports now than they used to be in women's sports. Responding to the complaints of downsized wrestlers, Marra says, dismissively, "Why can't they accept that people don't want to play the same sports they did 100 years ago?"

Ironically, Title IX's very success is being used as an argument for its dismantlement. As with affirmative action, the law's opponents argue that the job is done—women have reached equality and no longer need special attention. This argument resonates with girls of the post-Title IX generation, who feel pangs of guilt when Title IX is blamed for the elimination of minor men's sports. "I'm in favor of Title IX, but not for cutting guys' sports," says Kym Hubing, a sprinter at Wisconsin.

Indeed, many students now take women's athletics for granted. Male and female athletes hang out together and support each other. This is one of the most profound, positive effects of Title IX. "You're friends. You're equals," says Greta Bauer, a UW hurdler. "When you walk into a party, the guys will see you and punch you in the arm and say, 'Hey, how are you doing?' The other girls will look at you like, 'How did you get inside the circle?'"

Being "inside the circle" means that women in Division I sports are envied just like the men. There is an aura of exclusivity about hanging out in the expensive sports facilities, studying in the athletes' study hall, living in jock housing. Like breaking into any formerly segregated club, being part of the sports scene on campus means gaining privilege.

If the Education Department heeds the Commission on Opportunity in Athletics, the march toward equality will stall. High schools and colleges across the nation will stop counting heads and start taking interest surveys. That may sound fair to young athletes like Hubing. But when Title IX started, most girls couldn't imagine themselves as serious athletes. An interest survey at that time would have determined that only a few real tomboys deserved a chance to play. It was the opportunities offered under the law that created such a radical change in the culture. Women now make up 42 percent of college athletes—maybe not equality, but an enormous leap, thanks to the law. Interest surveys would freeze that progress where it is today.

25 And this would be a loss not only to girl athletes but to the culture of sports as a whole. Title IX has become one of the last bastions of amateur sports. While there are no limits on the amount of money a school can shift from other men's programs to football, Title IX insists they keep open athletic opportunities for women. Women's sports—often praised for their "purity," for the sheer joy of the athletes and for the fact that players get decent grades—have kept alive the ideal of the scholar-athlete.

But maybe not for long.

Engaging the Text

1. What gets established about the pending fate of Title IX in the first two paragraphs of the essay? Does the author deliver information objectively here, or is it possible to determine her position in the debate? Provide textual evidence to support your answer.

2. List the names of all the organizations mentioned over the course of the essay. How does the author use these references to evoke ethos (ethical appeal) for her argument? Conniff quotes individuals affiliated with some of these groups. Taken as a whole, which of their statements do you find most informative on the issues surrounding Title IX and why?

3. Summarize the case for and against Title IX as articulated by Conniff. According to the author, who has benefited from the law and in what ways? Whom does she believe would lose or gain if Title IX is dismantled?

4. Highlight all the statistics cited in the essay. What purpose do these examples serve? How effective are they in appealing to your sense of logos (logic)? Which do you find most convincing and why?

5. Explain what the author means by "being 'inside the inner circle'" of sports. Based on your experiences or observations, do you agree or disagree with Conniff's position that "[m]ale and female athletes hang out together and support each other" (paragraph 22)? Use specific examples to support your view.

The Shame of Boxing

JACK NEWFIELD

Viewed as both a beautiful and a brutal competition, boxing has been an inspiration to artists, writers, musicians, and filmmakers for nearly a century. While legendary boxers such as Jack Dempsey, Joe Louis, and Muhammad Ali seized the popular imagination during their championship reigns, more often fighters languish in obscurity, suffering lifelong ailments as a consequence of constant blows to the brain. Jack Newfield, who has written about boxing since 1964, views the mostly African-American and Latino fighters as exploited workers with few rights. Though a $500-million-a-year business, boxing remains unregulated—the only professional sport without a union, as Newfield documents in this essay. Arguing that the sport needs radical reform, he proposes "A Bill of Rights for Boxers."

Newfield has been a reporter for several New York City newspapers, including the *Village Voice*, the *Daily News*, and the *Post*. His documentary film *Don King: Unauthorized* won an Emmy in 1991. Newfield's memoir, *Somebody's Gotta Tell It*, was published in 2002. "The Shame of Boxing" originally appeared in the *Nation*.

—————————— ◆ ——————————

Despite its dark side—or more likely because of its dark side—boxing has always been the sport most stimulating and attractive to serious writers, filmmakers, painters and songwriters. It is deeply embedded in the American culture. It appeals to the blood-lust in human nature.

Boxing has been an inspiration to writers of the caliber of Norman Mailer, Albert Camus, Ernest Hemingway, Joyce Carol Oates, Gerald Early, A.J. Liebling, Jack London, Pete Hamill, James Elroy, Budd Schulberg, Nick Tosches, Leonard Gardner, W.C. Heinz, Gay Talese, Ted Hoagland and David Remnick.

More outstanding movies have been made about boxing than any other game or racket: *Body and Soul, Champion, Raging Bull, The Set-Up, Requiem for a Heavyweight, The Harder They Fall*, the first *Rocky* film, *Fat City* and *On the Waterfront* (in which Marlon Brando plays Terry Malloy, a boxer who took a dive for the mob). Two of Bob Dylan's best songs are about fighters: "Who Killed Davey Moore?" and "The Hurricane."

Even now, in an era without a Jack Dempsey/Joe Louis/Muhammad Ali-level star who is bigger than boxing, the sport is still a $500-million-a-year big business. It is still the ticket out of slum poverty, still what Joyce Carol Oates called "America's tragic theater."

5 HBO's annual budget for boxing is $75 million. Showtime's budget is $25 million. The second Holyfield-Tyson fight grossed $100 million in one night, because of pay-per-view technology. The mega-fight is still key to the Las Vegas casino economy of high rollers. HBO (AOL-Time Warner), Showtime (Viacom) and ESPN (Disney) make a lot of money off boxing programming. Boxing feeds the corporate system.

The problem is that the sport is unregulated. Except for Nevada and Pennsylvania, the state commissions are jokes, run by small-time politicians interested in free seats facing the TV cameras.

Boxing is like no other sport. It has no national commissioner to set standards for health and safety. In boxing there are no leagues or schedules. Every match is a separate deal. There is no rational structure. The chaos itself becomes an impediment to reform. The casual fan does not understand how the sport is run.

In baseball, the standings reflect a quantifiable reality. In boxing, the ratings (which supposedly rank fighters according to ability, from one to ten with a number-one ranking guaranteeing a lucrative fight for the title) are at best impressionistic, and at worst totally corrupt—sold for cash. Everyone in boxing knows that the three sanctioning bodies that issue the ratings—the World Boxing Association, the World Boxing Council and the International Boxing Federation—have no legitimacy. They force champions to pay huge sanction fees for the right to defend their titles. They strip champions of their titles if they don't go along with the sport's back-room politics. They manipulate the ratings and exclude merit from consideration. They assign incompetent judges to fights. They are more like bandits than regulators.

In basketball, the score is obvious. The ball has to go through the hoop. In boxing, nothing is clear, victory and defeat are matters of interpretation by judges. A number-one rating can be auctioned. Fighters sometimes don't get paid what they are promised in a contract. Nobody audits the money. There are conflicts of interest that would never be tolerated in predominantly white sports like tennis, golf or stock-car racing.

All the dominant fighters since the 1960s have been black or Latino—Ali, Duran, Roy Jones Jr., Leonard, Hagler, Pryor, Bernard Hopkins, Alexis Arguello, Thomas Herns, Chavez, Trinidad, Mosley, De La Hoya, Whitaker, Holmes, Holyfield. This has created a pathetic yearning for a white boxing star among white fans. This tribal inferiority complex is what helped make the *Rocky* movies a box-office bonanza. There is a huge market for this sort of therapeutic racial-revenge fantasy.

This past June I saw boxer Beethoven Scottland get killed during a fight in New York City because of medical and regulatory negligence. I've seen other fighters crumble into a fatal coma, most famously Benny "Kid" Paret in 1962. But this one got to me because I felt it was especially preventable. The political hacks who rule the New York boxing commission failed to perform their job. The doctors present failed to intervene when it was obvious that a one-sided beating was going on. Brooding about this needless death, I reached the internal tipping point, where my guilt started to outweigh my pleasure. I now feel that boxing must be cleaned up, or I don't want to watch it anymore.

I have known a lot of fighters and liked almost all of them. They have no pension, no union, no health insurance, no voice. For every George Foreman who gets rich, there are

1,000 you never hear of who end up with slurred speech, failing memory and an empty bank account.

I once asked a gallant old champion from the 1950s, Boston's Tony DeMarco, why so many ex-fighters I knew were such modest, quiet, sweet men, appreciative of any attention.

"Because we've had all the anger punched out of us," Tony replied.

15   I have been around gyms and pugilists since the early 1960s. I have seen the greatest fighters end up living in rooming houses, picking up cans to get the deposits. I have seen champions who are now indigent, depressed, deranged, emotionally troubled, in need of professional help.

It almost seems like a curse of the gods, or maybe a message. The three greatest champions who ever lived all ended up with the most tragic medical problems. They all boxed too long. All three made ill-advised comebacks; they got hit too much at the end.

Joe Louis suffered from paranoia and dementia, and was confined to a mental hospital for a time. His declining years were spent hearing voices and covering up the air vents in hotels.

Sugar Ray Robinson suffered from Alzheimer's disease the last fifteen years of his life. Fans cherished the memory of his knockouts of LaMotta, Graziano, Turpin and Fullmer, but he had no memory of them. He could not recognize his sister or his grandchildren and stared at the wall with a faint smile on his lips.

The causal relationship between thousands of blows to the brain and diseases like Alzheimer's and Parkinson's is accepted by most doctors involved in sports medicine. In 1993, a detailed report was published in the *American Journal of Sports Medicine* that analyzed all the existing information on brain damage to boxers. The study concluded that "dementia pugilistica" (the scientific term for the layman's "punch drunk") afflicts 9–25 percent of all professional boxers. The symptoms include tremor, memory loss, inattention, impaired hearing, paranoid ideas and "a decrease in general cognitive functions." Doctors believe that repeated blows to the head are one of the triggers of Alzheimer's.

"Dementia pugilistica" is more likely to affect boxers with 20 longer careers because they absorb more punches, and heavy weights because the blows arrive with greater force. It is less likely to affect amateur boxers, who wear headguards and box fewer rounds.

We have all seen Muhammad Ali and winced. We saw his trembling hand light the Olympic torch in Atlanta. The Greatest has become our mute, iconic, bloated Buddha. The man with the fastest hands and legs in sports now moves as slowly as though he were under water. The wittiest athlete now whispers inaudibly. His body is ravaged by Parkinson's, a disease that is degenerative and will never get better.

Watching Ali on a dais being lovingly fed by his wife, Lonnie, hurts my heart and makes me question my own fandom, my own complicity in his debilitation. Seeing a tape of his epic fight with Joe Frazier in Manila has become a bittersweet experience for me. While it was happening in 1975, I was drenched with sweat, hoarse from screaming and emotionally spent from the ebb-and-flow drama. But today, seeing the aftereffects on both men has made the greatest fight I ever saw no longer such a powerful argument for the sport it once exalted.

If this is the fate of the greatest boxers, what happens to all the local club fighters around the country? What happens to the tough kid from Mexico or Philly who has thirty hard fights over six years, and never becomes famous or a champion?

How does he take a vacation? What chance do his children have of going to college? Who pays his medical bills? Who pays for his funeral?

A BILL OF RIGHTS FOR BOXERS

The preconditions for any meaningful reform of boxing are: 25

1. Create a national commission with enforcement power to regulate the sport. Every other major sport has a national commissioner, and boxing reform depends on some central authority that can administer and enforce improvements. The current system of state commissions, dominated by political appointees, cannot do the job.

2. End all recognition of the international sanctioning organizations—the WBA, WBC, WBO and IBF. "They serve no useful purpose," Attorney General Spitzer[1] told me. "Their only function is to sell title belts and issue false rankings."

3. Create a poll of boxing writers and broadcasters to generate impartial ratings. This is the way it works in college football and basketball. The writers covering the games vote on the best teams. There is no reason boxing ratings can't be compiled the same way—as long as it is a truly international poll. If a few popular champions recognized these rankings, that would be the final interment of the sanctioning bodies.

4. Establish a pension system for boxers that includes a health plan and death benefits. This could be accomplished if the fighters, promoters, cable TV networks and casinos agree to allocate just 2 percent of the revenue from all the mega-matches on pay per view to underwrite this endowment. Three such fights in one year would start a fund of $5 million or $6 million. A top accounting firm should audit and administer the fund. Any boxer who has been active for four years, or has had twenty bouts, should qualify for the system. But nobody who has taken a lot of beatings should be allowed to keep boxing just to qualify.

30 5. Health and safety standards must be improved. Ringside doctors should be competent and well trained, and should not be assigned or hired through politics. They should be qualified neurological experts.

Any boxer who has lost more than ten fights over two years, or has been knocked out three times in a row, should have his license revoked. This would retire punching bags like Samson Cohen, who has been knocked out fourteen times—even by Richie Melito in 1998.

Every boxer should have a CT scan and MRI every year. A prefight drug test can detect steroid abuse, which Dr. Margaret Goodman says can make a boxer "more susceptible to blood clots and a brain hemorrhage."

---

[1]Attorney General for the State of New York.

6. Organize a labor union, or guild, of all boxers. Paul Johnson and ex-champ José Torres have been agitating for a union for years. The best model is probably the Screenwriters Guild, since fighters are independent contractors. Traditional union solidarity and collective bargaining may not be practical among men who have to fight each other. But a union could provide a collective voice for individual rights. A union could audit pay-per-view revenues and the expenses promoters bill to fighters that often seem illegitimate or padded. A union could also demand a higher minimum payment for preliminary fighters.

7. When I talk to fighters, their most emotional complaint is about biased and unfair decisions by judges. This angers them even more than the inadequate safety precautions. It demoralizes them to know they won a fight but did not get the decision.

   A special panel should monitor the performance of judges. Those who are biased or engage in favoritism should lose their licenses. Judges should be required to make full financial disclosure to this licensing panel.

8. Boxers should be encouraged to have their own lawyers and accountants in all dealings with promoters over contracts and compensation. Any promoter who does not comply should lose his license.

9. Until a national commission over boxing is set up, the state commissions should hire inspectors who know what they are doing, not the usual political drones. These inspectors should be posted in the gyms, which are now unregulated. Fighters who get knocked out in a gym should be suspended for medical reasons, just like a fighter in an arena; the brain damage is the same. A lot of boxing's injuries occur in unsupervised gyms and are never reported to any medical authority.

10. Make the promoters or the casinos—not the fighters—pay the exorbitant "sanction fees" to the bogus sanctioning bodies. Under the current system, champions have to pay 3 percent of their earnings to the WBC, WBA and IBF for the privilege of risking their title against a challenger approved by these worthless outfits.

When Evander Holyfield testified before the Senate in August 1992, he said that he had to pay $590,000 in sanction fees after his previous title defense. The sanctioning groups will strip a champion of his title and declare it vacant if he doesn't pay. This is close to extortion. Over the course of his career, Holyfield has paid about $20 million of his earnings in sanction fees. Maybe that's one reason he's still fighting as he nears 40, well past his prime.

40   If a doctor could shine a penlight into the swollen eyes of boxing now, he would detect evidence of internal bleeding. This Darwinian racket has descended into a crisis of credibility.

My conscience won't let me remain a passive spectator to scandal any longer. I think too much about Bee Scottland being strapped onto a stretcher. I dream about Ali's tremor. I am haunted by the Alzheimer's stare in Ray Robinson's eyes. I think about underdog David Tiberi, and how he fought the fight of his life but was cheated out of the decision against James Toney, and how he retired in disgust after that spirit-breaking injustice.

Boxing has to be changed, even though there is no lobby for fighters and no constituency for reform. It is the moral thing to do. I know Congress has more serious and universal priorities—the war on terrorism, the economy, the minimum wage, campaign finance reform, preventing the confirmation of right-wing judges and preserving the environment. I know it's difficult to legislate more regulation in an era of deregulation. But attention must be paid, the effort must be made. The fighters are powerless workers of color, waiting for the arrival of their Cesar Chavez, their A. Philip Randolph.[2] They need representation, rights and a collective voice.

The fact that almost all boxers are black and Latino makes it easier for respectable people to shrug and look away. It would not cost the taxpayers anything to regulate boxing at the same level every other professional sport is policed. Only the will is lacking. Nobody important cares enough.

But the rest of us should, whether we are boxing fans or not. It's easy to avert your eyes and say, "Abolish the sport."

---

[2]Noted twentieth-century labor union founders.

But that won't happen. Instead, we should help these voiceless workers obtain the justice they deserve.

Engaging the Text

1. Newfield opens the essay by attributing the deep appeal of boxing in America culture to the sport's "dark side." How do you interpret the author's use of the word "dark" in this context? What might it mean in relation to other strands of the discussion; for example, when Newfield compares boxing to "predominantly white sports like tennis, golf or stock-car racing" (paragraph 9)?

2. Rather than the actual competitors, whom does Newfield imply has benefited from professional boxing? In what ways does Newfield appeal to logos (logic) in offering this view, and how does the evidence he presents support his argument overall?

3. In offering anecdotes and observations in the first person (beginning with paragraph 11), how successful is Newfield at evoking ethos (ethics) and establishing his own credibility as a critic of boxing?

4. Make a list of the medical problems associated with boxing that are named in the text. How familiar were you with these side effects before reading the essay? How persuasive is this information in underscoring the need to reform boxing?

5. The second half of the essay, "A Bill of Rights for Boxers" contains a list of proposed recommendations aimed at ending the exploitation of competitive fighters. How effective is this listing strategy? Is there a relationship between Newfield's allusion to the bill of rights and the fighters whom he labels "powerless workers of color" in need of "representation, rights and a collective voice" (paragraph 42)? Explain your answer.

Responding in Writing

1. Write a narrative essay modeled on either Anna Quindlen's "How Reading Changed My Life" or Hunki Yun's "Trail Blazer" in which you use memory, description, observation, and personal knowledge to support a claim about initiation into a particular school subject or sporting activity. As an alternative to the assignment, write a poem about initiation, referring to Naomi Shihab Nye's "Biography of an Armenian Schoolgirl" for inspiration. According to *Webster's Collegiate Dictionary*, "initiate" means "to bring into practice or use; to introduce by first doing or using; to start." Paralleling Quindlen, you might describe learning to read, introducing and describing influential books from your childhood. In composing such a paper, try exploring some of the following questions: Why do particular literary works stand out in your memory? What did they teach you about cultures and geographies different from the ones in which you were raised? How has reading shaped your character? If you decide to write a case history about learning and playing a particular sport, pay attention to settings, rules, procedures, routines, and rituals, as Yun does in his profile of golf pro Choi.

2. Nathan McCall, Francisco Jiménez, and Darcy Frey all use the first day of school or a new school year as a narrative device. Write a narrative essay about your own first day or beginning weeks of school or college, modeling rhetorical strategies that you find effective in these essays. In gathering details for your paper, consider the following questions and ideas: What rituals and procedures do you associate with this rite of passage? Riding a school bus or living away from home for the first time? Meeting new teachers, friends, and acquaintances? Learning to appreciate or tolerate dormitory life? Standing in a long line to register for classes or to purchase supplies at the campus bookstore? Do you recall cultural differences playing a part in the proceedings? If so, explain in what ways. Create a list of potential characters to appear in your essay, such as family members, teachers, or fellow students. How might your conversations serve as dialogue for your essay? What do you want your audience to understand about the common rituals you are exploring and their relevance to society overall?

3. Choose a sport or an athletic activity and describe how it is played or performed in a process-analysis paper (a step-by-step explanation of a procedure, activity, or task). Use descriptions of athletic movement found in essays by Darcy Frey, Timothy Harper, and Colette Dowling as examples. Also notice how each of these authors employs sensory images—those that allude to sight, sound, smell, taste, or touch—to illuminate his or her descriptions. For instance, Frey begins "The Last Shot" with a description of Russell Thomas, a teenage basketball star, "gauging air currents." Harper describes aging basketball sensation Allan Dalton "checking the breeze" at the conclu-

sion of "The Best Pickup-Basketball Player in America" in order to arrive at an epiphany (a sudden revelation or showing forth of the divine in a piece of writing). Dowling, in "Throwing Like a Guy: The Mystique of Innate Ability," relays the importance of "negotiating the wind" to tennis pro Martina Hingis in order to explain how "different motor abilities are specific to particular tasks" (paragraph 3).

4. Based on your reading and analysis of Colette Dowling's "Throwing Like a Guy," as well as Ruth Conniff's "Title IX: Political Football," generate a list of adjectives that suggest what Dowling calls "historical assumptions" about differences in physical abilities between women and men. Next, go to or watch a broadcast of both a women's and a men's (two altogether) sporting event and engage in criteria matching, noting any correspondences between the words on your list and the athletic abilities of the participants. Based on your research, what conclusions can you draw about gender and differing athletic abilities? Use your findings to write an essay in which you argue for or against the proposition that women and men possess the ability to participate in sports equally, or to argue for keeping or abolishing Title IX in the circumstance of funding school athletics.

5. Consider underlying implications about the use of standard English or English only in school settings as articulated in Lois-Ann Yamanaka's "Pidgin Politics" and Francisco Jiménez's "The Circuit." Based on information found in the readings as well as your own observations and experiences, write an essay arguing for or against standard English or English-only schooling. Mirroring Yamanaka and Jiménez, consider using code switching in your essay. If you share the narrator of "The Circuit," Panchito's, experience of entering or assimilating into the American education system without knowing English well, consider how your identity changed, if at all, as a consequence of schooling.

6. Using Jack Newfield's "The Shame of Boxing" as a model, choose a sport or leisure time activity in need of reform and write an essay in which you propose concrete changes. Try modeling the closing section of your paper on Newfield's by constructing a "Bill of Rights" relative to your subject.

7. Select a set of paired readings from Part I—such as Darcy Frey's "The Last Shot" and Timothy Harper's "The Best Pickup-Basketball Player in America"—and write a paper in which you compare and contrast the central components, rhetorical strategies, and effectiveness of each author's argument. In framing your discussion, identify categories or points of comparison, such as references to race, gender, geographic location, or other sites of cultural difference.

PART II

Representation
Media and Visibility

In 2001, Halle Berry made film history as the first African-American woman to ever win the Academy of Motion Pictures Award for best actress, earned for her role as Leticia, a rural Georgia waitress in *Monster's Ball*. Denzel Washington shared the limelight, nominated for the third time and finally earning best actor (only the second African-American man to ever achieve that honor) for his turn as Los Angeles police officer Alonzo Harris in *Training Day*. Despite their victories, some observers have criticized their Oscar-winning roles as reinforcing ethnic stereotypes about blacks as low-wage earners. Media critics in general have noted that actors of color often achieve widespread visibility by portraying denigrating characters alongside white actors, as in the film comedy *Bringing Down the Noise* (2003), starring Queen Latifah as a sassy black woman entangled with an uptight white guy, played by Steve Martin. And what about the fact that white rapper Eminem brought mainstream visibility to black hip-hop subculture through his media-hyped role as Jimmy Smith, a.k.a. Bunny Rabbit, in the movie *8 Mile* (2002)? How well do Hollywood and other mass-media outlets represent people from diverse cultural backgrounds, and what are the consequences for the United States as a nation?

To discuss the inclusion or exclusion of particular groups in Hollywood films, or to analyze the quality of the onscreen roles they play, is to make assertions and draw conclusions about "representation." When considered in terms of media—the focus of Chapter 3 in Part II—representation refers to the degree to which an image or a likeness found in a print, an image, a broadcast, or an electronic system accurately or authentically portrays reality. Several writers included in Part II analyze media representations of gender, race, class, or nationality in their respective selections. These observers believe that representations can influence our ideas about what is "real" or "true," shaping our sense of cultural identity in the process.

Speaking about the quantity or quality of a particular group's representation in the media, some of the authors in this part embrace the concept of "visibility" as an interpretive tool. The focus of Chapter 4, visibility often refers to a person's recognizable presence in social life or institutions. For example, who are our leaders in government or anchors on the nightly television news? How and why does their presence in society become visible to mass audiences? In contrast, why do some groups or individuals remain "invisible"? Ideas surrounding representation extend not only to visibility in the media but also to other aspects of daily life, as several selections in Part II illustrate.

Ward Churchill leads off Part II with *"Smoke Signals* in Context," an overview of Native American visibility and invisibility in U.S. cinema. His critique of representation in film is followed by Julia Alvarez's memoir about watching the annual Miss America Pageant during the early days of the competition's television début. Alvarez questions how well the contestants truly represent America based on overall looks and skin color. Taking a more global view of media representation, Michael Massing in "Press Watch" warns that television news as well as its viewers should pay closer attention to Middle Eastern countries, such as Afghanistan. In contrast, John Nichols' "Huey Freeman: American Hero" profiles cartoonist Aaron McGruder, applauding this graphic artist's willingness to represent unpopular positions on race and class in his politically incorrect comic strip *The Boondocks*. Rounding out the media chapter by likewise questioning representation in news reporting, Tim Wise serves up "Blinded by the White: Crime, Race and Denial at Columbine High," an unabashed look at recent high-school mass shootings reminiscent of Michael Moore's 2002 Academy Award-winning documentary film *Bowling for Columbine*.

Setting the stage for the visibility chapter by echoing the purpose of Churchill's essay, cultural observer Michael Bronski critiques the prospect of gay-and-lesbian television channels in "Queering the Vast Wasteland." Though conceding that "visibility has been a hallmark of American social-justice movements over the past half-century," Bronski also cautions that "increased public visibility" may not necessarily equate to "a minority's liberation." Peggy McIntosh, another contributor to this chapter, establishes the reality of institutional racism by likening so-called white privilege to an "invisible knapsack" in which unearned social advantages are transported. McIntosh's central project is to examine how unacknowledged representation affects social conscience. Has representation in the mass media or social life also instigated or encouraged positive changes for people of diverse backgrounds? In "The New Intellectuals," Robert S. Boynton argues that an impressive group of African-American public intellectuals has indeed emerged, "sought out by the electronic media" and afforded "extraordinary visibility" as a result. Exploring visibility politics from a different angle, Ali Hossaini in a letter to the editor of the *Nation* considers how his Arab-American identity, not apparent by his appearance, affords him a "hyphenated perspective" of cultural differences.

Like people, physical landmarks can become visible and acquire meaning as a consequence of representation, whether in newspapers, travel brochures, or in the course of conversations about them. Rudolph Chelminski explores this notion in the "Turning Point," which documents how public regard for the World Trade Center changed after a French high-wire artist named Phillippe Petit walked a tightrope between its twin towers. Chelminski likewise raises questions about how the symbolic meaning of a landmark may shift in the wake of large-scale events. Is it ironic that the twin towers of the WTC became the most talked about buildings in U.S. history after they were no longer physically visible? In the chapter's final selection, which invites readers to navigate the internet to "The Peters Projection World Map," historian Arno Peters creates a visual representation of global boundaries and territories that invites viewers to shift perspectives about nationhood and world affairs.

Taken as a whole, the selections in Part II share thematic and rhetorical resonances. Wise, McIntosh, and Boynton confront "whiteness" or "blackness" as socioeconomic categories on which cultural differences are predicated. Bronski joins McIntosh and Boynton in embracing "visibility" as both a social construct and an interpretative tool. Churchill, Alvarez, Massing, and Nichols meanwhile all criticize mass-media outlets for their exclusive nature. Finally, Hossaini, Chelminski, and Peters use geographic and spatial concepts to bring unexamined cultural differences into sharper relief.

How closely do you pay attention to representation when watching television, taking in a film, reading a magazine, touring a city, or otherwise engaging mass culture? Is the race, class, gender, ethnicity, or geographic location with which you most identify visible or invisible in the mass media? Do you see your cultural identity fully represented in daily life, and if so, to what degree? Must sites of social struggle or advancement be represented in media and society in order to bring about responsible or necessary change?

CHAPTER 3

Media

Smoke Signals in Context
WARD CHURCHILL

The first feature film written, directed, produced, and acted entirely by Native Americans, *Smoke Signals* won the Filmmaker's Trophy as well as an Audience Award at the 1998 Sundance Film Festival. Coproducer Sherman Alexie authored the screenplay, a coming-of-age story based on his book, *The Lone Ranger and Tonto Fist Fight in Heaven* (1994), about two adolescent boys who have grown up on the Coeur d'Alene reservation in Idaho. In this essay, Ward Churchill considers the place of *Smoke Signals* in the history of U.S. cinema, arguing that the presence of Native Americans on the big screen and behind the scenes in the filmmaking industry has been conspicuously sparse during the past century.

Churchill, a Creek and Cherokee Métis and longtime Native American activist, is a professor of Ethnic Studies at the University of Colorado, Boulder, and coordinator of the American Indian Movement for the state of Colorado. The author of *Fantasies of the Master Race: Literature, Cinema and the Colonization of American Indians* (1992), *Struggle for the Land: Indigenous Resistance to Genocide, Ecocide and Expropriation in Contemporary North America* (1993), *From a Native Son: Selected Essays on Indigenism, 1985–1995* (1996), and other works, he is a frequent contributor to *Z Magazine,* in which this essay first appeared.

———————————— ◆ ————————————

In 1911, James Young Deer, a Winnebago Indian, directed the film *Yacqui Girl,* one of several commercially successful productions he completed before going off to make documentaries in France during World War I. On resuming in 1919, Young Deer found his once-promising career had inexplicably come to an abrupt halt. Conspicuously disemployed in his chosen trade for nearly 15 years, he was finally picked up as a second-unit director on Hollywood's "Poverty Row" during the mid-30s, grinding out B-westerns and serials.

Meanwhile, Edwin Carewe, a Chickasaw, had completed *The Trail of the Shadow* in 1917. The film was distinguished enough to land him the director's berth in a whole string of movies over the next decade, culminating in the sensitive and critically-acclaimed 1928 screen version of Helen Hunt Jackson's *Ramona.* With that, Carewe's career ended just as suddenly as Young Deer's, and with even greater finality. He was never hired to work in cinema again.

For the next 70 years, with the exception of a brief flurry of self-produced releases by Cherokee comedian/radio commentator/actor Will Rogers, no American Indian was allowed to direct a major motion picture. For that matter, despite Rogers's monumental success and the Penobscot Molly Spotted Elk's having carried her weight as the lead in *Silent Enemy* (1930), no Indian actor was slotted in a significant film role until 1970, when Arthur Penn cast the Squamish leader, Chief Dan George, as Old Lodge Skins in *Little Big Man.*

Nor were things better for native people trying to work in filmdom's "background" capacities. Cherokee Lynn Riggs, for example, was cited by no less than Bette Davis as being among Hollywood's "most important contributors" to screenplay development. In 1930, Riggs completed the stage play *Green Grow the Lilacs* which most people have never heard of, mainly because it became famous as *Oklahoma!* after Rodgers and Hammerstein glommed on to it.

5   So bleached-out had America's cinematic sensibilities become that when Cherokee actor Victor Daniels ("Chief Thunder Cloud") was hired for the non-speaking title role in the 1939 version of *Geronimo,* he was required to don heavy make-up so that he'd more closely resemble the white actors

audiences had grown accustomed to see portraying Indians during Saturday matinees.

All told, more than 350 "name brand" Euroamericans had made their mark appearing in redface by 1970. They included women like Mary Pickford and Lillian Gish, Debra Paget and Donna Reed, Jennifer Jones and Julie Newmar, Delores Del Rio and Linda Darnel. The roster of men included Jeff Chandler and Rock Hudson, Sal Mineo and Anthony Quinn, Burt Lancaster and Tony Curtis, Chuck Connors and Ricardo Montalban. Fortunately, although he was cast as the Mongol leader Genghis Khan in *The Conqueror* (1956), John Wayne was never selected to fill the bill as a Hollywood Indian.

During the near half-century when real native people were all but frozen out of the movies, the studios cranked out something in the order of 2,000 films dealing with what are called "Indian themes." Another 2,500 or so were made as TV segments between 1950 and 1970. Given this saturation of imagery, it is fair to say that three consecutive generations of Americans were conditioned to see native people in certain ways, for clearly definable purposes.

While most of what was produced consisted of squalid potboilers in which Indians served, as Oneida comic Charlie Hill puts it, as "pop-up targets to give the cowboys and the cavalry something to shoot at," some of the films at issue must be considered as serious cinema in that they convey a deeply virulent message of racial triumphalism.

Being perfected was what Cherokee aesthetician Jimmie Durham terms "America's Master Narrative"—that is, indoctrination of the populace with a mythic (mis)understanding that nothing really wrong had transpired in the course of U.S. history. On the contrary, it had all been a noble undertaking, carried out by a combination of gallant leaders and brave settlers forging a better future. If anyone had gotten hurt along the way, namely Indians, it was because they'd "brought it on themselves" by being essentially subhuman in the first place and then compounding the defect with persistent and aggressive attempts to prevent whites from making things "work out for the best."

Not all Indians were seen as bad, of course. Some were even depicted as noble. These were the ones who perceived a   10

"tragic inevitability" in being overrun by a self-anointedly superior race/culture, and who evidenced the good taste to "vanish" with dignity rather than complaining about it. Even better
were those who not only accepted the innateness of white su-
premacy, but who used their insights to provide service to Euroamerica, helping the invaders get on with it. Such notions
are not unfamiliar to colonial literature, as even the most cur-
sory reading of Joseph Conrad will reveal. The Lone Ranger's
Tonto is, after all, simply Rudyard Kipling's Gunga Din recast
in feathers, as is Chingachgook in *Last of the Mohicans*.

Although one can readily imagine the response had Hollywood opted to depict the 1940s European Holocaust in a similar fashion, albeit Steven Spielberg comes uncomfortably
close with *Schindler's List*, the convention has been adhered
to, vis-à-vis the American Holocaust, with seamless precision
for the past 25 years. Most recently, it has been evident in
Kevin Costner's 1990 epic *Dances With Wolves*, as well as
Michael Apthed's *Thunderheart* and such mid-1990s teletrash
as *Dr. Quinn, Medicine Woman*.

The propaganda function served by the revisionist for-
mula is to allow constituents of America's dominant settler society to avoid confronting the institutional and cultural realities which led unerringly to the historical genocide of
American Indians. In first being led to demonize men like
Custer, then helped to separate themselves from them via
characters like Jack Crabbe, Christa Lee, and Lt. Dunbar,
white audiences are made to feel simultaneously "enlightened" (for being "open" enough to concede that something
ugly had occurred) and "good about themselves" (for being
different from the perpetrators).

At the same time, contemporary Native Americans, from
whom much of the wealth supporting the Euroamerican standard of living continues to be extracted, are maintained in a
state of near-total disempowerment, and correspondingly
deep destitution. As Cherokee analyst Rennard Strickland has
observed, one result is that the "Indian health level is the lowest and the disease rate the highest of all major population
groups in the United States. . . . The incidence of tuberculosis
is over 400 percent higher than the national average. Similar

statistics show that the incidence of strep infections is 1,000 percent, meningitis is 2,000 percent higher, and dysentery is 10,000 percent higher. Death rates from disease are shocking when Indian and non-Indian populations are compared. Influenza and pneumonia are 300 percent greater killers among Indians. Diseases such as hepatitis are at epidemic proportions, with an 800 percent higher chance of death. Diabetes is almost a plague. And the suicide rate for Indian youths ranges from 1,000 to 10,000 higher than for non-Indian youths."

Faced with such ongoing conditions, American Indians could never have made films reinforcing the dominant society's coveted sense of smugly self-satisfied "I'm okay, you're okay" complacency about itself. Things for Indians are obviously not okay, and, in setting out to explain why that is, we're not about to accept critic John Lenihan's "modest proposal," advanced in 1980, that the proper role of cinema should be to lead audiences to a "mature" interpretation of history in which "ain't none of us right."

Collectively, we're more inclined to follow Navajo activist   15
John Redhouse's suggestion, offered a few years before Lenihan's, that such ideas will make sense when Euroamerica finds it as "harmless" for its children to play "Nazis and Jews" as it always has "Cowboys and Indians." American Indian understandings are, by definition, counterhegemonic, and that's why Hollywood has frozen us out so completely from such crucial functions as directing and scriptwriting.

Even with respect to acting, the one area in which revisionist cinema's ever-increasing need to "authenticate" itself has allowed native people to bleed into the industry, we continue to suffer a virtual eclipse in some very important respects. While Jeff Chandler received the Academy Award for Best Supporting Actor because of his stilted portrayal of Cochise in *Broken Arrow* (1950), the Creek actor Will Sampson was not even nominated for his far more accomplished performance as Chief Broom in *One Flew Over the Cuckoo's Nest* (1975). "Why should an Indian receive an award for playing an Indian?" demanded one director at the time. By the same token, why should Robert DeNiro, of Italian descent, have received a award for his portrayal of another Italian American, Jake La Motta in *Ruging Bull* (1980)?

Although there is an entry for "Bugs Bunny" in the latest edition of Ephraim Katz's definitive *Film Encyclopedia,* there is none for Will Sampson, despite his prominent roles in more than a score of major movies, including such box office hits as *The Outlaw Josey Wales* (1976), *The White Buffalo* (1977), *Orca* (1977), and *Fish Hawk* (1980). Nor is there mention of Graham Greene, the fine Oneida actor who actually won the Academy's supporting actor award for his work in *Dances With Wolves,* and whose accomplishments include remarkable performances in *Clearcut* (1991), *Thunderheart* (1992), and other films. Missing, too, is Gary Farmer, another Oneida, who has turned in equally exemplary efforts in *Powwow Highway* (1989) and *Dead Man* (1996), among others.

If these virtuosos can still be slighted in this manner, what does it say for the prospects of somewhat less visible but genuinely talented native actors like Irene Bedard, Eric Schweig, Sheila Tousey, Adam Beach, Tantoo Cardinal, Evan Adams, Tina Keeper, Michael Greyeyes, Elaine Miles, Tom Jackson, Sonny Landham, Molly Cheek, Larry Littlebird, Cody Lightening, Michelle St. John, and Michael Horse? Native North America can't rely on the cinematic establishment's posthumous acknowledgments of Chief Dan George and the *Lone Ranger*'s Jay Silverheels forever.

This is why the recent debut of *Smoke Signals* (1998), the first release of a major motion picture directed by an Indian since Will Rogers, is such a vitally important event. Not only that, but the screenplay was also written by an Indian, adapted from a book of his short stories, and virtually the entire cast is composed of Indians. To top things off, the director, Chris Eyre, an Arapaho, teamed up with the scriptwriter, Spokane author Sherman Alexie, to coproduce the venture. *Smoke Signals* is thus, from top to bottom, an American Indian production, and that makes it historically unprecedented.

20 Critical reaction to the film has been, in large part, chatter concerning its limitations and technical deficiencies rather than the profound social significance of its very existence. Such responses can be met head on. *Smoke Signals* is not

great cinema. Trite in places, cliched in others, it is much too obvious in its efforts to come off as something explicitly, even stereotypically, "Indian" at nearly every step along the way.

But, with that said, so what? *Smoke Signals* is nonetheless a good movie in that it hangs together just fine, far better than most in that endless gush of relatively uncriticized clodhoppers aired on TV every night. Chris Eyre may not (yet) have attained the level of sophistication evidenced by a Francis Ford Coppola or a Martin Scorsese in communicating ethnic content, but he's not an overindulgent twit like Michael Camino either. More importantly, he shows no signs of being a subtextual racist like Arthur Penn, or one of the more overt variety, like John Ford and John Huston.

Above all, let it be said that a "critical" establishment such as that in the U.S., which has demonstrated a truly astonishing capacity to let pass, with nothing resembling a probing analysis, the likes of Stallone and Steven Seagal—or to embrace as "legitimate entertainment" such extravagant wastes as *Air Force One, Titanic, Armageddon,* and *Godzilla,* all in the past year [1997]—has no business criticizing anybody's cinematic achievements, no matter how meager.

Yet there is nothing in the least meager about what Chris Eyre has accomplished. In his first attempt at the "big time" he has established his talents quite solidly. Given that this should serve as a license for him to stretch out a little, it seems likely that Eyre's commercial efforts will evolve into works evidencing an aesthetic stature surpassing that embodied in the art films he created as a graduate student at New York University. Indeed, the extent to which he has already succeeded should stand to pry open doors for other native directors aspiring to break into the trade.

One cannot reasonably avoid concluding that *Smoke Signals* is a singularly important movie, not just a milestone but a pivot point for Native North America in terms of our long and sorry (mis)representation on the silver screen. The assessment is doubly valid in view of another recent and momentous development, this one in Indian Country. Based on a near half-billion dollars in annual gambling revenues over the past dozen years, the Mashantucket Pequots have begun to invest in—and have the capacity to fully underwrite and, if necessary, distribute—the endeavors of native filmmakers. Several other peoples have arrived in more-or-less the same financial situation and have demonstrated an inclination to follow suit.

25   Correspondingly, Hollywood no longer controls the indigenous image. An autonomous native cinema can thus be forged, whether the titans of tinseltown like it or not. As a consequence, Eyre and his peers find themselves, uniquely, in a position to begin unraveling the codes of domination on which the portrayals of Indians in film have heretofore been constructed, reinterpreting the meaning of America in a far more accurate manner than their white counterparts, and generally crushing Hollywood's fantasies of the master race under the heel of a different future.

Whether they will measure up to the task remains to be seen, but at last the promise is at hand. One wishes that James Young Deer, Molly Spotted Elk, Lynn Riggs, Will Sampson and all the others could be here to see it, or, better yet, to participate. On second thought, they did participate. So, I guess maybe they're watching. And I'm sure they're proud.

Engaging the Text

1. Explain Churchill's purpose for opening the essay with an overview of Native Americans in U.S. cinema. How would you describe the tone the author embraces to establish his point of view? Assertive? Sarcastic? Optimistic? Support your answer by indicating specific language.
2. What does Churchill claim has resulted in our society as a consequence of "Indian themes" and imagery "cranked out" by studios that for much of the twentieth century systematically excluded "real native people" (paragraph 7)? Does Churchill appear to present a realistic point of view in delivering this verdict? Why or why not? Use examples from the text to explain your answers.
3. Underline all the statistics that Churchill cites in this essay. How well does this information convince you of the author's position through appeals to logos (logic)? How do statistics specifically related to the current Native American standard of living fit into his argument overall?

4. Churchill presents analogies, such as between playing "Nazis and Jews" and "Cowboys and Indians" (paragraph 15). In small groups, identify and discuss the analogies he offers. What is his purpose in drawing these comparisons? How effective are they in lending credibility to Churchill's argument? Explain your answer.
5. Summarize what Churchill has to say about the film *Smoke Signals*. Then indicate why he characterizes the release of this major motion picture as "a vitally important event" (paragraph 19) in the history of U.S. cinema.

I Want to Be Miss América

JULIA ALVAREZ

Inaugurated on a beach boardwalk in 1921 to promote tourism in Atlantic City, New Jersey, the Miss America Pageant began airing live on television during the 1950s. Julia Alvarez grew up watching the annual broadcast as a family event, as she recounts in this memoir. Young immigrants, she and her sisters studied the fifty contestants for clues about "American looks" and how to "belong" in the United States. To what extent does the media shape or distort your own ideas about standards of beauty in our culture? What do you make of the fact that only five African Americans have ever won the Miss America title (the first in 1984), or that no Latino, Asian American, or Arab American has worn the crown?

A noted poet, novelist, essayist, and frequent chronicler of bicultural experience, Alvarez is the author of eight books, including the novel *How the Garcia Girls Lost Their Accents* (1991) and the nonfiction volume *Something to Declare* (1998), from which "I Want to Be Miss América" is reprinted. A contributor to many anthologies and the winner of numerous literary awards and prizes, she has been a professor of English at the University of Illinois at Urbana and also at Middlebury College in Vermont.

◆

As young teenagers in our new country, my three sisters and I searched for clues on how to look as if we belonged here. We collected magazines, studied our classmates and our new TV, which was where we discovered the Miss America contest.

Watching the pageant became an annual event in our family. Once a year, we all plopped down in our parents' bedroom, with Mami and Papi presiding from their bed. In our nightgowns, we watched the fifty young women who had the American look we longed for.

The beginning was always the best part—all fifty contestants came on for one and only one appearance. In alphabetical order, they stepped forward and enthusiastically introduced themselves by name and state. "Hi! I'm! Susie! Martin! Miss! Alaska!" Their voices rang with false cheer. You could hear, not far off, years of high-school cheerleading, pom-poms, bleachers full of moon-eyed boys, and moms on phones, signing them up for all manner of lessons and making dentist appointments.

There they stood, fifty puzzle pieces forming the pretty face of America, so we thought, though most of the color had been left out, except for one, or possibly two, light-skinned black girls. If there was a "Hispanic," she usually looked all-American, and only the last name, López or Rodríguez, often mispronounced, showed a trace of a great-great-grandfather with a dark, curled mustache and a sombrero charging the Alamo. During the initial roll-call, what most amazed us was that some contestants were ever picked in the first place. There were homely girls with cross-eyed smiles or chipmunk cheeks. My mother would inevitably shake her head and say, "The truth is, these Americans believe in democracy—even in looks."

5   We were beginning to feel at home. Our acute homesickness had passed, and now we were like people recovered from a shipwreck, looking around at our new country, glad to be here. "I want to be in America,"[1] my mother hummed after we'd gone to see *West Side Story*, and her four daughters cho-

---

[1]Line from a popular song in the musical attributed to Puerto Ricans characters.

rused, "OK by me in America." We bought a house in Queens, New York, in a neighborhood that was mostly German and Irish, where we were the only "Hispanics." Actually, no one ever called us that. Our teachers and classmates at the local Catholic schools referred to us as "Porto Ricans" or "Spanish." No one knew where the Dominican Republic was on the map. "South of Florida," I explained, "in the same general vicinity as Bermuda and Jamaica." I could just as well have said west of Puerto Rico or east of Cuba or right next to Haiti, but I wanted us to sound like a vacation spot, not a Third World country, a place they would look down on.

Although we wanted to look like we belonged here, the four sisters, our looks didn't seem to fit in. We complained about how short we were, about how our hair frizzed, how our figures didn't curve like those of the bathing beauties we'd seen on TV.

"The grass always grows on the other side of the fence," my mother scolded. Her daughters looked fine just the way they were.

But how could we trust her opinion about what looked good when she couldn't even get the sayings of our new country right? No, we knew better. We would have to translate our looks into English, iron and tweeze them out, straighten them, mold them into Made-in-the-U.S.A. beauty.

So we painstakingly rolled our long, curly hair round and round, using our heads as giant rollers, ironing it until we had long, shining shanks, like our classmates and the contestants, only darker. Our skin was diagnosed by beauty consultants in department stores as sallow; we definitely needed a strong foundation to tone down that olive. We wore tights even in the summer to hide the legs Mami would not let us shave. We begged for permission, dreaming of the contestants' long, silky limbs. We were ten, fourteen, fifteen, and sixteen—merely children, Mami explained. We had long lives ahead of us in which to shave.

We defied her. Giggly and red-faced, we all pitched in to 10 buy a big tube of Nair at the local drugstore. We acted as if we were purchasing contraceptives. That night we crowded into the bathroom, and I, the most courageous along these lines, offered one of my legs as a guinea pig. When it didn't become gangrenous or fall off as Mami had predicted, we creamed the other seven legs. We beamed at each other; we were one step closer to that runway, those flashing cameras, those oohs and ahhs from the audience.

Mami didn't even notice our Naired legs; she was too busy disapproving of the other changes. Our clothes, for one. "You're going to wear *that* in public!" She'd gawk, as if to say, What will the Americans think of us?

"This *is* what the Americans wear," we would argue back.

But the dresses we had picked out made us look cheap, she said, like bad, fast girls—gringas without vergüenza, without shame. She preferred her choices: fuchsia skirts with matching vests, flowered dresses with bows at the neck or gathers where you wanted to look slim, everything bright and busy, like something someone might wear in a foreign country.

Our father didn't really notice our new look at all but, if called upon to comment, would say absently that we looked beautiful. "Like Marilina Monroe." Still, during the pageant, he would offer insights into what he thought made a winner. "Personality, Mami," my father would say from his post at the head of the bed, "Personality is the key," though his favorite contestants, whom he always championed in the name of personality, tended to be the fuller girls with big breasts who gushed shamelessly at Bert Parks. "Ay, Papi," we would groan, rolling our eyes at each other. Sometimes, as the girl sashayed back down the aisle, Papi would break out in a little Dominican song that he sang whenever a girl had a lot of swing in her walk:

> Yo no tumbo caña,
> Que la tumba el viento,
> Que la tumba Dora
> Con su movimiento!

> ("I don't have to cut the cane,
> The wind knocks it down,
> The wind of Dora's movement
> As she walks downtown.")

My father would stop on a New York City street when a young woman swung by and sing this song out loud to the great embarrassment of his daughters. We were sure that one day when we weren't around to make him look like the respectable father of four girls, he would be arrested.

My mother never seemed to have a favorite contestant. 15
She was an ex-beauty herself, and no one seemed to measure
up to her high standards. She liked the good girls who had
common sense and talked about their education and about
how they owed everything to their mothers. "Tell that to my
daughters," my mother would address the screen, as if none of
us were there to hear her. If we challenged her—how exactly
did we *not* appreciate her?—she'd maintain a wounded silence
for the rest of the evening. Until the very end of the show, that
is, when all our disagreements were forgotten and we waited
anxiously to see which of the two finalists holding hands on
that near-empty stage would be the next reigning queen of
beauty. How can they hold hands? I always wondered. Don't
they secretly wish the other person would, well, die?

My sisters and I always had plenty of commentary on all
the contestants. We were hardly strangers to this ritual of
picking the beauty. In our own family, we had a running competition as to who was the prettiest of the four girls. We coveted one another's best feature: the oldest's dark, almond-
shaped eyes, the youngest's great mane of hair, the third
oldest's height and figure. I didn't have a preferred feature, but
I was often voted the cutest, though my oldest sister liked to
remind me that I had the kind of looks that wouldn't age well.
Although she was only eleven months older than I was, she
seemed years older, ages wiser. She bragged about the new
kind of math she was learning in high school, called algebra,
which she said I would never be able to figure out. I believed
her. Dumb and ex-cute, that's what I would grow up to be.

As for the prettiest Miss America, we sisters kept our choices
secret until the very end. The range was limited—pretty white
women who all *really* wanted to be wives and mothers. But even
the small and inane set of options these girls represented seemed
boundless compared with what we were used to. We were being
groomed to go from being dutiful daughters to being dutiful
wives with hymens intact. No stops along the way that might en-
danger the latter; no careers, no colleges, no shared apartments
with girlfriends, no boyfriends, no social lives. But the young
women onscreen, who were being held up as models in this new
country, were in college, or at least headed there. They wanted to
do this, they were going to do that with their lives. Everything in

our native culture had instructed us otherwise: girls were to have no aspirations beyond being good wives and mothers.

Sometimes there would even be a contestant headed for law school or medical school. "I wouldn't mind having an office visit with her," my father would say, smirking. The women who caught my attention were the prodigies who bounded onstage and danced to tapes of themselves playing original compositions on the piano, always dressed in costumes they had sewn, with a backdrop of easels holding paintings they'd painted. "Overkill," my older sister insisted. But if one good thing came out of our watching this yearly parade of American beauties, it was that subtle permission we all felt as a family: a girl could excel outside the home and still be a winner.

Every year, the queen came down the runway in her long gown with a sash like an old-world general's belt of ammunition. Down the walkway she paraded, smiling and waving while Bert sang his sappy song that made our eyes fill with tears. When she stopped at the very end of the stage and the camera zoomed in on her misty-eyed beauty and the credits began to appear on the screen, I always felt let down. I knew I would never be one of those girls, ever. It wasn't just the blond, blue-eyed looks or the beautiful, leggy figure. It was who she was—an American—and we were not. We were foreigners, dark-haired and dark-eyed with olive skin that could never, no matter the sun blocks or foundation makeup, be made into peaches and cream.

20   Had we been able to see into the future, beyond our noses, which we thought weren't the right shape; beyond our curly hair, which we wanted to be straight; and beyond the screen, which inspired us with a limited vision of what was considered beautiful in America, we would have been able to see the late sixties coming. Soon, ethnic looks would be in. Even Barbie, that quintessential white girl, would suddenly be available in different shades of skin color with bright, colorful outfits that looked like the ones Mami had picked out for us. Our classmates in college wore long braids like Native Americans and embroidered shawls and peasant blouses from South America, and long, diaphanous skirts and dangly earrings from India. They wanted to look exotic—they wanted to look like us.

We felt then a gratifying sense of inclusion, but it had unfortunately come too late. We had already acquired the habit of doubting ourselves as well as the place we came from. To this day, after three decades of living in America, I feel like a stranger in what I now consider my own country. I am still that young teenager sitting in front of the black-and-white TV in my parents' bedroom, knowing in my bones I will never be the beauty queen. There she is, Miss America, but even in my up-to-date, enlightened dreams, she never wears my face.

Engaging the Text

1. Beginning with its title, identify rhetorical devices used in the essay to establish the author's bicultural identity. Do you find these techniques effective? Focus on specific examples to explain why or why not.
2. Why does the Miss America contest's "initial roll-call" (paragraph 4) appeal to the Alvarez sisters? What do they also find perplexing about it and why? Does it sound like they would enter the competition if given the chance? Do you think that you would?
3. Compare and contrast each Alvarez family member's reaction to the televised broadcast of the annual pageant. How does "this ritual of picking the beauty" (paragraph 16) infiltrate their family life?
4. According to the essay, what were young women of Alvarez's native culture "instructed" to aspire to during the 1950s and 1960s? What did she find different about "young women onscreen, who were being held up as models in [her] new country" (paragraph 17)? What does the Miss America Pageant suggest about options for women in the United States today?
5. Alvarez concludes the memoir by claiming to "feel like a stranger" in her own country, though she has lived in the United States for more than three decades. Locate passages in the essay that help explain why the author makes this claim.

Press Watch

MICHAEL MASSING

In the days immediately following the terrorist attacks of September 11, 2001, many U.S. citizens stayed glued to their television sets, watching the news. How accurate are representations of countries that land on the media radar screen as a consequence of international conflict involving the United States? To what degree are our beliefs about cultures outside of our own borders shaped by television news broadcasts? In this commentary, Michael Massing analyzes the limitations and possibilities of television's potential to objectively portray international news.

Massing, a contributing editor to the *Columbia Journalism Review,* is author of *The Fix,* a study of U.S. drug policy during the 1960s, which won the *Washington Monthly's* Political Book Award in 1998. Massing regularly publishes in leading periodicals, including the *New York Times Magazine,* the *Washington Post, Rolling Stone,* the *New Republic,* and the *Nation,* in which this commentary first appeared. He was awarded an Alicia Patterson journalism fellowship in 1989 and named a MacArthur Fellow in 1992.

◆

A few minutes into ABC's *World News Tonight* on September 21—the night after George W. Bush's speech to Congress—Peter Jennings somberly noted that it was "time for all Americans to begin learning more about Afghanistan." I immediately perked up. Since the calamitous events of September 11, the networks had focused heavily on the human and physical toll of the attacks and on the nation's fitful efforts to come to terms with them. And they performed admirably in those initial days, consoling and comforting the public even as they were informing it. But as the days passed, and as the government prepared to strike at Osama bin Laden and his Afghan hosts, the need for some sharp political analysis became urgent, and here, on cue, was Jennings, promising a mini-tutorial.

Leaning forward, I looked expectantly at my TV screen—only to find it filled with the pale, bespectacled face of Tony Cordesman. Cordesman, of course, was a ubiquitous talking head during the Gulf War, and now he was back, holding forth in the same nasal monotone. He dutifully recited some basic facts about Afghanistan—the small size of the Taliban army, the limited number of tanks and aircraft at its disposal, the scarcity of bombing targets on the ground. "The job is extraordinarily difficult if not impossible if you set deadlines and demand instant success," Cordesman burbled. Then he was gone, and the program was back to its ongoing coverage of victims, heroes and terrorists. We learned nothing about the level of support for the Taliban, about the strength of the opposition, about America's long history of involvement in the region.

The segment was typical. As the nation prepares to go to war, the coverage on TV—the primary source of news for most Americans—has been appallingly superficial. Constantly clicking my remote in search of insight, I was stunned at the narrowness of the views offered, at the Soviet-style reliance on official and semi-official sources. On *Meet the Press*, for instance, Tim Russert's guests were Colin Powell and (as he proudly announced) the "four leaders of the United States Congress"—Dennis Hastert, Richard Gephardt, Trent Lott and Tom Daschle. "How did the events of September 11 change you?" the normally feisty Russert tremulously asked each. Seeking wisdom on the question of Why They Hate Us, Barbara Walters turned to former Bush communications director, now senior White House counselor, Karen Hughes.

"They hate the fact that we elect our leaders," Hughes vacuously replied. On NBC, Brian Williams leaned heavily on failed-drug-czar-turned-TV-consultant Barry McCaffrey ("Americans are natural fighters," McCaffrey fatuously informed us), while on *The Capital Gang* Mark Shields asked former Middle East diplomat Edward Walker, "Can the antiterrorism coalition really count this time on Saudi Arabia?"

To a degree, such deference reflects TV's customary rallying around the flag in times of national crisis. Such a stance is understandable; in light of the enormity of the attack, even atheists are singing "God Bless America." But the jingoistic displays on TV over the past two weeks—the repeated references to "we" and "us," the ostentatious sprouting of lapel flags, Dan Rather's startling declaration that "George Bush is the President, he makes the decisions and, you know, as just

5

one American, he wants me to line up, just tell me where"—
have violated every canon of good journalism. They have also
snuffed out any whiff of debate and dissent; the discussion
taking place within the Bush Administration is no doubt more
vigorous than that presented on TV.

But there's more than simple patriotism at work here. The
thinness of the coverage and the shallowness of the analysis
seem a direct outgrowth of the networks' steady disengage-
ment from the world in recent years. Since the end of the cold
war, overseas bureaus have been closed, foreign correspon-
dents recalled and the time allocated to international news
sharply pared. Having thus plucked out their eyes, the networks—suddenly faced with a global crisis—are lunging about
in the dark, trying desperately to find their footing.

No outlet has seemed more blinkered than CNN. The network that once emulated the BBC has instead become another
MSNBC, and while it can still count on Christiane Amanpour
to parachute into the world's hot zones, and on the game efforts of such on-the-ground assets as Nic Robertson in Kabul,
the network has seemed thoroughly flummoxed by the complex political forces set in motion by the events of September
11. Consider, for instance, that famous brief clip showing a
clutch of Palestinians celebrating the attack on the World
Trade Center. Within days, word began circulating on the Internet that the footage had actually been shot during the Gulf
War. The furor became so great that CNN eventually had to issue a statement describing where it got the tape (from a
Reuters cameraman in East Jerusalem who insisted that he
had not encouraged the celebration, as some claimed).

The real scandal, though, is that CNN repeatedly showed
the clip without commentary, without attempting to place it in
the broader context of reactions from the Islamic world. What
were people in Gaza and the West Bank actually saying? Where
were the interviews with clerics in Cairo, editorial writers in
Amman, shopkeepers in Jakarta and schoolteachers in Kuala
Lumpur? It was certainly not hard to obtain such views—wit-
ness Ian Fisher's sparkling dispatch from Gaza in the *New York
Times* ("In the Gaza Strip, Anger at the U.S. Still Smolders")
and Peter Waldman and Hugh Pope's excellent front-page

roundup in the *Wall Street Journal:* "Some Muslims Fear War on Terrorism Is Really a War on Them; West Undercuts Islam, They Say, by Backing Israel, Autocratic Mideast Rule."

Not all was bland on CNN. Jeff Greenfield, for one, made some genuine efforts to probe the Islamic world's complex love-hate relationship with the United States. On September 20, for instance, he had a spirited discussion with Afghanistan hands Barnett Rubin of New York University and Shibley Telhami of the University of Maryland, along with Farid Esack, a Muslim scholar at Auburn Theological Seminary. Far more representative, though, was "What Do We Know About Islam?" an exceedingly brief Sunday segment in which a Christian minister and a Muslim cleric offered very vague observations about relations between Christianity and Islam. It was followed by an interview with a Muslim American who assured us that "Islam means peace." Shot in Boston and New York, the segment drove home how CNN has lost that precious journalistic ability to work the streets of the world and discover what's really taking place there. Given CNN's critical part in keeping the world informed, one can only hope that it will soon regain its bearings.

Engaging the Text

1. According to the opening paragraphs of Massing's commentary, what role did television networks play in broadcasting to the public in the days following "the calamitous events of September 11"? Do you agree with Massing that the need to learn more about Afghanistan along with "sharp political analysis became urgent"? Explain why or why not.

2. Massing calls television news coverage of the events of September 11 "appallingly superficial" (paragraph 3). Summarize the examples he offers in substantiating this claim. Using your summary as well as your own observations of television news as a basis for discussion, argue for or against Massing's position.

3. List the reasons Massing gives for the purported demise of television news in recent years. What does he imply has resulted in our culture as a consequence? According to the author, how have these changes affected once respectable

news outlets, such as CNN? Use examples from the text to illustrate your answer.

4. In paragraphs 6 and 7, Massing criticizes CNN for falsely representing Palestinians in Gaza. Do you feel it is appropriate to show international news clips on television without commentary, or is a picture truly worth a thousand words?

5. Make a list or prepare a free write detailing what you now know about Afghanistan as a country and Islam as a religion. Do you feel more informed about either the country or the religion than you did prior to September 11, 2001? If so, how much of your recent knowledge has come about as a result of watching television news? Use specific examples to explain your answer.

Huey Freeman: American Hero

JOHN NICHOLS

Cartoonist Aaron McGruder created his edgy comic strip *The Boondocks* while majoring in Afro-American studies at the University of Maryland, where it first appeared in the student paper. Focusing on race relations, it follows the adventures of African-American siblings Huey Freeman (a black nationalist) and his hip-hop-obsessed younger brother Riley, who move from inner-city Chicago to a mostly white suburb. Debuting nationally in 1999, McGruder's strip drew criticism for its content. Now syndicated in more than 200 of America's leading newspapers and coming soon to television, *The Boondocks* stirs up controversy for millions of readers every day. John Nichols profiles McGruder's rise among the nation's leading political cartoonists.

A Washington, D.C. correspondent for the *Nation*, Nichols covers politics and activism in the United States. Coauthor with Bob McChesney of the book *It's the Media, Stupid* (2002), his articles appear in numerous newspapers and magazines, including the *Chicago Tribune*, the *New York Times*, and the *Progressive*.

◆

On Thanksgiving Day 2001, with the United States in the midst of what polls identify as one of the most popular wars in history and with President Bush's approval ratings hovering around 90 percent, more than 20 million American households opened their daily newspapers to see a little black kid named Huey Freeman leading the pre-turkey prayer.

"Ahem," began the unsmiling youth. "In this time of war against Osama bin Laden and the oppressive Taliban regime, we are thankful that OUR leader isn't the spoiled son of a powerful politician from a wealthy oil family who is supported by religious fundamentalists, operates through clandestine organizations, has no respect for the democratic electoral process, bombs innocents, and uses war to deny people their civil liberties. Amen."

In the whole of American media that day, Huey's was certainly the most pointed and, no doubt, the most effective dissent from the patriotism that dare not speak its mind. And it was not the only day when the self-proclaimed "radical scholar" skewered George W. Bush, Attorney General John Ashcroft, the Defense Department, dithering Democrats, frenzied flag-wavers and scaremongering television anchors in what since September 11 has been the most biting and consistent critique of the war and its discontents in the nation's mass media.

The creation of 27-year-old cartoonist Aaron McGruder, Huey Freeman appears daily in *The Boondocks,* a comic strip featured in 250 of America's largest newspapers, including the *Washington Post, Dallas Morning News, Chicago Tribune, Los Angeles Times* and *Philadelphia Inquirer.* "There are a lot of newspapers where Aaron's comic strip probably is the only consistent voice of dissent," says Pulitzer Prize-winning cartoonist Joel Pett, whose editorial-page cartoons for the Lexington, Kentucky, *Herald-Leader* have raised tough questions about the suffering of Afghan civilians and the role the United States has played in spreading terror. "I think that not only is he doing good stuff, the fact that he is on those comics pages makes it important in a way that none of the rest of us could accomplish. He's hooking a whole group of people. He's getting ideas out to people who don't always read the opinion pages. And he's influencing a lot of young people about how it's OK to question their government and the media. When you think about it, what he has done since September 11 has just been incredible."

5   In recent weeks, McGruder's Huey has grumbled about how it may no longer be legal in John Ashcroft's America to ask whether George W. Bush was actually elected; hiked atop a mountain to yell, "For goodness sake people, it's a recession! Save money this Christmas!"; and repeatedly expressed the view that "Dick Cheney is just plain creepy." And he has listened in disbelief to an "announcement" from the Attorney General that went: "I would like to reassure Congress that my proposed Turban Surveillance Act, which would allow the FBI to covertly plant listening devices in the headgear of suspected terrorists, is in no way meant to single out Arab or Muslim Americans."

At a time when most comedians are still pulling their punchlines, McGruder has gotten plenty of laughs at the expense of the Bush Administration and its policies. But not everyone has been amused. In early October the cartoonist had Huey call the FBI's antiterrorist hotline to report that he had the names of Americans who trained and financed Osama bin Laden. When the FBI agent said that, yes, he wanted the names, Huey began, "All right, let's see, the first one is Reagan.

That's R-E-A-G. . . ." This series of strips was pulled from the New York *Daily News* and *Newsday* and shuffled off comics pages at other papers. Editors were quick to deny they were censoring *The Boondocks*, claiming they simply thought Mc-Gruder had gotten a little too political. McGruder played the controversy into more laughs. He produced an inane new strip featuring talking patriotic symbols, launching it with a satirical editor's note: "Due to the inappropriate political content of this feature in recent weeks, it is being replaced by 'The Adventures of Flagee and Ribbon,' which we hope will help children understand the complexities of current events. United we stand." Ribbon then declares, "Hey, Flagee, there's a lot of evil out there," to which his compatriot replies, "That's right, Ribbon. Good thing America kicks a lot of *@#!"

McGruder, whose cartoon began appearing nationally in April 1999, says he did not set out to make Huey the nation's No. 1 dissenter. Yes, *The Boondocks*—which recounts the experiences of Huey and his younger brother, Riley, inner-city youths who move with great trepidation to the suburbs—has always been controversial. Bitingly blunt in its examination of race and class issues, *The Boondocks* has made more waves more often than any nationally syndicated comic strip since Garry Trudeau's *Doonesbury* characters declared Nixon aides "Guilty! Guilty! Guilty!" in the Watergate era. "It even got pulled from the Buffalo paper for something involving Santa Claus," recalls McGruder, who grew up listening to rap artists Public Enemy and KRS-One, idolized Berkeley Breathed's politically pointed *Bloom County* comic strip, took an African-American studies degree from the University of Maryland and started drawing cartoons for the hip-hop magazine *The Source*.

But the cartoonist knew that the controversy he would stir in the weeks after September 11 would be different from any he had provoked before. What he did not know was that, unlike Trudeau in the Watergate era, he and his preteen characters would challenge a popular President and his policies with little cover from allies in the media or Congress. "Sometimes, I do look around and say to myself, 'Gee, I'm the only one saying some of these things.' That can make you a little paranoid.

But I don't think that's a reflection on me so much as it is a reflection on how narrow the discussion has become in most of the media today. The media has become so conglomerated that there really are very few avenues left for people to express dissent," says McGruder. Well aware that he is a young cartoonist—as opposed to a senator or veteran television commentator—McGruder is the first to note, "I should not be the guy right now. I should not be the one who is standing out here saying, 'Hold it. This doesn't make any sense.' . . . There are a lot of people who do this so much better than I do. I just have the distribution and the opportunity."

When the terrorist planes hit the World Trade Center and the Pentagon, McGruder was not thinking about the next turn in his career path; rather, he was doing what Huey and the other *Boondocks* kids do a lot of: watching television. "I watched five straight days of television. I was shocked by what happened. But I was also shocked by the simplistic nature of a lot of the commentary—this whole 'good' versus 'evil' analysis that sounded like something from fifth grade. And I started to recognize that this was going to be a defining moment in my career," recalls McGruder, who acknowledges that Huey tends to channel his most passionately held views. "I decided that I was going to risk throwing my career away. I absolutely thought that was the risk I was taking."

10   Why take the risk?

"The Boondocks is not an alternative weekly strip. This is not a website strip. This is in the *Washington Post,*" he explains. "It just seemed like nobody else was going to say the things that needed to be said in the places where I had an opportunity to raise questions about the war—in newspapers that millions of people read every day."

McGruder is not the only cartoonist upholding the craft's honorable tradition of tweaking the powerful. Despite pressure from many editors to narrow the discourse—because, in the words of *Soup to Nutz* cartoonist and National Cartoonist Society spokesman Rick Stromoski, "sales and subscriptions are down, and papers are afraid of offending their communities and losing even more readers"—a number of editorial-page cartoonists have poked and prodded more than most mainstream journalists. Pulitzer Prize-winner Steve Benson has created a tremendous stir in Phoenix, where his cartoons for the conservative *Arizona Republic* have attacked "war fever" and mocked superpatriots; angry readers have condemned Benson for what one described as "a vile tirade upon the people of the United States." Kentucky's Joel Pett has wondered aloud whether the antiterrorist cause might be better served by more food drops and fewer bombs. The *Philadelphia Inquirer*'s Tony Auth, the *Philadelphia Daily News*'s Signe Wilkinson and the *Sacramento Bee*'s Rex Babin have savaged the Bush Administration's assaults on civil liberties and decision to rely on military tribunals. And, though far gentler than in his heyday, Trudeau has used his *Doonesbury* strip—which often appears on editorial pages—to address anti-Arab stereotyping, slack media coverage and the dubious alliances made between the United States and Afghan warlords.

Gary Huck and Mike Konopacki, whose cartoons frequently appear in labor-union publications, have dissected war profiteering by corporations. Ted Rall, who is published in alternative weeklies and a growing number of daily papers, has exposed the excesses of corporate America (one of his cartoons, titled "America's business leaders consider their role in the war," features an executive crowing, "I laid off thousands of people and scored a bailout"); in addition, Rall has filed some of the best war reporting from Afghanistan by an American journalist. And no one has skewered the mindless patriotism of the media better than Dan Perkins, whose Tom Tomorrow strip coined the phrase "We must dismantle our democracy in order to save it."

But while many editorial cartoons are syndicated, none reach the audience that *The Boondocks* does daily. Thus when Huey started raising a ruckus, a lot of people noticed. One night last fall, when the LA-based cartoonist was visiting his parents in Maryland, McGruder sat down with Mom and Dad to watch a segment on ABC's *Nightline* portray him as one of America's most controversial commentators. Despite his off-message message, offers keep coming McGruder's way from Hollywood; he's developing an animated version of *The Boondocks* that's expected to show up as a network series this fall, and he's writing movie scripts—including one about George W. Bush's theft of the 2000 election. "If we can get it made, it will be a miracle," jokes McGruder, who calls Bush "our almost-elected leader." Weighing the continued success of *The Boondocks* and his Hollywood options against the recent controversy, McGruder says, "I can't say I've suffered. A few papers pulled [the strip] but most of them haven't. And the publicity has just drawn attention to what I'm doing."

15   Indeed, McGruder wonders why so few successful artists speak out about race, class, war and Bush's court-ordered presidency. "I understand that in a capitalist society, anger at the system is a luxury. But some people are on top of the system. Why don't they speak out?" he asks. "The only time I really get upset is when I see someone like Oprah [Winfrey], who has the money, who has the power, and I think, 'What is holding you back from changing the world, from changing the world in a drastic way?' " Adds McGruder, who has frequently used *The Boondocks* to criticize African-American celebrities who take the cautious route, "Some of these people clearly decided, at some point, not to take any risks. I can't do that." So Huey Freeman refuses to shut up. "I'm going to stay cynical, resist this bandwagon war," the cartoon character told his pal Caesar in a recent strip. "Sure, my kind may be obsolete. But so what?"

Actually, McGruder says, he doesn't believe Huey's thinking—or his own—to be obsolete, or even all that radical. "I really think that what I am doing with *The Boondocks* is common sense. It's just that when no one in a position to be heard is speaking out, common sense seems radical," he says, sounding distinctly like Huey as he adds, "How's that for irony: We live in a time when common-sense statements seem radical."

Engaging the Text

1. Nichols begins the essay with a synopsis of the Thanksgiving Day 2001 installment of *The Boondocks*. How successful is this opening strategy in illustrating Nichols's contention that the comic strip offers "effective dissent from the patriotism that dare not speak its mind" (paragraph

3)? Do you agree with the author's assessment? Explain your answer by defining your own view of patriotism.

2. The essay overall describes how McGruder and other cartoonists have critiqued the U.S. government. Identify examples from the text that illustrate this idea. Does Nichols reinforce, explore, or challenge particular political viewpoints in these examples or does he maintain a neutral position?

3. Summarize *The Boondocks* creator McGruder's view of television coverage of September 11, 2001, in the days immediately following the terrorist attacks (paragraph 9). Recalling your own reaction to the initial media response to 9/11, compare and contrast it to the cartoonist's.

4. According to Nichols, "McGruder is not the only cartoonist upholding the craft's honorable tradition of tweaking the powerful" (paragraph 12). Explain what he means by this statement. What is Nichols's attitude toward political cartoonists overall? Refer to the text to support your answer.

5. Near the end of the essay, Nichols portrays McGruder as critical of "successful artists" and "African-American celebrities" who do not "speak out about race, class," or political issues. Do you think that individuals occupying the media spotlight have an obligation to publicly voice their views on controversial subjects? To support your conclusions, consider those who have done so since 9/11.

Blinded by the White: Crime, Race, and Denial at Columbine High

Tim Wise

On April 20, 1999, Eric Harris, 18, and Dylan Klebold, 17, armed with semiautomatic weapons, murdered a dozen classmates and a teacher at Columbine High School in Littleton, Colorado, before killing themselves; twenty-five other people were injured in the rampage. Did town residents and school officials ignore possible warning signs leading up to the massacre because Harris and Klebold were white students from affluent families? Would the Littleton community have paid more attention to these auguries, perhaps preventing the outcome, if the adolescents at the center of the tragedy were of a different race? When it comes to violent crime overall, what role does the media play in teaching us whom to fear? Imagining the events of Columbine if the student planners had been black, writer Tim Wise embraces "rhetorical reversal" to examine media representation through the prism of race.

Recipient of the 2001 British Diversity Award for best feature essay on race and a social justice activist for more than two decades, Wise has published in hundreds of newspapers and magazines throughout the world. Author of the essay collection *Speaking Treason Fluently: Anti-Racist Reflections from an Angry White Male* (2003), he is a frequent contributor to *Z Magazine*, in which this essay first appeared.

———————— ✦ ————————

Imagine a quiet, suburban community: the kind commonly referred to as a "nice place to live and raise kids." It's a community known for civic pride, affluent families, and schools where the students score well above average on aptitude tests. It's also 93% white.

Now imagine that at this community's high school, a handful of black students who say they feel like outcasts begin talking openly, about how they hate everyone. They start dressing alike—perhaps wearing the same colors, or jackets, or black berets—and referring to themselves as the "dashiki posse." Furthermore, they show off their gun collection in a video they produce for a class project. In this video, they act out the murders of dozens of students and teachers.

In addition, the students are known to operate a website which espouses violence, on which they have been known to post what amount to hit lists, letting everyone know who they hate most, and intend to kill first. One of the targets of their hatred discovers the list, tells his father, and the two of them inform police of the thinly veiled threat.

And let's imagine these black students are fond of a particularly "violent" form of music, say gangsta' rap, and are known to paint anti-white slogans and symbols on their clothing, and sing the praises of a particular black mass murderer (say Colin Ferguson[1] for lack of a better example). Now, let us answer the following question: How long would it take, given this information, for school officials, teachers, and parents to make sure these kids were expelled and even prosecuted? How long would it take for their families to be run out of town? Does anyone believe this scenario would have been met with apathy, indifference, or even amusement?

Of course not. But that's exactly what happened in the real   5
world when at this same school, in this same community, two white students from "good families" began dressing alike, saying they hated everyone, calling themselves the "Trenchcoat Mafia," listening to "shock-rock" and the sometimes violent lyrics of white musical artists, showing off their guns and murder fantasies on film, operating a website that praised Hitler and advocated violence, painting swastikas on their clothes, and naming the people they wanted to kill over the internet.

Still seen as "basically normal kids" by their families, friends and teachers, these two would be ignored. Ignored that is until last week, when they would go on a killing rampage reminiscent of the previous seven that have occurred at schools around the country in the past two years.

"No one really thought they'd do anything," said some classmates. "We thought it was all talk," said others. Of course. These were white kids, with BMW's, whose families make six figures or more. These are the beautiful people. They never do anything wrong. "We moved from the city to get away from things like this." The statement rings in my ears with a burning familiarity. It's the same thing heard after Paducah, Pearl, Fayetteville, Jonesboro, Edinboro, and Springfield; and now again, in the wake of Littleton.[2]

Some people never get it. Some people are so caught up in their race and class stereotypes about what "danger" looks like, they still insist, "things like this don't happen here."

---

[1]Man accused in 1993 of opening gunfire on a rush-hour commuter train headed from New York City to Long Island.

[2]List of small towns in the United States blighted by school massacres.

Oh yeah? Well where *do* they happen? I've yet to hear of one black or Latino kid in an inner-city school plotting or carrying out mass murder. Just where does an urban-dweller go to build sixty bombs anyway? . . . [I]f these kids had been black they would have been followed around the hardware store for so long that they would never have been able to buy any pipes, let alone the other ingredients needed for the kind of explosives Klebold and Harris concocted.

10   So in light of what's happened, not only in Littleton, but in "nice, quiet" suburbs all around the country lately, one must ask: just what were these folks trying to get away from in the cities? Must not have been violence. Must have been black and brown people (except, of course for the handful that can afford to live amongst them in style), and poor folks generally. How sad.

Once again, the racialization of deviance has allowed us to let down our guard to the greatest threats to our safety: not people of color (if we're white), but our own white children, white parents, white neighbors, white husbands, white lovers and white friends. We have been so conditioned to see deviant and destructive behavior as a by-product of melanin or "defective" black culture that commentators can, without any sense of irony, continue to remark about how, well, remarkable it is when things like this happen.

It reminds me of something James Baldwin[3] once said about the Holocaust—a much bigger paroxysm of white violence no doubt, but which nonetheless resonates here—"They did not know that they could act that way. But I doubt very much whether black people were astounded."

The white American myth of innocence, decency, morality, and the cowboys who never fired on an "injun" unless it was self-defense, have all been laid bare for those willing to see. That people of color always knew the myths to be [bull], while the dominant majority refused to look at themselves only makes the situation more tragic. But not a damn bit more shocking.

---

[3]Noted novelist and essayist.

Of course, that the school killers have all been white lately has gone without mention in the media. Oh sure, we hear about the similarities between the Columbine High tragedy and the others—well at least some of the similarities: all the shooters were boys; all the shooters used guns; all the shooters talked openly about violence; all the shooters played violent video games; all the shooters ate Cheerios at some point in the last ten years—you get the picture.

In other words, the racial similarities between these gun lovin', trash-talkin', dark-clothes wearin', 'Doom'-playin', Cheerios-eatin', Marilyn Manson-listenin' sacks of testosterone [were] irrelevant. 15

While we can rest assured these kids would have been "raced" had they come from black "ghetto matriarchs" in the 'hood, it seems as though no one can see the most obvious common characteristic among them: namely, their white skin. This, I guess is what folks mean when they say they're color-blind: they can see color all right, it's white they have a problem with. Typical.

White folks go off, killing wholesale like there's a . . . closeout on semi-automatic ammunition, and we get fifty-eleven "explanations" from the so-called experts who are called in by the media to make sense of it all. People of color do something horrific or commit random acts of retail violence and the whole world lines up to blame one of three things: their black families (particularly their black single mommas); their black DNA (as in the rantings of the *Bell Curve*)[4]; or their "defective" black culture and inverted value system. Whatever the case, their blackness never, and I mean never, gets overlooked.

Gang violence in the cities heats up and we've got *U.S. News and World Report* running a story entitled: "A Shocking Look at Blacks and Crime," and every nighttime news program running stories asking "what's wrong with *the black family* (as if there's only one); what's wrong with *these people* in the

---

[4]Controversial book on the purported relationship between IQ, race, and class, co-authored by Charles Murray and the late Richard J. Herrnstein.

ghetto underclass." But when Charles Manson, John Wayne Gacy, Ted Bundy and Jeffrey Dahmer[5] go out and do their thing, no one thinks to ask what it is about white folks that makes them cut babies out of their mothers' wombs, torture young men and bury them under the house, kill two dozen or more women for the hell of it, or consume human flesh.

White deviants are afforded the privilege of individualization ("that's just crazy Charlie, ignore him, he's a potted plant"), while those of color get to represent their whole community and become exhibit A in David Duke and Charles Murray's eugenic fantasy. You say 90% of modern serial killers have been white? Well isn't that puzzling? Next question.

20   You'll never even hear the term "white crime" uttered in polite conversation. White *collar* crime, maybe: but to suggest that the collar might not be the only thing lacking color, would be dogma non grata in mainstream discussion. "White-on-white violence?" What the hell is that? Never heard of it. Even in the wake of these massacres. Even as white folks are killing other white folks in Kosovo[6] (and still *other* white folks are bombing them to get them to stop).

The media and politicians have done such a fine job making sure we know who to fear (namely the dark and poor) that we forget how whites are disproportionately likely to engage in all kinds of destructive behavior, from drunk driving, to drug use as teens, to animal mutilation, to fratricide, to cutting corners on occupational safety standards and pollution control, which then causes the deaths of twice as many people as are murdered annually.

We forget that when it comes to violent crime, whites are four times more likely to be victimized by another white person than by a person of color, and that only six-ten-thousandths of 1% of the white community will be killed by a black person in a given year.

---

[5]List of infamous U.S. mass murderers and serial killers, all Caucasian.

[6]Site of a late-twentieth-century civil war in Eastern Europe, characterized by "ethnic cleansing," according to media reports.

And it all leads one to wonder: how many of the white families with kids at Columbine would have moved, or at least taken their kids out of the school if, say, 100 black families had moved in and enrolled their children there?

If other suburbs and other whites are any indication, the answer is quite a few. Study after study for twenty-five years has found that whites begin to leave an area and disenroll their kids from the schools when the community becomes as little as 8% black. As the numbers get higher, the trickle becomes a mass exodus. And why? Well, to get away from crime of course, which in this case must rank as an especially disturbing textbook definition of irony.

Even more hilarious is the tendency to act as if young   25
white people were *ever* innocent, upstanding citizens compared to the rest of the country. Even as far back as 1966, a national survey of 15–17-year-old white males found that "virtually all" had committed numerous criminal offenses, from breaking and entering, to minor property destruction, to armed robbery.

I've decided that's why all those shows like *Leave It to Beaver, Father Knows Best,* and the *Brady Bunch* were so popular: not because many people actually lived like that but because they *didn't,* and could escape into this unreal fantasy life via the television. After all, why watch a program that looks just like your daily routine? That would be boring.

So just as with westerns that allowed mostly white kids to fantasize about a more exciting life, these wholesome family programs allowed (and still allow in syndication) mostly white viewers to ignore the dysfunction which is really all around them, and always has been, long before the first black kid set foot in their schools, and long before the "Godless" humanists bounced prayer from homeroom.

Engaging the Text

1. Explain Wise's purpose for opening "Blinded by the White" by inventing an imaginary community. What gets established in this profile both in terms of tone and theme?

Given what follows in the essay, is this an effective rhetorical strategy? Refer to the text to illustrate your answers.

2. Locate grounds within the essay for Wise's claim that people in American society are "conditioned to see deviant and destructive behavior as a by-product of melanin or 'defective' black culture" (paragraph 11). Do you agree or disagree with the author's assessment? Use your own personal knowledge and experience to support your answer.

3. Wise uses comparison and contrast in paragraphs 14–19 to make assertions about race and representation in the media. Summarize his viewpoints and analyze the examples he uses to support them. Do you find his line of reasoning here convincing? Why or why not?

4. Make a list of all the references to the word "color" in the essay. In small groups, discuss the author's use of this word as a motif or rhetorical device. Determine how you might embrace a similar strategy in your own writing in order to stimulate critical responses from your readers.

5. Underline all the statistics cited in the essay. What purpose do these facts and figures serve in illustrating or dispelling American attitudes about crime in relation to race?

CHAPTER 4

Visibility

Queering the Vast Wasteland

MICHAEL BRONSKI

In September of 2002, *Newsweek* reported that the *New York Times* had agreed to begin running announcements of same-sex weddings, a decision coinciding with the release of a television-reality series called *Gay Weddings*, created by Kirk Marcolina. The growing visibility of gay characters, themes, and programming in the media has attracted the attention of critics interested in analyzing this development as a reflection of evolving social norms in the United States. Surveying the representation of gay life in television programming, past and present, Michael Bronski debates the meaning and possible consequences of specialty gay-and-lesbian television channels.

A longtime champion of gay and feminist activism, Bronksi is a journalist and cultural critic whose topics include sex, AIDS, film, books, theater, television, and consumerism. The author of two books, *Culture Clash: The Making of Gay Sensibility* (1984) and *The Pleasure Principle: Sex, Backlash, and the Struggle for Gay Freedom* (1998), Bronski is a frequent contributor to the *Village Voice* and *Z Magazine*, in which this essay first appeared.

◆

Gay TV—clearly, this is an idea whose time has come. After all, in the words of the porn industry, it's a money shot. So on January 10 [2002] MTV and Showtime, cable outlets both owned by Viacom, announced that they were developing the first cable channel geared to a lesbian and gay audience. The proposed channel would operate as a pay channel along the lines of HBO or Showtime, but would cost subscribers possibly as little as $5 a month. A startup date has not yet been announced.

Just a week after Viacom's announcement, MDC Entertainment Group's Alt1-TV announced its own plans for a gay-and-lesbian channel that would premiere in early 2003. Alt1-TV's channel, unlike Viacom's, would be funded by advertising. The Canadian-based PrideVision, which premiered four months ago to very positive reviews, is seriously considering expanding into U.S. markets.

The Viacom and MDC announcements have given rise to lots of humor columns speculating about future programming (the *Washington Post's* Hank Stuever scored a laugh with "The Weakest Twink"). But media critics agree with the proposed channels' producers that success or failure will lie in the quality of its shows. "Programs and content make a network not the other way around," noted MDC's David McKillop.

While it is nice to know that television execs are interested in quality, the idea of a specialty gay-and-lesbian television channel raises issues that strike at the heart of how the gay movement generates and sets its agenda.

5   A popular myth holds that increased public visibility is crucial to a minority's liberation—even equivalent to it. In this tradition, Joan Garry, executive director of the Gay and Lesbian Alliance Against Defamation (GLAAD), greeted the unveiling of these homo-channels with the rousing battle cry, "The flag I'm carrying is for visibility, the more the better." Indeed, visibility has been a hallmark of American social-justice movements over the past half-century. African Americans, Latinos, Native Americans, Asians, women, homosexuals, and other marginalized groups have long demanded that they be represented more frequently and more accurately in the media, which was accustomed to blatantly, and often grotesquely, stereotyping "minorities"—or ignoring them al-

together in what was essentially a white and male-dominated landscape.

There's no question that visibility in the entertainment and news media introduces minorities into the fabric of everyday life. Shows like *The Jeffersons* and *The Cosby Show* broke through some of the stereotypes of African Americans as depicted on television and, by extension, they influenced to some degree how African Americans were perceived by the broader white-majority culture. So it is probably better to have black sit-coms on television than not. It is probably better to have *Will and Grace* and *Ellen* on TV than not. Just as it is better to have non-biased coverage of the Matthew Shepard murder or more racially sensitive coverage of African Americans than not. Though it is a vast wasteland, television is also a great equalizer and through the increased exposure it offers it helps render minorities more ordinary. The late wit and arch-queen Quentin Crisp referred to this truism, only half jokingly, as "liberation through banalization."

But this version of liberation, which places a high premium on visibility, isn't universally embraced. For as long and hard as some have fought to increase visibility, there have been others who claim that such visibility comes at too high a price—that the "banalization" inherent in the mainstreaming of minority images presents nothing but false, easily accessible and acceptable stereotypes that ultimately cause more harm than good. Did *The Cosby Show* help eliminate white racism or did it just present a portrait of upper-middle-class blacks who had almost nothing to do with the reality in which most African Americans (most Americans, for that matter) live?

Critics of liberation-through-visibility politics also note that increased media exposure does not ensure that the actual lives of gay men and lesbians are better. According to government statistics, hate crimes against gay men and lesbians are on the rise, even though *Will and Grace* continues to win Emmy Awards. Hillary Swank's Oscar-winning performance in *Boys Don't Cry* certainly didn't end violence against, or guarantee acceptance of, transgendered people.

The debate over the politics of visibility is laid out neatly by Suzanna Danuta Walters in her new book *All the Rage: The*

Story of Gay Visibility in America. But as fascinating as this discussion may be, it is largely beside the point.

10   To understand the political stakes for gay people in gay cable channels, you have to begin with the recognition that, by and large, the U.S. media is conceived and run by commercial interests that have little intention of making anyone's lives better. Television, along with the other arms of the entertainment industry, exists to make money. To that end, as media conglomeration proceeds at an unprecedented rate, programming has grown dangerously homogeneous. For gay liberation, the implications are alarming.

Sure, there's a lot of talk about the "responsibility" of the media and the important role it plays in shaping opinion and keeping the public informed. But this, for the most part, is nonsense. Although there have been a few instances—the *Pentagon Papers,* Watergate, and, if we're lucky, the ongoing and unfolding Enron scandal—when media has played the role of good citizen, they have been few and far between.

After September 11, there was a lot of talk about serious and sustained reconsideration of media priorities. The September 11 attacks were alleged to be the new millennium's wake-up call to an urgent sense of fresh responsibility. No more wallowing in scandals like the Bill-and-Monica affair, no more sleazy tabloid speculation about the whereabouts of Chandra Levy or the intricacies of the Rudy G. and Donna Hanover divorce. But these sentiments vaporized before they could be properly realized. Winnona Ryder's arrest and the collapse of Mariah Carey's record deal have replaced frisky and missing White House interns.

It is just as bad now as it was before. Of course, the entertainment is not much better. The major networks' magazine-format news shows are just this side of *Entertainment Tonight,* and *Survivor* is beginning to look like a scripted TV drama.

The bottom line is that the media is driven by bottom-line commercialization and generally relies on the lowest possible standards. Hey, you didn't hear throngs of gay men and lesbians clamoring for a gay television channel. It was the idea of corporate media marketing engineers. The opening sentence of the *New York Times* report on MTV's decision to develop a gay and lesbian channel states clearly: "Looking to take advantage of what they say is a large and lucrative niche audience untapped by television programmers. . . ." While the corporation promoting these ventures is not claiming to be helping, or even to be interested in, the gay and lesbian community or its political struggles, there is always lurking in their rhetoric the notion that the increased visibility afforded by gay television would "be good for the gays." The reality is that gay cable TV channels are going to represent corporate interests, not those of the community. Can you imagine a gay network giving any more time than do current network news shows to such non-mainstream groups as queeruption, the Lesbian Avengers, groups focusing on gay people of color, or NAMBLA? Sure there will be coverage of the Human Rights Campaign, the Log Cabin Club, GLAAD, and Lambda Legal Defense—all of whom already get some coverage in the mainstream media—but for the most part, the wide spectrum of community organizations and interests will be ignored, particularly if they don't cater to acceptable mainstream sensibilities.

Or consider this. Will the entertainment coverage on gay [15] channels include queer avant-garde artists, writers, or performers? Will we see interviews with Dennis Cooper? The Five Lesbian Brothers? Or Jennifer Miller, the famous lesbian bearded woman who performs in circuses and alternative venues?

Don't bet on it. Like recycled *Entertainment Tonight* and E-Network fare, the bulk of gay television will focus on the new film where a noted Hollywood male celeb goes "gay for pay" or on which straight celebs show up for an AIDS benefit.

The idea of a gay and lesbian channel became possible because over the past two decades queer content on TV and other media outlets has increased. From the early days of the famous drag-queen episodes of *All in the Family* and the lesbian subplot on *Golden Girls* to the far more central and explicit queerness of *Will and Grace*, gay-and-lesbian characters and themes have become something of a staple on network television. This development has been an indicator of changes in American mainstream culture, which raises the question, wouldn't gay TV be redundant?

After all, if current gay programming were politically ineffective altogether, why would the Christian right continually call for boycotts of gay-themed shows, holding them up as signs of moral decay? But let us not forget that their popularity generates substantial revenue. Gay-themed programming is certainly not aired because the networks have a commitment to gay visibility or intend to engineer positive social change for gay people.

But there is a terrible irony here. It is clear that an audience exists—with a gay and lesbian viewership at its core—to support these shows on network television. It is quite possible, however, that a gay cable television channel would actually have an adverse effect on widespread visibility. It could function as a drain to take the gay and lesbian content out of network television and to re-ghettoize it. Why should networks continue with gay content if that core—and relatively small—audience is getting it elsewhere? In the end, the question about gay cable television channels is not how much they will help gay people, but how much they might hurt them.

Engaging the Text

1. How do the opening paragraphs of the essay evoke both ethical and logical appeal in introducing the pending launch of specialty gay-and-lesbian television channels? Is this an effective rhetorical strategy? Why or why not?

2. Underline all the references to "visibility" in paragraphs 5–9. Referring to the author's use of the word in each context, determine the central positions that Bronksi explores in the "liberation-through-visibility politics" (paragraph 8) debate. Next, engage in criteria matching, assigning the titles of television shows named in these paragraphs to specific sides of the issue.

3. Summarize what Bronski considers "the political stakes for gay people in gay cable channels" (paragraph 10), using examples from the text to support your answer.

4. What type of programming does Bronski predict will dominate gay-and-lesbian television channels and why? Do you find the author's logic well supported here? In formulating your answer, refer to your own knowledge of gay

and lesbian characters and themes currently integrated into television programming as a whole.

5. The penultimate paragraph of the article addresses whether or not "networks have a commitment to gay visibility or intend to engineer positive social change for gay people." Summarize the central points in the article that lead to the author's take on this idea.

White Privilege: Unpacking the Invisible Knapsack

PEGGY McINTOSH

Cultural anthropologists consider "whiteness" a socioeconomic condition that identifies people who have been granted significant legal, political, or cultural value because of skin color. "White privilege" refers to special advantages or benefits enjoyed by these same people as a consequence of their whiteness. As Peggy McIntosh suggests in this essay, its beneficiaries are often oblivious to white privilege, conditioned to think of their lives as neutral or as representing a standard that other groups should aspire to or imitate. McIntosh compares this unacknowledged state of consciousness to transporting an "invisible knapsack," using her own life circumstances to illustrate.

McIntosh is associate director of Wellesley College Center for Research on Women, where she codirects the National SEED Project on Inclusive Curriculum: Seeking Educational Equity and Diversity. An advocate of multicultural education, her scholarly articles have appeared in *Journal of Pedagogy, Pluralism and Practice* and other publications.

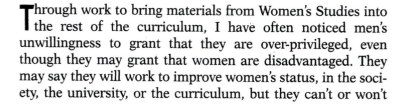

Through work to bring materials from Women's Studies into the rest of the curriculum, I have often noticed men's unwillingness to grant that they are over-privileged, even though they may grant that women are disadvantaged. They may say they will work to improve women's status, in the society, the university, or the curriculum, but they can't or won't support the idea of lessening men's. Denials which amount to taboos surround the subject of advantages which men gain from women's disadvantages. These denials protect male privilege from being fully acknowledged, lessened or ended.

Thinking through unacknowledged male privilege as a phenomenon, I realized that since hierarchies in our society are interlocking, there was most likely a phenomenon of white privilege which was similarly denied and protected. As a white person, I realized I had been taught about racism as something which puts others at a disadvantage, but had been taught not to see one of its corollary aspects, white privilege, which puts me at an advantage.

I think whites are carefully taught not to recognize white privilege, as males are taught not to recognize male privilege. So I have begun in an untutored way to ask what it is like to have white privilege. I have come to see white privilege as an invisible package of unearned assets which I can count on cashing in each day, but about which I was "meant" to remain oblivious. White privilege is like an invisible weightless knapsack of special provisions, maps, passports, codebooks, visas, clothes, tools and blank checks.

Describing white privilege makes one newly accountable. As we in Women's Studies work to reveal male privilege and ask men to give up some of their power, so one who writes about having white privilege must ask, "Having described it, what will I do to lessen or end it?"

5   After I realized the extent to which men work from a base of unacknowledged privilege, I understood that much of their oppressiveness was unconscious. Then I remembered the frequent charges from women of color that white women whom they encounter are oppressive. I began to understand why we are justly seen as oppressive, even when we don't see ourselves that way. I began to count the ways in which I enjoy unearned skin privilege and have been conditioned into oblivion about its existence.

My schooling gave me no training in seeing myself as an oppressor, as an unfairly advantaged person, or as a participant in a damaged culture. I was taught to see myself as an individual whose moral state depended on her individual moral will. My schooling followed the pattern my colleague Elizabeth Minnich has pointed out: whites are taught to think of their lives as morally neutral, normative, and average, and also ideal, so that when we work to benefit others, this is seen as work which will allow "them" to be more like "us."

I decided to try to work on myself at least by identifying some of the daily effects of white privilege in my life. I have chosen those conditions which I think in my case *attach somewhat more to skin-color privilege* than to class, religion, ethnic status, or geographical location, though of course all these other factors are intricately intertwined. As far as I can see, my African-American co-workers, friends and acquaintances with whom I come into daily or frequent contact in this particular time, place, and line of work cannot count on most of these conditions.

1. I can if I wish arrange to be in the company of people of my race most of the time.
2. If I should need to move, I can be pretty sure of renting or purchasing housing in an area which I can afford and in which I would want to live.
3. I can be pretty sure that my neighbors in such a location will be neutral or pleasant to me.
4. I can go shopping alone most of the time, pretty well assured that I will not be followed or harassed.
5. I can turn on the television or open to the front page of the paper and see people of my race widely represented.
6. When I am told about our national heritage or about "civilization," I am shown that people of my color made it what it is.
7. I can be sure that my children will be given curricular materials that testify to the existence of their race.
8. If I want to, I can be pretty sure of finding a publisher for this piece on white privilege.
9. I can go into a music shop and count on finding the music of my race represented, into a supermarket and find the staple foods which fit with my cultural traditions, into a hairdresser's shop and find someone who can cut my hair.
10. Whether I use checks, credit cards, or cash, I can count on my skin color not to work against the appearance of financial reliability.

11. I can arrange to protect my children most of the time from people who might not like them.

12. I can swear, or dress in secondhand clothes, or not answer letters, without having people attribute these choices to the bad morals, the poverty, or the illiteracy of my race.

13. I can speak in public to a powerful male group without putting my race on trial.

14. I can do well in a challenging situation without being called a credit to my race.

15. I am never asked to speak for all the people of my racial group.

16. I can remain oblivious of the language and customs of persons of color who constitute the world's majority without feeling in my culture any penalty for such oblivion.

17. I can criticize our government and talk about how much I fear its policies and behavior without being seen as a cultural outsider.

18. I can be pretty sure that if I ask to talk to "the person in charge," I will be facing a person of my race.

19. If a traffic cop pulls me over or if the IRS audits my tax return, I can be sure I haven't been singled out because of my race.

20. I can easily buy posters, postcards, picture books, greeting cards, dolls, toys, and children's magazines featuring people of my race.

21. I can go home from most meetings of organizations I belong to feeling somewhat tied in, rather than isolated, out-of-place, outnumbered, unheard, held at a distance, or feared.

22. I can take a job with an affirmative action employer without having co-workers on the job suspect that I got it because of race.

23. I can choose public accommodation without fearing that people of my race cannot get in or will be mistreated in the places I have chosen.

24. I can be sure that if I need legal or medical help, my race will not work against me.

25. If my day, week, or year is going badly, I need not ask of each negative episode or situation whether it has racial overtones.

26. I can choose blemish cover or bandages in "flesh" color and have them more or less match my skin.

I repeatedly forgot each of the realizations on this list until I wrote it down. For me white privilege has turned out to be an elusive and fugitive subject. The pressure to avoid it is great, for in facing it I must give up the myth of meritocracy. If these things are true, this is not such a free country; one's life is not what one makes it; many doors open for certain people through no virtues of their own.

In unpacking this invisible backpack of white privilege, I have listed conditions of daily experience which I once took for granted. Nor did I think of any of these perquisites as bad for the holder. I now think that we need a more finely differentiated taxonomy of privilege, for some of these varieties are only what one would want for everyone in a just society, and others give licence to be ignorant, oblivious, arrogant and destructive.

I see a pattern running through the matrix of white privilege, a pattern of assumptions which were passed on to me as a white person. There was one main piece of cultural turf; it was my own turf, and I was among those who could control the turf. *My skin color was an asset for any move I was educated to want to make.* I could think of myself as belonging in major ways, and of making social systems work for me. I could freely disparage, fear, neglect, or be oblivious to anything outside of the dominant cultural forms. Being of the main culture, I could also criticize it fairly freely. 10

In proportion as my racial group was being made confident, comfortable, and oblivious, other groups were likely being made inconfident, uncomfortable, and alienated. Whiteness protected me from many kinds of hostility, distress, and violence, which I was being subtly trained to visit in turn upon people of color.

For this reason, the word "privilege" now seems to me misleading. We usually think of privilege as being a favored state, whether earned or conferred by birth or luck. Yet some of the conditions I have described here work to systematically overempower certain groups. Such privilege simply *confers dominance* because of one's race or sex.

I want, then, to distinguish between earned strength and unearned power conferred systematically. Power from unearned privilege can look like strength when it is in fact permission to escape or to dominate. But not all of the privileges on my list are inevitably damaging. Some, like the expectation that neighbors will be decent to you, or that your race will not count against you in court, should be the norm in a just society. Others, like the privilege to ignore less powerful people, distort the humanity of the holders as well as the ignored groups.

We might at least start by distinguishing between positive advantages which we can work to spread, and negative types of advantages which unless rejected will always reinforce our present hierarchies. For example, the feeling that one belongs within the human circle, as Native Americans say, should not be seen as privilege for a few. Ideally it is an *unearned entitlement*. At present, since only a few have it, it is an *unearned advantage* for them. This paper results from a process of coming to see that some of the power which I originally saw as attendant on being a human being in the U.S. consisted in *unearned advantage* and *conferred dominance*.

15   I have met very few men who are truly distressed about systemic, unearned male advantage and conferred dominance. And so one question for me and others like me is whether we will be like them, or whether we will get truly distressed, even outraged, about unearned race advantage and conferred dominance and if so, what we will do to lessen them. In any case, we need to do more work in identifying how they actually affect our daily lives. Many, perhaps most, of our white students in the U.S. think that racism doesn't affect them because they are not people of color; they do not see "whiteness" as a racial identity. In addition, since race and sex are not the only advantaging systems at work, we need similarly to examine the daily experience of having age advantage, or ethnic advantage, or physical ability, or advantage related to nationality, religion, or sexual orientation.

It seems to me that obliviousness about white advantage, like obliviousness about male advantage, is kept strongly inculturated in the United States so as to maintain the myth of meritocracy, the myth that democratic choice is equally available to all. Keeping most people unaware that freedom of confident action is there for just a small number of people props up those in power, and serves to keep power in the hands of the same groups that have most of it already.

Though systematic change takes many decades, there are pressing questions for me and I imagine for some others like me if we raise our daily consciousness on the perquisites of being light-skinned. What will we do with such knowledge? As we know from watching men, it is an open question whether we will choose to use unearned advantage to weaken hidden systems of advantage, and whether we will use any of our arbitrarily-awarded power to try to reconstruct power systems on a broader base.

Engaging the Text

1. What was your initial response to this essay? Interest? Surprise? Discomfort? Underline passages in the essay that drew your strongest reactions and discuss their impact on your thinking in small groups.

2. In paragraph 6, McIntosh explains that she was taught to see herself as an "individual." Paraphrase what the author means here. Has your own education led you to perceive of yourself as an individual, or as part of a group that, according to the essay, could be unconsciously labeled as "them"?

3. McIntosh identifies twenty-six conditions that she believes represent "the daily effects of white privilege," which she experiences in contrast to her African-American colleagues in her place and line of work. Which of these conditions can you probably count on for yourself and why? Which, if any, do you believe "should be the norm in a just society," as McIntosh says in paragraph 13?

4. According to the article, many "white students in the U.S. think that racism doesn't affect them" and "do not see 'whiteness' as a racial identity" (paragraph 15). Do you agree or disagree with these charges? Draw from real-life examples or experience to support your point of view.

5. In identifying and confronting a list of conditions such as those mentioned in this essay, what might people learn

about the circumstance of race in relation to socioeconomic privilege? In gaining insight from this exercise, how
might you answer the question raised in the essay's final
paragraph: "What will we do with such knowledge"?

The New Intellectuals
ROBERT S. BOYNTON

Public intellectuals are people who translate complex, academic ideas into everyday language in order to reach wide audiences. They may write for mass-media newspapers and journals, appear on popular television shows, or sound off on talk
radio. Historically associated with a group of Jewish literary
critics and social commentators who made their mark in New
York City during the mid-twentieth century, public intellectuals seemed close to extinction a generation ago. But as Robert
S. Boynton declared in a 1995 *Atlantic Monthly* cover story, excerpted below, a new breed has arisen in recent times. "And,
most significant, they are black," he writes. Which spokespeo-
ple or commentators do you recognize as framing large social,
cultural, or political debates? Whom among them would you
name as a representative of ordinary people and why? Have
you encountered the ideas of contemporary African-American
intellectuals in newspapers and magazines, or on television
and radio? If so, how would you describe their public voices?

Director of New York University's graduate magazine-
journalism program, Boynton is a widely published cultural
critic whose work has appeared in the *New Yorker, Lingua
Franca*, the *Los Angeles Times Book Review*, and elsewhere. His
areas of expertise include race, religion, and politics.

——————— ◆ ———————

One of the few things most intellectuals will agree on in public is that the age of the public intellectual is over. By and
large, American intellectuals are private figures, their difficult
books written for colleagues only, their critical judgments con-

strained by the boundaries of well-defined disciplines. Think of an intellectual today, and chances are he is a college professor whose "public" barely extends beyond the campus walls.

Today our image of the public intellectual is locked safely in the past, associated almost exclusively with the literary and social critics who gathered around the *Partisan Review* in the 1930s, 1940s, and 1950s. Such writers as Philip Rahv, Edmund Wilson, Lionel Trilling, Alfred Kazin, Irving Howe, and Daniel Bell formed the core of the New York Intellectuals, a group famous for its brazen style, which Howe once described as a combination of "free-lance dash, peacock strut [and] knockout synthesis."

Chronicled and romanticized in a flood of biographies and memoirs, the New York clan has become a veritable gold standard for public intellectuals. Now more praised than read, its members are literary curiosities in the museum of culture; even their most important works—Wilson's *To the Finland Station*, Trilling's *Liberal Imagination*, Kazin's *On Native Grounds*, Bell's *The End of Ideology*, Rahv's *Image and Idea*—are largely ignored or out of print.

The public intellectual's death knell was sounded by Russell Jacoby in his book *The Last Intellectuals* (1987), an indictment of contemporary academic irrelevance which argued that the New Yorkers were not only America's greatest public thinkers but also its last. Academic specialists, rather than sophisticated generalists, now dominated intellectual life, leaving us duller for the loss. "One thousand radical sociologists, but no [C. Wright] Mills; three hundred critical literary theorists but no Wilson," Jacoby lamented. "If the western frontier closed in the 1890s, the cultural frontier closed in the 1950s." With its fashionably apocalyptic title and nostalgic tone, Jacoby's book was a hit, sparking a heated debate ("Hey, what about *us*?" cried an army of radical academics of every political stripe). Yet even though individual thinkers here and there were cited against Jacoby's thesis, a consensus soon formed that the era of the public intellectual was indeed over.

But no sooner had the last opinion piece about Jacoby's book been written than another group of intellectuals began getting quite a bit of attention. If they didn't conform precisely 5 to Jacoby's ideal of the public intellectual—which bears so close a resemblance to the New Yorkers that it is difficult to use as a general definition—they were at the very least developing a significant presence by consistently and publicly addressing some of the most heavily contested issues of the day. The differences were striking, though: Whereas Jacoby's intellectuals were freelance writers based in New York, most of this group is ensconced in elite universities across the country. Whereas the New Yorkers were predominantly male and Jewish, this group includes women and is entirely gentile. In contrast to the New Yorkers, who were formed by their encounters with socialism and European culture, these intellectuals work solidly within the American grain, and are products of the political upheaval of the 1950s and 1960s. And, most significant, they are black.

When the best-selling author Cornel West, now a Harvard professor, and the critic Stanley Crouch appeared on *The Charlie Rose Show* to discuss the connection between race and cities during the Los Angeles riots,[1] they contributed to a tradition of urban social philosophy which originated with Lewis Mumford. When Henry Louis Gates Jr., also of Harvard, denounced black anti-Semitism on the *New York Times* op-ed page, he no doubt reached a wider audience than Norman Podhoretz ever did with similar pieces on black-Jewish relations. When Stephen Carter, of Yale, appeared on the *Today* show to talk about the intricacies of competing affirmative-action policies in the wake of Justice Clarence Thomas's nomination, he took his place alongside Lionel Trilling and Alfred Kazin in explaining the travails of a successful minority figure in a WASP-dominated culture.

Toni Morrison, whose fiction and criticism regularly (and simultaneously) sit on best-seller lists, wins both Nobel and Pulitzer prizes; the Harvard sociologist Orlando Patterson's study of freedom wins the National Book Award; Shelby Steele

---

[1]Aftermath of the acquittal of Los Angeles police officers videotaped beating motorist Rodney King in 1992.

receives the National Book Critics Circle Award for his best-selling meditation on race; David Levering Lewis wins a Pulitzer Prize for his biography of W.E.B. Du Bois; the essayist Stanley Crouch receives a MacArthur "genius" grant; West, Gates, Morrison, and Steele all get six-figure offers for their next books. Add to these names thinkers such as Patricia Williams, William Julius Wilson, bell hooks, Houston Baker, Randall Kennedy, Michael Eric Dyson, Gerald Early, Jerry Watts, Robert Gooding-Williams, Nell Painter, Thomas Sowell, Ellis Cose, Juan Williams, Lani Guinier, Glenn Loury, Michele Wallace, Manning Marable, Adolph Reed, June Jordan, Walter Williams, and Derrick Bell, among others, who appear in magazines and newspapers and on television programs around the country, and one begins to suspect that we are witnessing something bigger than a random blip on the screen of public intellectual culture.

In addressing a large and attentive audience about today's most pressing issues, these thinkers have begun taking their places as the legitimate inheritors of the mantle of the New York Intellectuals. Street-smart, often combative, and equipped with a strong moral sense, they, too, have a talent for shaking things up. This is not at all to say that the current constellation represents America's first black public intellectuals, which would be to ignore the tremendous contributions of such figures as Alain Locke, W.E.B. Du Bois, St. Clair Drake, E. Franklin Frazier, John Hope Franklin, and many others. Rather, the claim is that although opinions may differ about the work of individual contemporary authors, *as a group* they are indisputably receiving extraordinary attention, especially considering the marginal role of the intellectual in America. Nearly all between the ages of roughly thirty-five and fifty-five, the new black intellectuals have achieved a level of recognition usually reserved for near-emeritus figures with numerous books behind them and few years ahead.

How have they become so popular? In addition to their individual achievements and talent, a number of external factors have helped give them prominence. Four are particularly important: They have unprecedented access to the mass-circulation print media. They have been sought out by the electronic media, and shows like *Nightline, Today,* and *The Oprah Winfrey Show* give them extraordinary visibility. Those who are professors—and most are—have used their prestigious university positions to extend their influence beyond the academy. And, finally, they have benefited from America's current concern about race, serving as experts on everything from the L.A. riots and affirmative action to the nominations of Clarence Thomas and Lani Guinier, and *anything* having to do with Louis Farrakhan.[2] They have, indeed, benefited from post-Cold War America's shift in attention from ideological movements abroad to racial issues at home. The central place that the New Yorkers held by virtue of Cold War America's fixation on communism is now occupied by black intellectuals in a society obsessed with race.

10   Surprisingly, given their newfound prominence, a number of contemporary black thinkers who aspire to be public intellectuals find themselves in a genuine quandary. Having distinguished themselves by their analysis of racial subjects, they must now widen their scope and address broader political questions; having received accolades as academic specialists, they must now address a general audience. Secure in their place at the center of mainstream intellectual culture, they must now endure the criticisms of those who accuse them of having shed their "authentic" minority identification and of selling out. Today's African-American public intellectuals are juggling a dizzying number of often conflicting identities and allegiances.

Black intellectuals are important not only because they address an emerging set of public concerns but also because they provide a viable, if radically different, image of what a public intellectual can be.

Recently several black intellectuals have been redirecting their attention from race-based identity politics to the impor-

---

[2]Lani Guinier was a one-time candidate to the U.S. Supreme Court, on which Thomas now serves. Louis Farrakhan is a leader in the Nation of Islam, a pro-black religious movement in the United States.

tance of American citizenship for race relations. That is, they have thought less exclusively about the meaning of "blackness" and more inclusively about what it means to be an African-American—taking pains to scrutinize both sides of the hyphen. Most important, by pointing out the pitfalls of rigid identity politics, they have sought to distance themselves from the notion of victimization that has so dominated race- and ethnicity-specific rhetoric whether formulated by blacks or by whites.

This shift is reminiscent of one Ralph Ellison[3] described as having taken place in Jewish literature. "What the Jewish American writer had to learn before he could find his place was the American-ness of his experience," Ellison wrote. "He had to see himself as American and project his Jewish experience as an experience unfolding within this pluralistic society." Only then, Ellison explained, could the Jewish writer "project this variant of the American experience as a metaphor for the whole." He predicted that black writers would eventually do the same. If Ellison was right and contemporary black intellectuals are moving toward a more pluralistic model, then perhaps a figure like Irving Howe, rather than one like Malcolm X, is standing at the end of the road that black thinkers are now traveling—leading one to wonder whether black and Jewish public thinkers have more in common than is ordinarily thought.

Anyone who steeps himself in the writings of these groups knows that there is no such person as *the* New York Intellectual or *the* black intellectual; the designations are necessarily crude and describe certain figures much better than others. Any broad assumptions one makes about the ideological agreement within either group quickly dissolve once one begins unpacking individual substantive positions. But for all their imprecision, these broad groupings are important, if only because they provide a cultural context for a particular thinker's work; at some level his or her thought will always be perceived as being distinctly black or Jewish. Whereas a university professor can locate himself with some precision

---

[3]Novelist and intellectual (1914–1994) best known for his masterpiece *Invisible Man* (1952), which won the National Book Award in fiction.

within a disciplinary matrix, a public intellectual must often wear a label not of his own choosing.

15   For contemporary black intellectuals, the defining event of their lives was unquestionably the civil-rights movement. Playing a role that Marx believed was the exclusive property of the proletariat, African Americans in the 1950s and 1960s were nothing less than the revolutionary subjects of history. However else one judges the legacy of those decades, one must surely agree with Stephen Carter when he argues that "the massive change in the legal and social status of black Americans was perhaps the most revolutionary aspect of the sixties." Although many members of today's generation of intellectuals were too young to take an active part in the protests and marches, their belief in the necessary and intimate connection between race and politics was gleaned from these events.

Shaped in response to a movement that explicitly used the rhetoric of citizenship to articulate its demands for political equality, this generation's conscious racial identity was qualitatively different from those of the generations that preceded it. Although this group's fate as Americans was still complex, it was a complexity in which the ideas of blackness and American citizenship sat in a determinate—if uneasy—relationship to each other. The *Brown* decision in 1954, the Civil Rights Act of 1964, the Voting Rights Act of 1965, and other legislation combined to create the conditions for a notion of African-American citizenship that was a radical break from the past. Even in the face of brutal and persistent racism, to be black and American was now also to be legally empowered. The very concept of rights, the legal scholar Patricia Williams argues, "feels new in the mouths of most black people. The concept of rights, both positive and negative, is the marker of our citizenship, our relation to others." In this sense, young black intellectuals in the early 1970s understood the possibly beneficial and augmenting connection between their ethnic and American identities.

Post–Malcolm X, post–Martin Luther King, Jr., the younger among them came of age at a distinctive period in the history of race relations: between the time of an inclusive movement, which appealed to what Stanley Crouch calls the "commonality of American concern," and that of a separatist one, which held that blacks could survive only apart from white society. So situated, they enjoyed the fruits of both the civil-rights and the black-nationalist vision without being entirely beholden to either. In this context they developed a hybrid form of racial rhetoric that brought together the lessons of black self-esteem and a belief in the importance of citizens' rights.

This link provided a unique context for a number of political and intellectual developments. One has been the inclination of black thinkers—regardless of their training—to become "race experts" by virtue of their being black. This has been encouraged by those in the media (and elsewhere) who ask them to represent the "black perspective" on any given issue, the assumption being that all black experience has an essential nature—a simplistic assumption that would never be applied to whites.

The belief that there exists an organic connection between one's intellectual sensibility and one's race has not been uncommon. Henry Louis Gates recalls how, as a graduate student in English, he felt a responsibility to study black literature by analyzing what he "thought it was saying to me about the nature of my experiences as a black person living in a historically racist Western culture. . . . [as if I had] embarked upon a mission for all black people."

Among the most striking characteristics one notices in the work of many black intellectuals is how much is written in a deeply personal style, a style usually eschewed by academics. Coming from very different ideological perspectives, Stephen Carter, Shelby Steele, bell hooks, Patricia Williams, Derrick Bell, and others have devoted much of their work to exploring what the literary theorist Houston Baker calls "the African-American autobiographical moment"—in a genre dubbed "autocritography" by Gates, whose most recent book, *Colored People*, is, fittingly, a memoir.

"It is the birthright of the black writer," Gates suggests in a review for *The New Yorker* of the journalist Nathan McCall's memoir, *Makes Me Wanna Holler*, "that his experiences, however personal, are automatically historical." In the work of the most talented writers, this personal style carries a certain revelatory power, as in James Baldwin's marvelously introspective, brooding essays. But not all intellectuals are gifted writers, and for many black thinkers this historical burden is simply too much, resulting in a personal writing style that is merely self-involved. Starting from the fact of their racial identity, some have been reluctant to move much beyond it—an aesthetic that is more admirable in a belletrist than in a wide-ranging public intellectual.

As elite private universities finally opened their doors to black students, in the late sixties and early seventies, blacks' previously token representation suddenly soared—from three at Harvard in the class graduating in 1948, for example, to forty in the class of 1969, to nearly a hundred in the freshman class entering the following year. Afro-American studies programs were established on campuses across the country in response to student protests, thereby sending out a signal that universities were willing to transform themselves by taking into account the perspectives of different racial and ethnic groups.

Arriving on campus as the influence of the radical Black Panthers was cresting, today's younger black intellectuals were more moved than formed by their nationalist ideology. By the time they were old enough to engage the Black Power movement themselves, the arguments were beginning to sound a little old. After flirting with the debate over various ideas of "comparative blackness," Gates came to the conclusion that for him, blackness was "not a material object, an absolute, or an event" but only "a trope." He expands on this insight in *Colored People:* "I want to be black, to know black, to luxuriate in whatever I might be calling blackness at any particular time, but to do so in order to come out the other side, to experience a humanity that is neither colorless nor reducible to color." With the rhetoric of civil rights as a first language, many black thinkers developed a sophisticated sense of their racial identity, more informed by history and politics than by racial metaphysics. "'Race' is *only* a sociopolitical category," Gates writes, "nothing more."

The birth of black studies was a particularly important development, because it provided the institutional as well as the intellectual power base that would later prove helpful when black intellectuals began teaching at the elite universities they had attended. This was the first generation of black scholars to progress almost entirely outside traditionally black institutions like Howard and Morehouse, and it adopted a more optimistic attitude toward the possibilities afforded by an academic life. Whereas the New Yorkers had once feared that university affiliation would deprive them of their intellectual independence, they had come to see that it also gave them tremendous freedom and benefits. Today's black intellectuals have learned from the New Yorkers' experiences. Presented with few intellectually rewarding alternatives, black intellectuals sensed from the beginning that the university, despite its flaws, could be valuable in helping them gain respectability for their views in a credential-obsessed society and in extending their intellectual authority beyond the academic world.

Although black intellectuals have received an enormous amount of attention in the media, the academy, and beyond, it remains to be seen whether they will have an enduring impact on American culture at large. In a thoroughly consumerist society, where anything can be marketed, it must be asked how much of their prominence is due to the cynical exploitation of the same kind of multicultural advertising niche that gave us the "United Colors of Benetton." 25

Have black thinkers been so assimilated that they will find it difficult to keep from becoming mere pundits or intellectual celebrities? In securing places for themselves at the center of the elite academic world and in the mainstream media, have they forfeited their claim on the public intellectual's traditional oppositional stance? Having gained wide recognition through the disposable media of op-ed pieces and talk shows, will they leave enough substantial work behind?

Have black thinkers compromised their legacy with "academic hucksterism and instant-expert witnessing," as Houston Baker suggests? Have they inadvertently traded principled

Kulturkampf[4] for appearances on *Nightline*? As public intellectuals gain greater access to mainstream culture, do they become more important thinkers, or only better known?

Perhaps the style of black public intellectuals can best be appreciated in light of the distinction Daniel Bell once drew between the scholar and the intellectual. The scholar, he wrote, finds his place in an established tradition, adding to it piece by piece as one might to an elaborate mosaic. In contrast, the intellectual "begins with *his* experience, *his* individual perceptions of the world, *his* privileges and deprivations, and judges the world by these sensibilities"—and in so doing uses himself as a litmus test for the way society regards its citizens.

Engaging the Text

1. According to Boynton, how did mid-twentieth-century public intellectuals emerge in the United States and what part did ethnicity play in their rise? What does he find similar and different about the emergence of contemporary public intellectuals today? Why does he emphasize the role of colleges and universities in drawing distinctions?

2. In paragraph 7, Boynton lists many prominent African Americans who are professors, writers, or thinkers, and in many cases all three. Which of these names do you recognize, if any? Can you identify any of their books, articles, radio broadcasts, or television appearances? What do your answers suggest about Boynton's overall argument?

3. According to Boynton, how did today's public intellectuals become popular? In what ways does he consider their "extraordinary visibility" (paragraph 9) an important development in U.S. society? Do you agree or disagree with his reasoning? Focus on specific passages in the text to explain your position.

4. List the "social upheavals" and historical events named in the essay as defining the lives of contemporary black

---

[4]A conflict between civil government and religious authorities, especially over control of education and church appointments.

intellectuals. What connections does the author make between this history and the "rhetoric of citizenship" (paragraph 16)? In your own words, explain what the author means a paragraph later when he writes that black intellectuals "developed a hybrid form of racial rhetoric that brought together the lessons of black self-esteem and a belief in the importance of citizens' rights."

5. In paragraph 23 of the article, Henry Louis Gates, Jr. is quoted as characterizing "blackness" as a "trope" (figure of speech). " 'Race' is *only* a sociopolitical category, nothing more," he concludes. In small groups, discuss the meaning of his claim.

A "Hyphenated Perspective"
Ali Hossaini

In the wake of the attacks on the United States on September 11, 2001, many commentators as well as ordinary citizens have tried to understand the events in terms of our nation's cultural differences. In particular, many people of Arab-American heritage within the United States have found themselves in conflicted circumstances. For instance, individuals may wish to speak about cultural extremists while still promoting a positive worldview of Islam. Ali Hossaini articulates his own unique position in a letter to the editor published in the *Nation* during October of 2001, before the U.S. government went to war in the Middle East. His letter, included here, has since been reprinted in Canadian and German magazines and textbooks.

One of the pioneers of interactive television and electronic media, Hossaini, who received a doctorate in philosophy from the University of Texas in 1994, helped launch MSNBC, WorldLink TV, and other electronic partnerships. A freelance writer and photographer, he has earned fellowships to produce poetry, photography, and philosophy.

———————— ✦ ————————

New York City

Can I be at war with myself? Watching the World Trade Center collapse, then living through the aftermath, I ask that absurd question. I'm American with a Muslim name but nondescript appearance. No one takes me for Middle Eastern—I was born in West Virginia, and I'm only a quarter Arab. But thanks to the peculiarities of history, and naming, I have an Arab-American identity.

The attack on the World Trade Center puts me in an awful place. Like everyone else, I am horrified and angered. I could have been there, munching a bagel on the observation deck. I can't imagine how someone could have planned such an attack, and my shock is turning into anger and mourning. At the same time, I feel excluded from the national unity. Why? As an Arab American, I'm subject to reprisals, I'm nervous, wondering if I will somehow share the blame. Slurs, threats and even violence have been leveled against anyone associated with Islam, and I wonder what will happen to me. I'm looking for work—will I be denied a job? What if a wider war breaks out? Will I lose my liberty?

Some friends have said I should go to Egypt. They meant well, but their comments betrayed a misunderstanding that verges on racism. Hard as it is for the safely white to comprehend, there is only one place for me and other hyphenated Americans: the United States. America produced me. My grandparents hail from four different countries. Where else could they have created a family? If I'm out of place here thanks to my name, I'm certainly out of place in the Middle East, where I stick out as an American. What is left for me? Do we have to pick sides in the end? And what can I do if neither side will have me, if both treat me as the enemy? Some of my fellow citizens are striking out at American Muslims. Some are even calling for a firestorm to be rained upon Islamic nations. Don't they see that the terrorists had the same inspiration? The Afghans were caught between the Soviet Union and the United States for decades. Their country has been reduced to rubble. They have no hope. Violence occurs in cycles, and, if we respond senselessly, striking innocent people in our search for criminals, we'll create more radicals, more suicide bombers who embody the despair of poverty and war. The monopoly on violence is broken, and I shudder to think what comes next.

My situation brings a special clarity, one that opposes   5
choosing sides. What do I see from my hyphenated perspective? The absurdity of labels, indeed, of the whole idea that race, religion or flags divide humanity. I have a Muslim name, but my grandfather was Serbian. How would that fly in the Balkans? Is the world becoming a vast Balkan state?

I've wondered if I will have to choose a side. If I do, here is my choice: pacifism and dialogue. I choose love, I choose humanity. I may symbolize Islam to some and America to others, but I transcend these distinctions. I am proof that love conquers hate. My grandparents conquered tradition to found my family, and I stand tall as an American born from a unique and tolerant soil. What race produced me? The human race. I plead for understanding and compassion. Chase the criminals, but let us then begin to fight. Let us fight not for oil, money or revenge but for a world where hatred and weapons belong to a distant, barbaric past.

Engaging the Text

1. Representing himself in the opening paragraph as "American with a Muslim name but nondescript appearance," what does Hossaini imply about the often invisible circumstances surrounding ethnic identity or cultural differences in the United States?
2. What emotions does the author claim to share with other citizens regarding the September 11, 2001, attack on the World Trade Center? Why does he also "feel excluded from the national unity" (paragraph 2)?
3. Hossaini perceives of well-intended advice dispensed by his "safely white" friends as verging "on racism" (paragraph 3). In what ways do their comments illustrate the idea of white-skin privilege explored by Peggy McIntosh in this chapter?
4. Does the author believe war is a reasonable response to large-scale acts of violence perpetrated by terrorists? How does a "hyphenated perspective" (paragraph 5) influence

his point of view? Given the course of action the U.S. government ultimately chose following 9/11, how insightful do you find Hossaini's position?

5. According to the letter, Americans with hyphenated identities are often faced with "choosing sides." Is this a unique position in American life? Why or why not? To support your answer, discuss a time when your socioeconomic identity or circumstances led you to choose sides in an issue or activity.

Turning Point

RUDOLPH CHELMINSKI

Awe-inspiring and iconic, the twin towers of the World Trade Center, designed by architect Minoru Yamasaki of Detroit, were briefly the world's tallest buildings. When they opened in 1973, many New Yorkers criticized them as both ostentatious and bland. But one August morning a year later, when French high-wire artist Philippe Petit suddenly appeared crossing between them on a tightrope, the WTC became visible in a new way. In the human-interest story that follows, freelance writer Rudolph Chelminski chronicles Petit's career, focusing on the act that transformed Manhattan's skyline. How does a physical landmark acquire meaning through controversy? Has public regard for the WTC again shifted since its destruction by terrorists? What connections do you see between monuments and national memory?

The author of four books and formerly a *Life* staff correspondent in Paris and Moscow, Chelminski has written for numerous American and French publications, including *Time, Fortune, People, Reader's Digest, Wired, France Today,* and *Le Monde*. First published in *Smithsonian*, "Turning Point" appeared in *Best American Essays 2002*.

───────────── ✦ ─────────────

What turned the tide of public regard [for the World Trade Center] was not the bigness of the place but the way it could be momentar-

*ily captured by fanciful gestures on a human scale. It was the
French high-wire artist Philippe Petit crossing between the towers
on a tightrope in 1974. . . .*

—*The New York Times,* September 13, 2001

Was it only 27 years ago? it seems at least a lifetime, or
two, has passed since that August morning in 1974 when
Philippe Petit, a slim, young Frenchman, upstaged Richard
Nixon by performing one of the few acts more sensational—in
those faraway times—than resigning the Presidency of the
United States.

A week before his 26th birthday, the nimble Petit clandes-
tinely strung a cable between the not-yet-completed twin towers, already dominating lower Manhattan's skyline, and for the
better part of an hour walked back and forth over the void,
demonstrating his astonishing obsession to 100,000 or so
wide-eyed gawkers gathered so far below.

I missed that performance, but last summer, just two
weeks before the 1,360-foot-tall towers would come to symbolize a ghastly new reality, I persuaded Petit to accompany me
to the top and show me how he did it and, perhaps, explain
why. I was driven by a long-standing curiosity. Ever since
reading about his exploit in New York, I had felt a kind of familiarity with this remarkable fellow. Years before, I had
watched him at close range and much lower altitude, in another city on the other side of the pond.

In the 1960s, the Montparnasse area of Paris was animated by a colorful fauna of celebrities, eccentrics and artistic
characters. On any given day, you might run into Giacometti
walking bent forward like one of his skinny statues, Raymond
Duncan (Isadora's brother) in his goofy sandals and Roman
toga, or Jean-Paul Sartre morosely seeking the decline of capitalism in the Communist daily, *L'Humanite*. And after nightfall, if you hung around long enough, you were almost certain
to see Philippe Petit.

When he might appear was anyone's guess, but his hang- 5
outs were pretty well known: the corner of rue de Buci and
Boulevard St. Germain; the sidewalk outside Les Deux
Magots, or directly under the terrace windows of La Coupole.

Silent and mysterious, this skinny, pasty-faced kid dressed in black would materialize unannounced on his unicycle, a shock of pale blond hair escaping from under a battered top hat. He would draw a circle of white chalk on the sidewalk, string a rope between two trees, hop up onto it and, impassive and mute as a carp, go into an improvised show that combined mime, juggling, prestidigitation and the precarious balancing act of loose-rope walking. After an hour or so he would pass the hat and, as wordlessly as he had arrived, disappear into the night.

Then, on a drizzly morning in June 1971, the kid in black suddenly showed up dancing on a barely perceptible wire between the massive towers of Notre Dame Cathedral. For nearly three hours, he walked back and forth, mugged, saluted and juggled Indian clubs while angry gendarmes waited for him to come down. When he finally did, they arrested him for disturbing the peace.

Disturbing the peace was a good part of what it was all about, of course, because Petit was out to prove something. Notre Dame was his first great coup, the sensational stunt that was to become his trademark. It was also his first declaration of status: he was not a mere street entertainer but a performer, an artiste. Ever since that June morning, he has dedicated himself to demonstrating his passionate belief that the high wire—his approach to the high wire, that is—transcends the cheap hype of circus "daredevil" routines to become a creative statement of true theater, as valid as ballet or modern dance.

Getting that point across has never been easy. After gratifying Petit with a few front-page pictures, the French establishment gave a Gallic shrug, dismissed him as a youthful crank and returned to more serious matters—like having lunch and talking politics. There was a very interesting story to be told about this young loner who had learned the art of the *funambule* (literally, "rope walker") all by himself as a teenager, but the Parisian press ignored it. Within a couple of days, his Notre Dame stunt was largely forgotten.

Stung, Petit resolved to take his art elsewhere and began a long vagabondage around the world, returning to Paris for brief spells before setting off again. Traveling as light as a medieval minstrel and living hand to mouth, he carried his mute personage from city to city, juggling for his supper. None of his onlookers could know that back in his tiny Parisian studio—a rented broom closet he had somehow converted into a dwelling—he had a folder marked "projects."

Two years after the Notre Dame caper, the skinny figure in black appeared with his balancing pole between the gigantic northern pylons of the Sydney Harbour Bridge in Australia. Petit had strung his cable there just as furtively as he had done at Notre Dame, but this time the police reacted with brainless if predictable fury, attempting to force him down by cutting one of his cavalettis, the lateral guy ropes that hold a sky walker's cable steady. Flung a foot up in the air when the cavaletti sprang free, Petit managed to land square on the cable and keep his balance. He came in and was manacled, led to court and found guilty of the usual crimes. The owner of a Sydney circus offered to pay his $250 fine in return for a tightrope walk two days later over the lions' cage.

And then came the World Trade Center. Petit had been planning it ever since he was 19 when, in a dentist's waiting room, he saw an article with an artist's rendering of the gigantic towers planned for New York's financial district. ("When I see three oranges I juggle," he once said, "and when I see two towers I walk.") He ripped the article from the magazine and slipped it into his projects file.

The World Trade Center would be the ultimate test of Petit's fanatically meticulous planning. For Notre Dame and Sydney, he had copied keys to open certain locks, picked others and hacksawed his way through still others in order to sneak his heavy material up into place for the sky walk. But New York presented a much more complicated challenge. The World Trade Center buildings were fearfully higher than anything he had ever tackled, making it impossible to set up conventional cavalettis. And how to get a cable across the 140-foot gap between the south and north towers, anyway, in the face of omnipresent security crews?

There was one factor in Petit's favor: the buildings were still in the final stages of construction and trucks were regularly delivering all sorts of material to the basement docks, to be transferred to a freight elevator and brought up to the floors by workers of all descriptions. Wearing hard hats, Petit and an accomplice hauled his gear to the top of the south tower (his walking cable passed off as antenna equipment) while two other friends similarly made their way to the roof of the north tower, armed with a bow and arrow and a spool of stout fishing line. Come nightfall, they shot the arrow and line across the 140-foot gap between the towers. Petit retrieved the line, pulled it over until he was in possession of the stronger nylon cord attached to it, then tied on the heavy rope that would be used to carry his steel walking cable over to the other side.

As Petit paid out the rope, and then the cable, gravity took over. The cable ran wild, shooting uncontrollably through his hands and snaking down the side of the giant building before coming up short with a titanic *thwonk!* at the steel beam to which Petit had anchored it. On the north tower, holding fast to the other end of the heavy rope, his friends were pulled perilously close to the roof's edge. Gradually, the four regained control and spent the rest of the night hours pulling the cable up, double-cinching the anchor points, getting it nearly level, tensioning it to three tons with a ratchet and finally attaching a set of nearly horizontal cavalettis to the buildings. At a few minutes past 7 a.m., August 7, 1974, just as the first construction workers were arriving on the rooftop. Petit seized his balancing pole and stepped out over the void.

15   The conditions weren't exactly ideal. Petit had not slept for 48 hours and now he saw that the hurry-up rigging job he had carried out in the dark had resulted in a cable that zigzagged where the improvised cavalettis joined it. Sensitive to wind, temperature and any sway of the buildings, it was also alive— swooping, rolling and twisting. At slightly more than 26 feet, his balancing pole was longer and heavier—55 pounds—than any he had ever used before. Greater weight meant greater stability, but such a heavy load is hard enough to tote around on terra firma, let alone on a thin wire in midair at an insane altitude. It would require an uncommon debauch of nervous energy, but energy was the one thing Petit had plenty of.

With his eyes riveted to the edge of the far tower—wire walkers aren't supposed to look down—Petit glided his buffalo-hide slippers along the cable, feeling his way until he was halfway across. He knelt, put his weight on one knee and swung his right arm free. This was his "salute," the signature gesture of the high-wire artist. Each has his own, and each is an individual trademark creation. Arising, he continued to the north tower, hopped off the wire, double-checked the cable's anchoring points, made a few adjustments and hopped back on.

By now traffic had stopped in the environs of Wall Street, and Petit could already hear the first police and ambulance sirens as he nimbly set forth again. Off he went, humming and mumbling to himself, puffing grunts of concentration at tricky moments. Halfway across, he steadied, halted, then knelt again. And then, God in heaven, he lay down, placing his spine directly atop the cable and resting the balancing pole on his stomach. Breathless, in Zen-like calm, he lay there for a long moment, contemplating the red-eyed seabird hovering motionless above him.

Time to get up. But how do you do it, I asked Petit as we stood together on the roof of the south tower, when the only thing between you and certain death is a cable under your body and 55 extra pounds lying on your belly?

"All the weight on the right foot," he replied with a shrug. "I draw my right foot back along the cable and move the balancing bar lower down below my belt. I get a little lift from the wire, because it is moving up and down. Then I do a sit-up and rise to a standing position, with all the weight on my right foot. It takes some practice."

He got up. Unable to resist the pleasure of seeing New York 20 at his feet, he caressed the side of the building with a glance and slowly panned his eyes all the way down to the gridlocked traffic below. Then he flowed back to the south tower. "I could hear the horns of cars below me," he recalled, relishing the memory. "I could hear the applause too. The *rumeur* [clamor] of the crowd rose up to me from 400 meters below. No other show person has ever heard a sound like that."

Now, as he glided along north to south, a clutch of police officers, rescue crews and security men hovered with arms outstretched to pull him in. But Petit hadn't finished. Inches from their grasp, he did a wire walker's turnaround, slipping his feet 180 degrees and swinging his balancing bar around to face in the other direction. He did his elegant "torero's" walk and his "promenader's" walk; he knelt; he did another salute;

he sat in casual repose, lord of his domain; he stood and balanced on one foot.

After seven crossings and 45 minutes of air dancing, it began to rain. For his finale he ran along the cable to give himself up. "Running, ah! ah!" he had written in one of his early books. "That's the laughter of the wire walker." Then he ran into the arms of waiting police.

Petit's astonishing star turn created a sensation the likes of which few New Yorkers had ever seen. Years later, the art critic Calvin Tompkins was still so impressed by what Petit had done that he wrote in the *New Yorker:* "He achieved the almost unimaginable feat of investing the World Trade Center . . . with a thrilling and terrible beauty."

Ever resourceful, Petit worked out a deal with the Manhattan district attorney. In lieu of punishment or fine, and as penance for his artistic crime, he agreed to give a free performance in Central Park. The following week he strung a 600-foot wire across Turtle Pond, from a tree on one side to Belvedere Castle on the other. And this time he nearly fell. He was wearing the same walking slippers and using the same balancing pole, but security was relaxed among the 15,000 people who had come to watch him perform, and kids began climbing and jumping on his cavalettis. The wire twitched, and suddenly he felt himself going beyond the point of return.

25 But he didn't go all the way down. Instinctively squirming as he dropped, he hooked a leg over the wire. Somehow, he managed to swing himself back up, get vertical and carry on with the performance. The crowd applauded warmly, assuming it was all part of the act, but Petit doesn't enjoy the memory. Falling is the wire walker's shame, he says, and due only to a lack of concentration.

In the years since his World Trade Center triumph, Petit has disdainfully turned away all offers to profit from it. "I could have become a millionaire," he told me. "Everyone was after me to endorse their products, but I was not going to walk a wire dressed in a hamburger suit, and I was not going to say I succeeded because I was wearing such and such a shirt." Continuing to operate as a stubbornly independent freelance artist, he has organized and starred in more than 70 performances around the world, all without safety nets. They have included choreographed strolls across the Louisiana Superdome in New Orieans, between the towers of the Laon Cathedral in France, and a "Peace Walk" between the Jewish and Arab quarters of Jerusalem. In 1989, on the bicentennial of the French Revolution, he took center stage in Paris—legally and officially this time—by walking the 2,300-foot gap between the Trocadero esplanade on the Right Bank, over the Seine and up to the second tier of the Eiffel Tower.

Today, at 52, Petit is somewhat heavier than in his busking days in Paris, and his hair has turned a reddish blond, but neither his energy nor overpowering self-confidence has waned in the least. He shares a pleasantly rustic farmhouse at the edge of the Catskills near Woodstock, New York, with his longtime companion, Kathy O'Donnell, daughter of a former Manhattan publishing executive. She handles the planning, producing, problem-solving and money-raising aspects of Petit's enterprises while they both think up new high-wire projects and he painstakingly prepares them. Petit supplements his income from performances with, among other things, book royalties and fees from giving lectures and workshops.

His preferred place of study is his New York City office. Knowing what an artiste he is, you would not expect to find him in an ordinary building, and you would be right. Petit hangs out at the Cathedral of St. John the Divine, the world's biggest Gothic cathedral, at Amsterdam Avenue and 112th Street. His office is a balustraded aerie in the cathedral's triforium, the narrow gallery high above the vast nave. Behind a locked entryway, up a suitably medieval spiral staircase and then down a stone passageway, the rare visitor to his domain comes upon a sturdy door bearing a small framed sign: *Philippe Petit, Artist in Residence.* Behind that door, stowed as neatly as a yacht's navigational gear, lie his treasures: thousands of feet of rope coiled just so, all manner of rigging and tensioning equipment, floor to ceiling archives, maps and models of past and future walk projects, and shelves upon shelves of technical and reference books.

It was another of his coups that got him there. In 1980 he offered to walk the length of the nave to raise funds for the cathedral's building program. He was sure he had the perfect occasion for it: Ascension Day. The cathedral's then dean, the ebullient James Parks Morton, famous for his support of the arts, was enthusiastic, but his board of trustees vetoed the idea as too dangerous. Petit sneaked a cable crosswise over the nave and did his walk anyway. Once again the police came to arrest him, but Morton spoiled their day by announcing that Petit was artist in residence and the cathedral was his workplace. And so he came to be.

30   Over the years, taking his title seriously, Petit reciprocated by carrying out a dozen wire walks inside and outside the cathedral. He figures that by now he has raised half a million dollars for the still uncompleted cathedral's building program, and enjoys pointing out the small stone carving of a wire walker niched in among the saints in the main portal. "It is high art," Morton says of Petit's work. "There is a documented history of wire walkers in cathedrals and churches. It's not a new idea, but his walk here was his first in an American cathedral."

Sometimes after 6 p.m., when the lights go out, the big front door slams shut and the cathedral closes down for the night, Petit is left alone in the mineral gloom of St. John with his writing, sketches, calculations, chess problems, poetry and reveries. The comparison to Quasimodo is immediate and obvious, of course, but unlike Notre Dame's famous hunchback, Petit wants nothing more than to be seen, in the ever greater, more ambitious and spectacular shows that fill his dreams. One night after he took me up to his cathedral office, he gazed longingly at a print of the Brooklyn Bridge—what a walk that could be! But there is, he assured me, plenty more in his "projects" file. A walk on Easter Island, from the famous carved heads to the volcano. Or the half-mile stretch over open water between the Sydney Harbour Bridge and the celebrated Opera House.

Even more than all these, though, there is one walk—*the* walk, the ultimate, the masterpiece—that has filled his dreams for more than a decade. It's the Grand Canyon. Prospecting in the heart of the Navajo nation by air in 1988, Petit discovered the ideal spot for crowning his career: a ruggedly beautiful landscape off the road from Flagstaff to Grand Canyon Village, where a noble mesa soars at the far end of a 1,200-foot gap from the canyon's edge. The gap is deeper than it is wide, 1,600 feet straight down to the Little Colorado River.

Petit's eyes glowed as he went through the mass of blueprints, maps, drawings and models he has produced over all the years of planning the Canyon Walk. Only one thing is missing: money. Twice now, the money people have backed out at the last minute.

But none of that seemed to matter when I spoke to Petit a few days after the September 11 catastrophe struck. He could scarcely find words for his sorrow at the loss of so many lives, among them people he knew well—elevator operators, tour guides, maintenance workers. "I feel my house has been destroyed," he said. "Very often I would take family and friends there. It was my pride as a poet and a lover of beautiful things to show as many people as possible the audacity of those impossible monoliths."

Haunted, as we all are, by the images of the towers in their final moments, Petit told me it was his hope that they would be remembered not as they appeared then but as they were on that magical August day more than a generation ago, when he danced between them on a wire and made an entire city look up in awe. "In a very small way I helped frame them with glory," he said, "and I want to remember them in their glory." 35

Engaging the Text

1. Notice how Chelminski establishes a rhetorical pattern in the opening paragraphs of the essay by using dates, numbers, and historical references. Where else in the essay does the author repeat this strategy? Do you find it effective in engaging your attention? Analyze specific examples to support your answer.

2. Beginning with the essay's title, locate words and phrases that allude to Philippe Petit's visibility as "an artiste" (paragraph 7) and celebrity. According to the author, what distinguishes Petit's "trademark" (paragraph 7) style of performance and what "projects" (paragraph 9) helped him establish it?

3. Summarize the central narrative of the essay, which describes Petit's glide between the north and south towers of the World Trade Center. What key facts and details does the author choose to commemorate and why? Describe the role of direct quotations in lending credibility to Chelminski's account.

4. Chelminski uses nomenclature (a specialized vocabulary or system of naming) to introduce and describe "the art of *funambule*" (paragraph 8). Identify words and phrases throughout the essay that serve this purpose. Then, in small groups discuss how you might use special or technical language to write about an activity or process, such as playing a sport or musical instrument.
5. Early in the essay, the author suggests that the fallen WTC towers now "symbolize a ghastly reality." How does this observation relate to Petit's feelings about the events of September 11, summarized in the final two paragraphs of the profile? Discuss how the high-wire artist's walk between the twin towers itself claims new meaning since 9/11.

The Peters Projection World Map

Arno Peters

Although borders between states, countries, and continents are imaginary, maps allow us to visualize them, thus framing distinct areas of the planet within a geopolitical context. But German historian Arno Peters, who in 1974 introduced "The Peters Projection World Map," suggests that landmass dimensions as charted on maps may be inaccurate. In the context of mapping, "projection" refers to the process or technique of reproducing a curved surface, such as that of planet earth, upon a spatially flat plane. Although Peters was not a trained cartographer, his projection remains an area-accurate representation. During the 1980s, he published *Peters Atlas of the World*, then the only text of its kind to show all land areas at the same scale. Peters died in 2002.

To view or download "The Peters Projection World Map" via the internet, navigate to www.odt.org. Once the page opens, scroll down to the text describing "Peters World Atlas" and click on the link that reads "Free download of the Peters map." When the link opens, scroll down to the three visual versions of "The Peters Map" (sized small, medium, and large) and click on one to view a clear projection.

Engaging the Text

1. Describe your first impression of "The Peters Projection World Map." Did it appear inaccurately drawn to you and therefore opposing reality? Does the language you used to convey your initial reaction to the image in any way suggest how visual representation affects consciousness? Explain your answers.

2. In what ways does Peters's image invite you to view the world differently than traditional map projections? Explain how the Peters projection attempts to make an alternate world perspective visible.

3. Consider how Peters represents the Western hemisphere. Does his mapping technique focus your attention in a new way? Explain why or why not. Does your answer in any way relate to the viewpoint that places North America at the center of world power? Refer to specific images on the map to support your answers.

4. Interview classmates or other people on your college campus who were raised in countries other than the United States about the world maps they viewed while growing up. What countries were centrally located (i.e., positioned in the middle) on these maps and what does their placement suggest about global perceptions of cultural difference?

5. In small groups, consider ways in which maps are used in the mass media, such as in newspapers, magazines, or television newscasts. What do these representations illustrate or make visible about national and global boundaries? Do you think that maps play a part in organizing your own understanding of race, ethnicity, or nationhood? Explain why or why not.

Responding in Writing

1. Ward Churchill in "*Smoke Signals* in Context," Julia Alvarez in "I Want to Be Miss América," and Michael Bronski in "Queering the Vast Wasteland" describe how particular culture groups have been historically excluded or underrepresented in film, television, or magazines because of race or gender. Choose a specific culture group and track its current representation in a specific mass media. Arrive at a claim about how members of the culture group are represented in the medium and write a paper in which you argue your position. Use specific examples from primary texts to support your point of view. Taking a cue from Churchill, you might consider how frequently and in what contexts Native Americans appear in film. Are they cast in starring roles or do they simply make minor appearances? Drawing on ideas presented in Alvarez's essay, you may wish to study women characters played by Latinos on television shows. Are they successful professionals or low-wage workers? Additionally, you may want to consider whether or not actors, models, or personalities (such as newscasters) appearing in the representations that you are studying seem appropriate for the roles. For example, are openly gay men and lesbians cast to play homosexual characters on television?

2. Many people use mass media to keep in touch with national and world events. But how reliable, inclusive, or objective are the sources to which we turn for information? As Michael Massing ("Press Watch"), John Nichols ("Huey Freeman: American Hero"), and Ali Hossaini ("A 'Hyphenated Perspective' ") all conclude, the events of September 11, 2001 and the aftermath have been represented in a variety of ways—on television news, in comic strips, and through the words of ordinary citizens writing letters to the editors of magazines. Has your understanding of cultural differences evolved or changed since the events of 9/11? Do you consider yourself more informed about global politics since that point in time? Based on your own knowledge gained from a variety of mass-media sources, write a paper in which you thoughtfully analyze your own understanding of national or global differences as influenced by media coverage of 9/11 and related news stories.

3. The interrelated concepts of "invisibility," "whiteness," and "blackness" inform writings in Part II by Peggy McIntosh ("White Privilege: Unpacking the Invisible Knapsack"), Robert S. Boynton ("The New Intellectuals"), and Tim Wise ("Blinded by the White: Crime, Race and Denial at Columbine High"). Choosing racial differences as a starting point, McIntosh and Wise attempt to represent frequently unexamined conditions to which we may be "blind" or choose to render "invisible" that result in social advantages for some groups and disadvantages for others. At the same time, Boynton claims that African Americans with "newfound prominence" and now "at

the center of mainstream intellectual culture" may harbor "conflicting identities and allegiances" (paragraph 10). Write a paper in which you describe how your understanding of race relations in the United States has shifted or been reinforced as a result of reading these essays. For example, do you perceive of humanity's collective embrace of blindness or invisibility as a tool of racial power or domination that has resulted in your own social advantage or disadvantage? On the other hand, given the rise of successful public intellectuals, media personalities, and government officials named in Boynton's essay, do you believe racism is eroding? (Note for example Boynton's mention in paragraph 21 of journalist Nathan McCall's *Makes Me Wanna Holler,* also excerpted in this reader's chapter on schooling.) What do your own experiences and observations tell you?

For another approach to writing about race relations, begin by modeling the list found in McIntosh's article in order to construct your own set of social conditions that you believe you can or cannot count on as a consequence of your race. To narrow your scope, try focusing specifically on social conditions you have experienced or observed on your college campus. Make your list the centerpiece of an essay.

4. Robert S. Boynton in "The New Intellectuals," Ali Hossaini in "A 'Hyphenated Perspective,' " and Arno Peters in "The Peters Projection World Map" demonstrate how artificially constructed or imaginary borders can influence perspectives about cultural differences, including in relation to race and ethnicity, religion, or nationality. For instance, Boynton writes that contemporary black intellectuals "have thought less exclusively about the meaning of 'blackness' and more inclusively about what it means to be an African-American—taking pains to scrutinize both sides of the hyphen" (paragraph 12). Hossaini articulates the perplexities of his particular "hyphenated identity." Peters questions the implications for different cultural groups in visual representations of landmasses. Write an essay in which you compare and contrast how the authors use geographic and spatial concepts (whether words, images, or punctuation marks) to illustrate cultural difference.

As another approach to the assignment, you may wish to consider whether or not you have a bicultural or "hyphenated identity," explaining what it means to live in the United States on both sides of the rhetorical divide.

5. The now fallen twin towers of New York City's World Trade Center were once instantly recognizable icons that symbolized U.S. identity. In "Turning Point," Rudolph Chelminski examines how the meaning and visibility of the former site of the WTC took shape following high-wire artist Philippe Petit's tightrope walk between its towers in 1974. Choose an iconic historical site, building, monument, or physical landmark and write a paper in which you describe what it symbolizes or means to viewers. As an alternative assignment, consider how a mass-media personality or celebrity has raised the visibility of a specific location, discussing the effects of this coverage.

6. In the final sentence of "Turning Point," a quotation by high-wire artist Philippe Petit references the twin towers of the WTC. "I want to remember them in their glory," Petit says. Though architectural plans to rebuild two skyscrapers on the site are now underway, many people, including ordinary U.S. citizens, have conflicting opinions about this decision. How should the site be remembered? Develop an answer to this question by researching opinions on the issue posed in mass-media reports. Then write an argumentative essay in which you develop a position, using the outside sources to support your point of view.

   As an alternative assignment, determine an historical event you would like to see commemorated in a memorial and imagine what the site might look like. Try drawing a simple sketch of your design or use computer graphics to represent it visually. Then write a proposal or statement of purpose that explains your design criteria and purpose.

7. Attempting to represent unexamined conditions and consequences of cultural difference, both Tim Wise and Arno Peters embrace "rhetorical reversal" as a textual strategy. Wise asks readers to imagine what would have happened if the students responsible for the Columbine High School massacre had been black. Peters' map invites observers to imagine a world in which the sizes and shapes of landmasses express a reversal of traditional perspectives. Engage "rhetorical reversal" as a critical thinking strategy and use it to frame an essay that reexamines a recent news item, mass-media event, or visual artifact in which cultural difference plays a significant role.

PART III

Rights
Language and Workplace

Signed by the first Congress of the United States of America on July 4, 1776, The Declaration of Independence holds that individuals deserve unalienable rights, among them "life, liberty, and the pursuit of happiness." But does this doctrine translate into reality when it comes to language or workplace rights? Though the United States does not by law have an official language, those who live and work here generally are expected to speak English. And while the Fair Labor Standards Act enacted by the U.S. Congress in 1938 established the federal minimum wage, no law ensures that job earnings provide workers an adequate standard of living. In fact, as Barbara Ehrenreich reveals in the essay "Serving in Florida," many full-time, year-round workers in America earn poverty-level wages. Meanwhile, many of our lowest wage earners do not speak English. Others may experience job discrimination due to race, class, gender, or national origin, despite preventive measures sanctioned by Equal Employment Opportunity legislation enacted in 1965, commonly known as "affirmative action." Should English be the official language of the United States or should our right to a polyglot coexistence remain? Must people be required to speak and communicate in English in order to survive and prosper in the workplace? Given our racial and linguistic diversity, does affirmative action make sense? The ten selections in Part III address these questions by considering language and workplace rights, demonstrating how these two areas of life frequently overlap.

Part III begins with five selections devoted to controversies surrounding language. Judith Ortiz Cofer ("The Paterson Public Library") looks at how language differences collide, especially when challenged by the dominance of English. "Students' Right to

Their Own Language," a statement issued in 1974 by members of the Conference on College Composition and Communication (CCCC), argues for multilingualism, in schooling and in American life. The selections by Amy Tan ("Mother Tongue") and Luc Sante ("Living in Tongues") illustrate linguistic diversity, at the same time shedding light on the origins of specific dialects. Similar to the framers of the CCCC statement, Robert King considers multilingualism in "Should English Be the Law?" by drawing on linguistic research as well as historical precedent, recognizing the United States as a nation with a diverse "heritage of dialects."

Leading off the chapter on work, Ellis Cose exposes the mythic nature of equal opportunity employment in his essay "Affirmative Action and the Dilemma of the 'Qualified'." Cose suggests that cultural differences regarding race and class promote unfair advantages for some workers at the expense of others. Both Bob Muldoon's first-person account "White-Collar Man in a Blue-Collar World" and Martin Espada's narrative poem "The Foreman's Wallet" examine how the workplace can become a site where cultures clash. Next comes Ehrenreich's investigative report about minimum-wage workers, excerpted from her best-selling book *Nickled and Dimed: On (Not) Getting By in America*. Likewise exposing labor practices that exploit cultural differences among wage earners, in "The Insiders," Marc Peyser and a team of coauthors look at recent Wall Street business scandals that benefited the wealthiest of Americans at the expense of small-time investors.

Part III as a whole demonstrates how language and workplace rights intertwine. For example, in presenting the case for multilingualism, the CCCC authors question the wisdom of the "business world" and "employers" who demand a single-variety language, while Ehrenreich indicts the hotel industry's reliance on housekeepers "at the wrong end of some infallible ethnic equation" (paragraph 12), which encompasses their command of our "unofficial" language. Corroborating Ehrenreich's observations, novelist and essayist Tan suggests that proficiency in English extends to the career paths to which individuals in America are steered.

Do you believe that in exercising certain rights, immigrants or bilingual Americans must abandon their language of origin? Instead, might the ability to speak and communicate in a variety of languages and dialects help strengthen our country's national and global ties, including in matters related to business, industry, and commerce?

CHAPTER 5

Language

The Paterson Public Library
JUDITH ORTIZ COFER

In this retrospective narrative, Judith Ortiz Cofer reflects on mastering the English language as a Puerto Rican girl who sought refuge from her impoverished Paterson, New Jersey, neighborhood at the public library. Cofer suggests that low-income immigrant and minority children "living in large cities" often struggle to become fully literate in English due to challenges permeated on cultural differences. They may have parents who don't speak English, suffer racial stereotypes and prejudices at school, or exhaust their energy on avoiding what the author calls "enemy territory." Should children have the right to safety and a sense of belonging in gaining access to institutions that encourage mastery of English? Consider how Cofer's memoir addresses this question.

Born in Hormigueros, Puerto Rico, but raised primarily in New Jersey, poet, essayist, and novelist Cofer writes extensively about growing up Puerto Rican in the United States. Winner of numerous literary awards and prizes, she is the author or editor of twelve books, including *The Line of the Sun* (1989), *Silent Dancing: A Partial Remembrance of a Puerto Rican Childhood* (1990), and *The Latin Deli* (1993), in which this essay first appeared.

———————— ✦ ————————

It was a Greek temple in the ruins of an American city. To get to it I had to walk through neighborhoods where not even the carcasses of rusted cars on blocks nor the death traps of discarded appliances were parted with, so that the yards of the borderline poor, people who lived not in a huge building, as I did, but in their own decrepit little houses, looked like a reversed archaeological site, incongruous next to the pillared palace of the Paterson Public Library.

The library must have been built during Paterson's boom years as the model industrial city of the North. Enough marble was used in its construction to have kept several Michelangelos busily satisfied for a lifetime. Two roaring lions, taller than a grammar school girl, greeted those brave enough to seek answers there. Another memorable detail about the façade of this important place to me was the phrases carved deeply into the walls—perhaps the immortal words of Greek philosophers—I could not tell, since I was developing astigmatism at that time and could only make out the lovely geometric designs they made.

All during the school week I both anticipated and feared the long walk to the library because it took me through enemy territory. The black girl Lorraine, who had chosen me to hate and terrorize with threats at school, lived in one of the gloomy little houses that circled the library like beggars. Lorraine would eventually carry out her violence against me by beating me up in a confrontation formally announced through the school grapevine so that for days I lived with a panic that has rarely been equaled in my adult life, since now I can get grown-ups to listen to me, and at that time disasters had to be a fait accompli for a teacher or a parent to get involved. Why did Lorraine hate me? For reasons neither one of us fully understood at the time. All I remember was that our sixth grade teacher seemed to favor me, and her way of showing it was by having me tutor "slow" students in spelling and grammar. Lorraine, older and bigger than myself, since she was repeating the grade, was subjected to this ritual humiliation, which involved sitting in the hallway, obviously separated from the class—one of us for being smart, the other for the opposite reason. Lorraine resisted my efforts to teach her the basic rules of spelling. She would hiss her threats at me, addressing me as *You little spic.* Her hostility sent shudders through me. But baffling as it was, I also accepted it as inevitable. She would beat me up. I told my mother and the teacher, and they both reassured me in vague adult terms that a girl like Lorraine would not dare get in trouble again. She had a history of problems that made her a likely candidate for reform school. But Lorraine and I knew that the violence she harbored had found a target: me—the skinny Puerto Rican girl whose father was away with the navy most of the time and whose mother did not speak English; I was the perfect choice.

Thoughts like these occupied my mind as I walked to the library on Saturday mornings. But my need for books was strong enough to propel me down the dreary streets with their slush-covered sidewalks and the skinny trees of winter looking like dark figures from a distance: angry black girls waiting to attack me.

But the sight of the building was enough to reassure me   5
that sanctuary was within reach. Inside the glass doors was the inexhaustible treasure of books, and I made my way through the stacks like the beggar invited to the wedding feast. I remember the musty, organic smell of the library, so different from the air outside. It was the smell of an ancient forest, and since the first books that I read for pleasure were fairy tales, the aroma of transforming wood suited me as a prop.

With my pink library card I was allowed to check out two books from the first floor—the children's section. I would take the full hour my mother had given me (generously adding fifteen minutes to get home before she sent my brother after me) to choose the books I would take home for the week. I made my way first through the world's fairy tales. Here I discovered that there is a Cinderella in every culture, that she didn't necessarily have the white skin and rosy cheeks Walt Disney had given her, and that the prince they all waited for could appear in any color, shape, or form. The prince didn't even have to be a man.

It was the way I absorbed fantasy in those days that gave me the sense of inner freedom, a feeling of power and the ability to fly that is the main reward of the writer. As I read those stories I became not only the characters but their creator. I am still fascinated by the idea that fairy tales and fables are part of humankind's collective unconscious—a familiar theory that acquires concreteness in my own writing today, when I discover over and over that the character I create or the themes that recur in my poems and in my fiction are my own versions of the "types" I learned to recognize very early in my life in fairy tales.

There was also violence in these stories: villains decapitated in honorable battle, goblins and witches pursued, beaten, and burned at the stake by heroes with magic weapons, possessing the supernatural strength granted to the self-righteous in folklore. I understood those black-and-white duels between evil and justice. But Lorraine's blind hatred of my person and my knee-liquefying fear of her were not so clear to me at that time. It would be many years before I learned about the politics of race, before I internalized the awful reality of the struggle for territory that underscored the lives of blacks and Puerto Ricans in Paterson during my childhood. Each job given to a light-skinned Hispanic was one less job for a black man; every apartment leased to a Puerto Rican family was one less place available to blacks. Worst of all, though the Puerto Rican children had to master a new language in the schools and were often subjected to the scorn and impatience of teachers burdened with too many students making too many demands in a classroom, the blacks were obviously the ones singled out for "special" treatment. In other words, whenever possible they were assigned to special education classes in order to relieve the teacher's workload, mainly because their black English dialect sounded "ungrammatical" and "illiterate" to our white Seton Hall University and City College-educated instructors. I have on occasion become angry at being treated like I'm mentally deficient by persons who make that prejudgment upon hearing an unfamiliar accent. I can only imagine what it must have been like for children like Lorraine, whose skin color alone put her in a pigeonhole she felt she had to fight her way out of every day of her life.

I was one of the lucky ones; as an insatiable reader I quickly became more than adept at the use of the English language. My life as a navy brat, moving with my family from Paterson to Puerto Rico every few months as my father's tours of duty demanded, taught me to depend on knowledge as my main source of security. What I learned from books borrowed from the Greek temple among the ruins of the city I carried with me as the lightest of carry-on luggage. My teachers in both countries treated me well in general. The easiest way to become a teacher's pet, or *la favorita*, is to ask the teacher for books to read—and I was always looking for reading material. Even my mother's romantic novels by Corín Tellado and her *Buenhogar* (Spanish *Good Housekeeping* magazine) were not safe from my insatiable word hunger.

Since the days when I was stalked by Lorraine, libraries have always been an adventure for me. Fear of an ambush is no longer the reason why I feel my pulse quicken a little when I approach a library building, when I enter the stacks and inhale the familiar smell of old leather and paper. It may be the memory of the danger that heightens my senses, but it is really the expectation that I felt then and that I still feel now about books. They contained most of the information I needed to survive in two languages and in two worlds. When adults were too busy to answer my endless questions, I could always *look it up*; when I felt unbearably lonely, as I often did during those early gypsy years traveling with my family, I read to escape and also to connect: you can come back to a book as you cannot always to a person or place you miss. I read and reread favorite books until the characters seemed like relatives or friends I could see when I wanted or needed to see them.

10

I still feel that way about books. They represent my spiritual life. A library is my sanctuary, and I am always at home in one. It is not surprising that in recalling my first library, the Paterson Public Library, I have always described it as a temple.

Lorraine carried out her threat. One day after school, as several of our classmates, Puerto Rican and black, circled us to watch, Lorraine grabbed a handful of my long hair and forced me to my knees. Then she slapped my face hard enough that the sound echoed off the brick walls of the school building and ran off while I screamed at the sight of blood on my white knee socks and felt the throbbing on my scalp where I would have a bald spot advertising my shame for weeks to come.

No one intervened. To this crowd, it was one of many such violent scenes taking place among the adults and the children of people fighting over a rapidly shrinking territory. It happens in the jungle and it happens in the city. But another course of action other than "fight or flight" is open to those of us lucky enough to discover it, and that is channeling one's anger and energy into the development of a mental life. It requires something like obsessiveness for a young person growing up in an environment where physical labor and physical endurance are the marks of a survivor—as is the case with minority peoples living in large cities. But many of us do manage to discover books. In my case, it may have been what anthropologists call a cultural adaptation. Being physically small, non-English-speaking, and always the new kid on the block, I was forced to look for an alternative mode to survival in Paterson. Reading books empowered me.

Even now, a visit to the library recharges the batteries in my brain. Looking through the card catalog reassures me that there is no subject that I cannot investigate, no world I cannot explore. Everything that is is mine for the asking. Because I can read about it.

Engaging the Text

1. Notice the description of the Paterson Public Library and its surroundings in paragraphs 1–2 of the essay. Explain why Cofer calls the juxtaposition of the building and the neighborhood "incongruous." What does the library symbolize when compared to a "Greek temple"?

2. Why does the narrator fear walking to the library? Discuss her discomfort in relation to the statement, "It would be many years before I learned about the politics of race, before I internalized the awful reality of the struggle for territory that underscored the lives of blacks and Puerto Ricans in Paterson during my childhood" (paragraph 8). What does the narrative imply about "the struggle for territory" in terms of the mastery of English?

3. According to the essay, what "prejudgments" do people sometimes make about a speaker's intelligence upon hear-

ing his or her "black English dialect" or "an unfamiliar accent" (paragraph 8)? How might such stereotypic reactions undermine equality in a classroom setting?

4. According to the author, how did her "insatiable word hunger" (paragraph 9) help her "to survive in two languages and two worlds" (paragraph 10)? Discuss how Cofer's journey into the world of books compares to that described by Anna Quindlen in "How Reading Changed My Life," in the schooling chapter.

5. Consider the series of related claims that Cofer makes in the final paragraph of the essay. Do your own experiences with visiting and using libraries support her conclusions here? Explain why or why not.

Students' Right to Their Own Language
COMMITTEE ON CCCC LANGUAGE STATEMENT

According to many linguists and language scholars, a proper, unified way of pronouncing and using the English language in the United States, or a so-called "standard American dialect," does not exist. How then can school systems best serve the needs of students, including non-native speakers of English, whose language habits originate in diverse social, cultural, and economic circumstances? Responding to this question in 1974, a group of speech and writing teachers, all members of the Conference on College Composition and Communication (CCCC), drafted an historic document known as "Students' Right to Their Own Language." According to this CCCC special committee, students deserve the "right to their own patterns and varieties of language," that is, to "whatever dialects in which they find their own identity and style." Do you agree with this assertion or believe that students in twenty-first-century classrooms should adapt to a shared-language standard in speaking and writing? In furthering your thinking on the subject, consider the following excerpt, which contains the first four (of fifteen total) sections of "Students' Right to Their Own Language."

———————————— ✦ ————————————

American schools and colleges have, in the last decade, been forced to take a stand on a basic educational question: what should the schools do about the language habits of students who come from a wide variety of social, economic, and cultural backgrounds? The question is not new. Differences in language have always existed, and the schools have always wrestled with them, but the social upheavals of the 1960's, and the insistence of submerged minorities on a greater share in American society, have posed the question more insistently and have suggested the need for a shift in emphasis in providing answers. Should the schools try to uphold language variety, or to modify it, or to eradicate it?

The emotional nature of the controversy has obscured the complexities of the problem and hidden some of the assumptions that must be examined before any kind of rational policy can be adopted. The human use of language is not a simple phenomenon: sophisticated research in linguistics and sociology has demonstrated incontrovertibly that many long held and passionately cherished notions about language are misleading at best, and often completely erroneous. On the other hand, linguistic research, advanced as much of it is, has not yet produced any absolute, easily understood, explanation of how people acquire language or how habits acquired so early in life that they defy conscious analysis can be consciously changed. Nor is the linguistic information that is available very widely disseminated. The training of most English teachers has concentrated on the appreciation and analysis of literature, rather than on an understanding of the nature of language, and many teachers are, in consequence, forced to take a position on an aspect of their discipline about which they have little real information.

And if teachers are often uninformed, or misinformed, on the subject of language, the general public is even more ignorant. Lack of reliable information, however, seldom prevents people from discussing language questions with an air of absolute authority. Historians, mathematicians, and nurses all hold decided views on just what English teachers should be requiring. And through their representatives on Boards of Education and Boards of Regents, businessmen, politicians, parents, and the students themselves insist that the values taught by the schools must reflect the prejudices held by the public. The English profession, then, faces a dilemma: until public attitudes can be changed—and it is worth remembering that the past teaching in English classes has been largely responsible for those attitudes—shall we place our emphasis on what the vocal elements of the public think it wants or on what the actual available linguistic evidence indicates we should emphasize? Shall we blame the business world by saying, "Well, we realize that human beings use language in a wide variety of ways, but employers demand a single variety"?

Before these questions can be responsibly answered, English teachers at all levels, from kindergarten through college, must uncover and examine some of the assumptions on which our teaching has rested. Many of us have taught as though there existed somewhere a single American "standard English" which could be isolated, identified, and accurately defined. We need to know whether "standard English" is or is not in some sense a myth. We have ignored, many of us, the distinction between speech and writing and have taught the language as though the *talk* in any region, even the talk of speakers with prestige and power, were identical to edited *written* English.

We have also taught, many of us, as though the "English of   5 educated speakers," the language used by those in power in the community, had an inherent advantage over other dialects as a means of expressing thought or emotion, conveying information, or analyzing concepts. We need to discover whether our attitudes toward "educated English" are based on some inherent superiority of the dialect itself or on the social prestige of those who use it. We need to ask ourselves whether our rejection of students who do not adopt the dialect most familiar to us is based on any real merit in our dialect or whether we are actually rejecting the students themselves, rejecting them because of their racial, social, and cultural origins.

And many of us have taught as though the function of schools and colleges were to erase differences. Should we, on the one hand, urge creativity and individuality in the arts and the sciences, take pride in the diversity of our historical development, and, on the other hand, try to obliterate all the differences in the way Americans speak and write? Our major emphasis has been on uniformity, in both speech and writing; would we accomplish more, both educationally and ethically, if we shifted that emphasis to precise, effective, and appropriate communication in diverse ways, whatever the dialect?

It was with these concerns in mind that the Executive Committee of the Conference on College Composition and Communication, in 1972, passed the following resolution:

> We affirm the students' right to their own patterns and varieties of language—the dialects of their nurture or whatever dialects in which they find their own identity and style. Language scholars long ago denied that the myth of a standard American dialect has any validity. The claim that any one dialect is unacceptable amounts to an attempt of one social group to exert its dominance over another. Such a claim leads to false advice for speakers and writers, and immoral advice for humans. A nation proud of its diverse heritage and its cultural and racial variety will preserve its heritage of dialects. We affirm strongly that teachers must have the experiences and training that will enable them to respect diversity and uphold the right of students to their own language.

The members of the Committee realized that the resolution would create controversy and that without a clear explanation of the linguistic and social knowledge on which it rests, many people would find it incomprehensible. The members of the Executive Committee, therefore, requested a background statement which would examine some common misconceptions about language and dialect, define some key terms, and provide some suggestions for sounder, alternate approaches. What follows is not, then, an introductory course in linguistics, nor is it a teaching guide. It is, we hope, an answer to some of the questions the resolution will raise.

I. WHAT DO WE MEAN BY DIALECT?

A dialect is a variety of a language used by some definable group. Everyone has a personal version of language, an idiolect,[1] which is unique, and closely related groups of idiolects make up dialects. By custom, some dialects are spoken. Others are written. Some are shared by the community at large. Others are confined to small communities, neighborhoods, or social groups. Because of this, most speakers, consciously or unconsciously, use more than one dialect. The need for varying dialects may arise from a speaker's membership in different age or educational groups. Or, it may arise from membership in groups tied to physical localities. The explanation of what a dialect is becomes difficult when we recognize that dialects are developed in response to many kinds of communication needs. And further complications occur because the user of a specific dialect, as a function of habit, can choose alternate forms which seem effective for given situations.

A dialect is the variety of language used by a group whose   10
linguistic habit patterns both reflect and are determined by shared regional, social, or cultural perspectives. The user of a specific dialect employs the phonological (pronunciation), lexical (vocabulary), and syntactic patterns (word arrangement) and variations of the given "community." Because geographical and social isolation are among the causes of dialect differences, we can roughly speak about regional and social dialects. Regional differences in phonology[2] may become quite evident when one hears a Bostonian say "pahk the cah" where a Midwesterner would say "parrk the car." Regional differences in vocabulary are also quite noticeable as in the words

---

[1]The language or speech pattern of one individual at certain point in life.
[2]The study of speech sounds.

used throughout the country for a carbonated drink. Depending on where one is geographically, you can hear "soda," "soda water," "sweet soda," "soft drink," "tonic," "pop," or "cold drink." Regional differences in syntactic patterns are found in such statements as "The family is to home," and "The family is at home." Social differences can also be detected. Social differences in phonology are reflected in "goil" versus "girl." Social differences in vocabulary are reflected in the distinctions made between "restaurant" and "cafe." Syntactic phrases such as "those flowers" tend to have more prestige than "them flowers," and "their flowers" has more prestige than "they flowers."

It is not surprising to find two or more social dialects coexisting in a given region. In small towns where a clear social cleavage exists between the wealthier, more educated portion of the population and the mass of people, the difference may be reflected in their speechways. The local banker whose dialect reveals his group allegiance to the statewide financial community still is able to communicate easily with the local farmhand who may rarely cross the county line and whose linguistic habit patterns reveal different allegiances.

In many larger American cities people of the same ethnic origins tend to live in a single neighborhood and have a common culture and thus share a dialect. Through their clothing, games, and holidays they may preserve the values and customs of the "old country" or "back home." And in their restaurants, churches, schools, and homes, one may hear the linguistic values and customs of their heritage preserved. For example, a neighborhood group's cultural orientation may encourage its members to differentiate between action and intention in the immediate future and in a still-further immediate future through "I'm a-do it" and "I'm a'gonna do it." Yet, a neighborhood is not a country, so speakers of several dialects may mingle there and understand each other. Visitors with yet another heritage may render an approximation of such differentiation through "I'll do it now" and "I'll do it soon." Pride in cultural heritage and linguistic habit patterns need not lead either group to attack the other as they mingle and communicate.

II. WHY AND HOW DO DIALECTS DIFFER?

Differences in dialects derive from events in the history of the communities using the language, not from supposed differences in intelligence or physiology.[3] Although they vary in phonology, in vocabulary, and in surface grammatical patterns, the differences between neighboring dialects are not sufficiently wide to prevent full mutual comprehension among speakers of those dialects. That is to say, when speakers of a dialect of American English claim not to understand speakers of another dialect of the same language, the impediments are likely to be attitudinal. What is really the hearer's resistance to any unfamiliar form may be interpreted as the speaker's fault. For example, an unfamiliar speech rhythm and resulting pronunciation while ignoring the content of the message. When asked to respond to the content, they may be unable to do so and may accuse the speaker of being impossible to understand. In another situation, vocabulary differences may require that the hearers concentrate more carefully on contextual cues. If the word "bad" is being used as a term of praise, the auditor may have to pay unusual attention to context. Although the usual redundancies of speech ordinarily will provide sufficient cues to permit a correct interpretation, still the auditor has to work harder until he becomes accustomed to the differences. The initial difficulties of perception can be overcome and should not be confused with those psychological barriers to communication which may be generated by racial, cultural and social differences and attitudes.

III. HOW DO WE ACQUIRE OUR DIALECTS?

The manner in which children acquire language (and hence dialect) competence is unknown in spite of some research and much speculation on the subject. Theories ranging from the

---

[3]The branch of biology that deals with the internal workings of living things.

purely behavioristic to the highly metaphysical have been proposed. What is demonstrable, and hence known, is that children at very early ages begin to acquire performance skills in the dialect(s) used in their environment, and that this process is amazingly rapid compared to many other types of learning.

15   Before going to school, children possess basic competence in their dialects. For example, children of six know how to manipulate the rules for forming plurals in their dialects. In some dialects children add an "s" to the word to be pluralized as in "book/books." In some other dialects, plurality is signaled by the use of the preceding word as in "*one* book/*two* book." But in either instance children have mastered the forms of plurality and have learned a principle of linguistic competence. It is important to remember that plurality signals for the nurture dialect reflect children's reality and will be their first choice in performance; plurality rules for another dialect may simply represent to them the rituals of someone else's linguistic reality.

IV. WHY DO SOME DIALECTS HAVE MORE PRESTIGE THAN OTHERS?

In a specific setting, because of historical and other factors, certain dialects may be endowed with more prestige than others. Such dialects are sometimes called "standard" or "consensus" dialects. These designations of prestige are not inherent in the dialect itself, but are *externally imposed*, and the prestige of a dialect shifts as the power relationships of the speakers shift.

     The English language at the beginning of its recorded history was already divided into distinct regional dialects. These enjoyed fairly equal prestige for centuries. However, the centralization of English political and commercial life at London gradually gave the dialect spoken there a preeminence over other dialects. This process was far advanced when printing was invented; consequently, the London dialect became the dialect of the printing press, and the dialect of the printing press became the so-called "standard" even though a number of oral readings of one text would reveal different pronunciations and rhythmic patterns across dialects. When the early American settlers arrived on this continent, they brought their British dialects with them. Those dialects were altered both by regional separation from England and concentration into sub-groups within this country as well as by contact with the various languages spoken by the Indians [sic] they found here and with the various languages spoken by the immigrants who followed.

At the same time, social and political attitudes formed in the old world followed to the new, so Americans sought to achieve linguistic marks of success as exemplified in what they regarded as proper, cultivated usage. Thus the dialect used by prestigious New England speakers early became the "standard" the schools attempted to teach. It remains, during our own time, the dialect that style books encourage us to represent in writing. The diversity of our cultural heritage, however, has created a corresponding language diversity and, in the 20th century, most linguists agree that there is no single, homogeneous American "standard." They also agree that, although the amount of prestige and power possessed by a group can be recognized through its dialect, no dialect is inherently good or bad.

The need for a written dialect to serve the larger, public community has resulted in a general commitment to what may be called "edited American English," that prose which is meant to carry information about our representative problems and interests. To carry such information through aural-oral media, "broadcast English" or "network standard" has been developed and given precedence. Yet these dialects are subject to change, too. Even now habit patterns from other types of dialects are being incorporated into them. Our pluralistic society requires many varieties of language to meet our multiplicity of needs.

Engaging the Text

1. What attitudes about language use in American schools and colleges provoked the authors to write the CCCC statement? Consider the question by looking at paragraphs 1–6 of the document. How and why do the authors differentiate between "standard English," "written English," and "educated English"? How do these distinctions

connect to references to "differences" contained within the same paragraphs?

2. In section 1, how do the authors define and illustrate "dialect"? How do their examples of specific differences in vocabulary or phonology illustrate "the myth of standard American dialect" referred to in the CCCC resolution of 1972 (paragraph 7)?

3. Summarize the authors' explanation presented in section 2 for why and how dialects differ. How effective is the specialized vocabulary in conveying this information?

4. According to the authors, what can researchers tell us about how individuals acquire dialects?

5. In the final section, what do the authors mean when stating that "standard" or "consensus" dialects are "externally imposed," shifting "as the power relationships of speakers shift"? How does this idea support the final sentence of the excerpt? Do you agree or disagree with the authors' conclusion here? Support your position by referring to your own language habits.

Mother Tongue
AMY TAN

Born in Oakland, California, to Chinese-immigrant parents, Amy Tan grew up using what she calls "different Englishes," picking one kind over another depending on the circumstances. In this essay, Tan explores both the limitations and possibilities of her "mother tongue," the name she gives to the English spoken within her family. Do you find yourself speaking differently in and out of your college classes or notice a switch in the way you use language on campus versus back in the neighborhood where you were raised? How about when writing a required paper versus writing an email message to a friend? What does your code switching (to move back and forth between languages or dialects) suggest about language as a marker of cultural difference?

A best-selling fiction writer and essayist, Tan wrote the highly acclaimed novel *The Joy Luck Club* (1989), which was made into a film directed by Wayne Wang. Her other notable books include *The Kitchen God's Wife* (1991), *The Hundred Secret Senses* (1995), *The Bonesetter's Daughter* (2001), and the children's book *The Moon Lady* (1992). Originally published in the *Three Penny Review,* "Mother Tongue" appears in *The Best American Essays 1991.*

— — — — — — — ✦ — — — — — — —

I am not a scholar of English or literature. I cannot give you much more than personal opinions on the English language and its variations in this country or others.

I am a writer. And by that definition, I am someone who has always loved language. I am fascinated by language in daily life. I spend a great deal of my time thinking about the power of language—the way it can evoke an emotion, a visual image, a complex idea, or a simple truth. Language is the tool of my trade. And I use them all—all the Englishes I grew up with.

Recently, I was made keenly aware of the different Englishes I do use. I was giving a talk to a large group of people, the same talk I had already given to half a dozen other groups. The nature of the talk was about my writing, my life, and my book, *The Joy Luck Club.* The talk was going along well enough, until I remembered one major difference that made the whole talk sound wrong. My mother was in the room. And it was perhaps the first time she had heard me give a lengthy speech, using the kind of English I have never used with her. I was saying things like, "The intersection of memory upon imagination" and "There is an aspect of my fiction that relates to thus-and-thus"—a speech filled with carefully wrought grammatical phrases, burdened, it suddenly seemed to me, with nominalized forms, past perfect tenses, conditional phrases, all the forms of standard English that I had learned in school and through books, the forms of English I did not use at home with my mother.

Just last week, I was walking down the street with my mother, and I again found myself conscious of the English I was using, the English I do use with her. We were talking about the price of new and used furniture and I heard myself saying this: "Not waste money that way." My husband was with us as well, and he didn't notice any switch in my English. And then I realized why. It's because over the twenty years we've been together I've often used that same kind of English with him, and sometimes he even uses it with me. It has become our language of intimacy, a different sort of English that relates to family talk, the language I grew up with.

5   So you'll have some idea of what this family talk I heard sounds like, I'll quote what my mother said during a recent conversation which I videotaped and then transcribed. During this conversation, my mother was talking about a political gangster in Shanghai who had the same last name as her family's, Du, and how the gangster in his early years wanted to be adopted by her family, which was rich by comparison. Later, the gangster became more powerful, far richer than my mother's family, and one day showed up at my mother's wedding to pay his respects. Here's what she said in part:

"Du Yusong having business like fruit stand. Like off the street kind. He is Du like Du Zong—but not Tsung-ming Island people. The local people call putong, the river east side, he belong to that side local people. That man want to ask Du Zong father take him in like become own family. Du Zong father wasn't look down on him, but didn't take seriously, until that man big like become a mafia. Now important person, very hard to inviting him. Chinese way, came only to show respect, don't stay for dinner. Respect for making big celebration, he shows up. Mean gives lots of respect. Chinese custom. Chinese social life that way. If too important won't have to stay too long. He come to my wedding. I didn't see, I heard it. I gone to boy's side, they have YMCA dinner. Chinese age I was nineteen."

You should know that my mother's expressive command of English belies how much she actually understands. She reads the *Forbes* report, listens to *Wall Street Week*, converses daily with her stockbroker, reads all of Shirley MacLaine's books with ease—all kinds of things I can't begin to understand. Yet some of my friends tell me they understand 50 percent of what my mother says. Some say they understand

80 to 90 percent. Some say they understand none of it, as if she were speaking pure Chinese. But to me, my mother's English is perfectly clear, perfectly natural. It's my mother tongue. Her language, as I hear it, is vivid, direct, full of observation and imagery. That was the language that helped shape the way I saw things, expressed things, made sense of the world.

Lately, I've been giving more thought to the kind of English my mother speaks. Like others, I have described it to people as "broken" or "fractured" English. But I wince when I say that. It has always bothered me that I can think of no way to describe it other than "broken," as if it were damaged and needed to be fixed, as if it lacked a certain wholeness and soundness. I've heard other terms used, "limited English," for example. But they seem just as bad, as if everything is limited, including people's perceptions of the limited English speaker.

I know this for a fact, because when I was growing up, my mother's "limited" English limited *my* perception of her. I was ashamed of her English. I believed that her English reflected the quality of what she had to say. That is, because she expressed them imperfectly her thoughts were imperfect. And I had plenty of empirical evidence to support me: the fact that people in department stores, at banks, and at restaurants did not take her seriously, did not give her good service, pretended not to understand her, or even acted as if they did not hear her.

My mother has long realized the limitations of her English as well. When I was fifteen, she used to have me call people on the phone to pretend I was she. In this guise, I was forced to ask for information or even to complain and yell at people who had been rude to her. One time it was a call to her stockbroker in New York. She had cashed out her small portfolio and it just so happened we were going to go to New York the next week, our very first trip outside California. I had to get on the phone and say in an adolescent voice that was not very convincing, "This is Mrs. Tan." 10

And my mother was standing in the back whispering loudly, "Why he don't send me check, already two weeks late. So mad he lie to me, losing me money."

And then I said in perfect English, "Yes, I'm getting rather concerned. You had agreed to send the check two weeks ago, but it hasn't arrived." Then she began to talk more loudly. "What he want, I come to New York tell him front of his boss, you cheating me?" And I was trying to calm her down, make her be quiet while telling the stockbroker, "I can't tolerate any more excuses. If I don't receive the check immediately, I am going to have to speak to your manager when I'm in New York next week." And sure enough, the following week there we were in front of this astonished stockbroker, and I was sitting there red-faced and quiet, and my mother, the real Mrs. Tan, was shouting at his boss in her impeccable broken English.

We used a similar routine just five days ago, for a situation that was far less humorous. My mother had gone to the hospital for an appointment, to find out about a benign brain tumor a CAT scan had revealed a month ago. She said she had spoken very good English, her best English, no mistakes. Still, she said, the hospital did not apologize when they said they had lost the CAT scan and she had come for nothing. She said they did not seem to have any sympathy when she told them she was anxious to know the exact diagnosis, since her husband and son had both died of brain tumors. She said they would not give her any more information until the next time and she would have to make another appointment for that. So she said she would not leave until the doctor called her daughter. She wouldn't budge. And when the doctor finally called her daughter, me, who spoke in perfect English—lo and behold—we had assurances the CAT scan would be found, promises that a conference call on Monday would be held, and apologies for any suffering my mother had gone through for a most regrettable mistake.

15   I think my mother's English almost had an effect on limiting my possibilities in life as well. Sociologists and linguists probably will tell you that a person's developing language skills are more influenced by peers. But I do think that the language spoken in the family, especially in immigrant families which are more insular, plays a large role in shaping the language of the child. And I believe that it affected my results on achievement tests, IQ tests, and the SAT. While my English

skills were never judged as poor, compared to math, English could not be considered my strong suit. In grade school I did moderately well, getting perhaps B's, sometimes B-pluses, in English and scoring perhaps in the sixtieth or seventieth percentile on achievement tests. But those scores were not good enough to override the opinion that my true abilities lay in math and science, because in those areas I achieved A's and scored in the ninetieth percentile or higher.

This was understandable. Math is precise; there is only one correct answer. Whereas, for me at least, the answers on English tests were always a judgment call, a matter of opinion and personal experience. Those tests were constructed around items like fill-in-the-blank sentence completion, such as, "Even though Tom was _____, Mary thought he was _____." And the correct answer always seemed to be the most bland combinations of thoughts, for example, "Even though Tom was shy, Mary thought he was charming," with the grammatical structure "even though" limiting the correct answer to some sort of semantic opposites, so you wouldn't get answers like, "Even though Tom was foolish, Mary thought he was ridiculous." Well, according to my mother, there were very few limitations as to what Tom could have been and what Mary might have thought of him. So I never did well on tests like that.

The same was true with word analogies, pairs of words in which you were supposed to find some sort of logical, semantic relationship—for example, "*Sunset* is to *nightfall* as _____ is to _____." And here you would be presented with a list of four possible pairs, one of which showed the same kind of relationship: *red* is to *stoplight*, *bus* is to *arrival*, *chills* is to *fever*, *yawn* is to *boring*. Well, I could never think that way. I knew what the tests were asking, but I could not block out of my mind the images already created by the first pair, "*sunset* is to *nightfall*"—and I would see a burst of colors against a darkening sky, the moon rising, the lowering of a curtain of stars. And all the other pairs of words—red, bus, stoplight, boring— just threw up a mass of confusing images, making it impossible for me to sort out something as logical as saying: "A sunset precedes nightfall" is the same as "a chill precedes a fever." The only way I would have gotten that answer right would have been to imagine an associative situation, for example, my being disobedient and staying out past sunset, catching a chill at night, which turns into feverish pneumonia as punishment, which indeed did happen to me.

I have been thinking about all this lately, about my mother's English, about achievement tests. Because lately I've been asked, as a writer, why there are not more Asian Americans represented in American literature. Why are there few Asian Americans enrolled in creative writing programs? Why do so many Chinese students go into engineering? Well, these are broad sociological questions I can't begin to answer. But I have noticed in surveys— in fact, just last week—that Asian students, as a whole, always do significantly better on math achievement tests than in English. And this makes me think that there are other Asian-American students whose English spoken in the home might also be described as "broken" or "limited." And perhaps they also have teachers who are steering them away from writing and into math and science, which is what happened to me.

Fortunately, I happen to be rebellious in nature and enjoy the challenge of disproving assumptions made about me. I became an English major my first year in college, after being enrolled as pre-med. I started writing nonfiction as a freelancer the week after I was told by my former boss that writing was my worst skill and I should hone my talents toward account management.

20   But it wasn't until 1985 that I finally began to write fiction. And at first I wrote using what I thought to be wittily crafted sentences, sentences that would finally prove I had mastery over the English language. Here's an example from the first draft of a story that later made its way into *The Joy Luck Club*, but without this line: "That was my mental quandary in its nascent state." A terrible line, which I can barely pronounce.

Fortunately, for reasons I won't get into today, I later decided I should envision a reader for the stories I would write. And the reader I decided upon was my mother, because these were stories about mothers. So with this reader in mind—and in fact she did read my early drafts—I began to write stories using all the Englishes I grew up with: the English I spoke to my mother, which for lack of a better term might be described as "simple"; the English she used with me, which for lack of a better term might be described as "broken"; my translation of her Chinese, which could certainly be described as "watered down"; and what I imagined to be her translation of her Chinese if she could speak in perfect English, her internal language, and for that I sought to preserve the essence, but neither an English nor a Chinese structure. I wanted to capture what language ability tests can never reveal: her intent, her passion, her imagery, the rhythms of her speech and the nature of her thoughts.

Apart from what any critic had to say about my writing, I knew I had succeeded where it counted when my mother finished reading my book and gave me her verdict: "So easy to read."

Engaging the Text

1. Describe how the author becomes "keenly aware of the different Englishes" (paragraph 3) that she uses. What is her attitude toward this realization and why?
2. According to Tan, how have people described the type of English spoken by her mother? Why is the author critical of this phrasing? What words would you use to characterize the conversational speech of Mrs. Tan quoted in paragraph 6? In framing your response, consider linguistic vocabulary presented in the selection "Students' Rights to Their Own Language."
3. Throughout the essay, Tan presents facts and anecdotes about her mother's proficiency in English. How does Mrs. Tan's "expressive command of English" (paragraph 7) sometimes falsely affect other people's perceptions of her? What is the author's purpose in presenting their reactions? How does it relate to Judith Ortiz Cofer's observation, contained earlier in this chapter that "black English dialect sounded 'ungrammatical' and 'illiterate'" (paragraph 8) to the white school teachers of her childhood?
4. What connections does the author make between "the language spoken in the family, especially immigrant families"

(paragraph 15) and academic testing? How well do the sample test questions presented in paragraphs 17 and 18 support her line of reasoning here?

5. Why does Tan believe that few Asian-American college students enroll in creative writing programs, instead choosing math, science, or engineering? According to the author, how can growing up using different Englishes in fact enable a writer? How might such a writer ultimately expand and enrich American literature?

Living in Tongues
Luc Sante

Born in a Belgium factory town, Luc Sante immigrated to the United States with his family in 1959. In this memoir, Sante reflects on how the experience of growing up fluent in English, French, and a Belgian dialect called Walloon influenced the person he came to be, "not rootless but multiply rooted" as he concludes. How does language shape who we are as individuals? What role does language play in influencing our perceptions of U.S. culture as well as our place within it?

"Living in Tongues," excerpted from Sante's 1998 memoir *The Factory of Facts*, was selected for *The Best American Essays 1997*. The author of several other books, including *Low Life: Lures and Snares of Old New York* (1991), *Evidence* (1992), and *Walker Evans* (1998), he recently wrote the introduction to *Gangs of New York: Making the Movie* (2003). A frequent contributor of reviews and commentaries on art, film, and photography to many national publications, he has taught at Bard College and Princeton University.

———————— ✦ ————————

The first thing you have to understand about my childhood is that it mostly took place in another language. I was raised speaking French, and did not begin learning English until I was nearly seven years old. Even after that, French continued to be the language I spoke at home with my parents. (I still speak only French with them to this day.) This fact inevitably affects my recall and evocation of my childhood, since I am writing and primarily thinking in English. There are states of mind, even people and events, that seem inaccessible in English, since they are defined by the character of the language through which I perceived them. My second language has turned out to be my principal tool, my means for making a living, and it lies close to the core of my self-definition. My first language, however, is coiled underneath, governing a more primal realm.

French is a pipeline to my infant self, to its unguarded emotions and even to its preserved sensory impressions. I can, for example, use language as a measure of pain. If I stub my toe, I may profanely exclaim, in English, "Jesus!" But in agony, such as when I am passing a kidney stone, I become uncharacteristically reverent, which is only possible for me in French. "*Petit Jésus!*" I will cry, in the tones of nursery religion. When I babble in the delirium of fever or talk aloud in my sleep, I have been told by others, I do so in French. But French is also capable of summoning up a world of lost pleasures. The same idea, expressed in different languages, can have vastly different psychological meanings. If, for example, someone says in English, "Let's go visit Mr. and Mrs. X," the concept is neutral, my reaction determined by what I think of Mr. and Mrs. X. On the other hand, if the suggestion is broached in French, "*Allons dire bonjour,*" the phrasing affects me more powerfully than the specifics. "*Dire bonjour*" calls up a train of associations: for some reason, I see my great-uncle Jules Stelmes, dead at least thirty years, with his fedora and his enormous white mustache and his soft dark eyes. I smell coffee and the raisin bread called *cramique,* hear the muffled bong of a parlor clock and the repetitive commonplaces of chitchat in the drawling accent of the Ardennes, people rolling their *s*'s and leaning hard on their initial *h*'s. I feel a rush-caned chair under me, see white curtains and starched tablecloths, can almost tap my feet on the cold ceramic tiles, perhaps the trompe-l'oeil pattern that covered the entire floor surface of my great-uncle Albert Remacle's farmhouse in Viville. I am sated, sleepy, bored out of my mind.

A large number of French words and turns of phrase come similarly equipped with dense associative catalogues, which may contain a ghostly impression of the first time I understood their use in speech. On the other hand, nearly all English words and phrases have a definite point of origin, which I can usually recall despite the overlaying patina acquired through years of use. Take that word "patina," for example. I don't remember how old I was when I first encountered it, but I know that I immediately linked it to the French *patiner,* meaning "to skate," so that its use calls up an image of a cross-hatched pond surface.

Other English words have even more specific histories. There is "coffee," which I spotted on a can of Chock Full o' Nuts in our kitchen in Westfield, New Jersey, in 1960, when I was six. I learned to spell it right away because I was impressed by its insistent doubling of *f*'s and *e*'s. The creative spellings reveled in by commerce in the early 1960s tended to be unhelpful. I didn't know what to make of "kleen" or "Sta-Prest," and it took me some time to appreciate the penguin's invitation on the glass door of the pharmacy: "Come in, it's KOOL inside." Then there was the local dry-cleaning establishment whose signs promised "one-hour Martinizing." I struggled for years to try and plumb that one, coming up with increasingly baroque scenarios.

5   When I started first grade, my first year of American schooling—I had begun school in Belgium at three and a half, in a pre-kindergarten program that taught basic reading, writing, and arithmetic—I knew various words in English, but not how to construct a sentence. My first day remains vivid in its discomfort: I didn't know how to ask to go to the toilet. In addition, my mother had dressed me in a yellow pullover over a white shirt-collar dickey. It was a warm day, and the nun in charge suggested I take off my sweater. Since I didn't understand, she came over and yanked it off me, revealing my sleeveless undershirt.

As the weeks and months went on, I gradually learned how to speak and comprehend the new language, but between home and school, and school and home, I would pass through a sort of fugue state lasting an hour or two during which I could not use either language. For a while, my mother tackled this problem by tutoring me in French grammar and vocabulary as soon as I got home. It never crossed my parents' minds that we should begin employing English as the household tongue. For one thing, my parents' command of it was then rudimentary—I was rapidly outpacing them—and for another, they were never certain that our American sojourn was to be permanent. We were economic refugees, to use the current expression, victims of the collapse of the centuries-old textile industry centered in my native city of Verviers, but my parents' loyalty to their own country was unquestioned.

Our household was a European outpost. My parents made earnest attempts to replicate Belgian food, a pursuit that involved long car trips to the then rural middle of Staten Island to purchase leeks from Italian farmers, and expeditions to German butcher shops in Union and Irvington, New Jersey, to find a version of *sirop*—a dense concentrate of pears and apples that is the color and texture of heavy-gauge motor oil and is spread on bread—and various unsatisfactory substitutions. Neither cottage cheese nor ricotta could really pass for the farmer cheese called *makée* (*sirop* and *makée* together make *caca de poule*), but we had little choice in the matter, just as club soda had to stand in for *eau gazeuse,* since we lived in suburbs far from the seltzer belt, and parsley could only ever be a distant cousin to chervil. Desires for gooseberries and red currants, for familiar varieties of apricots and strawberries and potatoes and lettuce, for "real" bread and "real" cheese and "real" beer, simply had to be suppressed.

It wasn't easy constructing a version of Belgium in an apartment in a wooden house, with wood floors and Salvation Army furniture and sash windows and no cellar—not that the situation didn't present certain advantages, such as central heating, hot running water, and numerous appliances, none of which my parents could afford in Belgium, where we had actually been more prosperous. "Belgium" became a mental construct, its principal constituent material being language. We spoke French, thought in French, prayed in French, dreamed in French. Relatives kept us supplied with a steady stream of books and periodicals, my father with his Marabout paperbacks, my mother with the magazine *Femme d'Aujourd'hui* (Woman of Today), and me with history books for kids and comic magazines, in particular *Spirou*, which I received every week. Comics occupy a place in Belgian popular culture roughly comparable to that held in America by rock-and-roll, and like every other Belgian child, I first aspired to become a cartoonist. The comics I produced were always in French and clearly set in Belgium. (I couldn't abide American superhero adventures, although I did love *Mad* and the Sunday funnies, which were more commensurate with a Belgian turn of mind.) Somehow, though, I decided I wanted to become a writer when I was ten, and having made that decision never thought of writing in any language but English. Even so, I continued to conduct my internal monologues in French until late adolescence. For me the French language long corresponded to the soul, while English was the world.

My parents learned the language of their adopted country not without some difficulty. My father could draw on what remained of his high school English, complete with pronunciation rules that wavered between Rhenish German and the BBC, but otherwise my parents had arrived equipped only with the 1945 edition of a conversation manual entitled *L'Anglais sans peine* (English Without Toil). The book could not have been much help, especially since its vocabulary and references were attuned not to 1960s America but to Britain in the 1930s: "The Smiths had wired ahead the time of their arrival, and were expected for lunch at Fairview."

10   Sometimes, especially under pressure, my parents would reach for one tongue or the other and find themselves instead speaking Walloon, the native patois of southern Belgium. Walloon, now moribund, is usually identified as a dialect of French, whereas it is actually as old as the patois of Île-de-France, which became the official language—the eleventh edition of the *Encyclopedia Britannica* in fact describes it as the northernmost Romance language. Like English, Walloon incorporates a substantial body of words that derives from Old Low German, so that it could, if unconsciously, seem like the middle ground between English and French. An often-told

story in my family related how Lucy Dosquet, when her GI suitor arrived looking like a slob, angrily ordered him in Walloon, *"Louke-tu el mireu!"* He understood perfectly, and studied his reflection.

Walloon was the household tongue of all the relatives of my grandparents' generation. Their parents in turn might have spoken nothing else; that no one bothered to establish rules for the writing of Walloon until the very beginning of this century, just in time for its decline in currency, partly accounts for the fact that nearly everyone in the family tree before my grandparents' time was illiterate. Walloon enjoyed a brief literary flowering that started in the 1890s but was largely killed off by World War I. My paternal grandfather acted in the Walloon theater in Verviers during its heyday, and my father followed in his footsteps after World War II, but by then it had largely become an exercise in nostalgia. Today, only old people still speak Walloon, and poor ones at that, since its use is considered rude by merchants, businessmen, and the middle class in general, and young people simply don't care. Young Walloons nowadays have been formed by television, movies, and pop music, much of it emanating from France, and they have seemingly acquired the Parisian accent *en bloc.*

I was raised in a Belgian bubble, though, which means, among other things, that my speech is marked by the old Verviers Walloon accent, which causes observant Belgians some confusion. They can't reconcile that accent with the American flavor that has inevitably crept in, nor with my age and apparent class status. My French speech is also peppered with archaisms; I find myself unconsciously saying, for example, *"auto"* instead of *"voiture"* to mean "car," or *"illustre"* instead of *"revue"* to mean "magazine," expressions redolent of the thirties and forties, if not earlier.

The sound of Walloon, on those rare occasions when I hear it, affects me emotionally with even more force than French does. Hearing, as I did a few months ago, an old man simply greeting his friend by saying, *"Bôdjou, Djôsef,"* can move me nearly to tears. But, of course, I hear much more than just "Hiya, Joe"—I hear a ghostly echo of my maternal grandfather greeting his older brother, Joseph Nandrin, for

one thing, and I also hear the table talk of countless generations of workers and farmers and their wives, not that I particularly wish to subscribe to notions of collective ethnic memory. Walloon is a good-humored, long-suffering language of
the poor, naturally epigrammatic, ideal for both choleric fer-
vor and calm reflection, wry and often psychologically acute—
reminiscent in some ways of Scottish and in some ways of
Yiddish. Walloon is often my language of choice when, for instance, I am sizing up people at a party, but I have no one to
speak it with at home. (My wife hails from Akron, Ohio.) I
sometimes boast that, among the seven million people in New
York City, I am the only Walloon speaker, which may or may
not be true.

My three languages revolve around and inform one another. I live in an English-speaking world, of course, and for
months on end I may speak nothing else. I do talk with my
parents once a week by phone, but over the years we have developed a family dialect that is so motley it amounts to a Creole. I cannot snap back and forth between languages with
ease, but need to be surrounded by French for several days before I can properly recover its rhythm, and so recover my id-
iomatic vocabulary—a way of thinking rather than just a set of
words—and not merely translate English idioms. This means
that I am never completely present at any given moment, since
different aspects of myself are contained in different rooms of
language, and a complicated apparatus of air locks prevents
the doors from being flung open all at once. Still, there
are subterranean correspondences between the linguistic
domains that keep them from stagnating. The classical order
of French, the Latin-Germanic dialectic of English, and the
onomatopoeic-peasant lucidity of Walloon work on one
another critically, help enhance precision, and reduce cant.

15   I like to think that this system helps fortify me in areas beyond the merely linguistic. I am not rootless but multiply
rooted. This makes it impossible for me to fence off a plot of
the world and decide that everyone dwelling outside those
boundaries is "other." I am grateful to the accidents of my displaced upbringing, which taught me several kinds of irony.
Ethnically, I am about as homogeneous as it is possible to be:

aside from one great-grandmother who came from Luxem-
bourg, my gene pool derives entirely from an area smaller
than the five boroughs of New York City. I was born in the
same town as every one of my Sante forebears at least as far
back as the mid-sixteenth century, which is as far back as the
records go. Having been transplanted from my native soil,
though, and having had to construct an identity in response to
a double set of demands, one from my background and one
from my environment, I have become permanently "other."
The choice I am faced with is simple: either I am at home
everywhere or I am nowhere at all; either I realize my ties to
human beings of every race and nationality or I will die, as-
phyxiated by the vacuum. Mere tolerance is idle and useless—
if I can't recognize myself in others, no matter how remote in
origin or behavior they might appear, I might as well declare
war upon myself.

Engaging the Text

1. Reflecting on his bilingual upbringing in the opening
   paragraph of the essay, Sante says that his recall of childhood events is defined by the language (English or
   French) in which he perceives them. Locate and discuss
   examples throughout the essay that support this claim. Do
   Sante's experiences with language and memory in any way
   resemble your own? If so, support your answer by referring to specific words and phrases that trigger people,
   places, or events from earlier in your life.
2. Once Sante began American schooling, how did his parents
   attempt to preserve his European heritage? What struggles
   did they themselves encounter in attempting to construct
   "a version of Belgium" (paragraph 8) in the United States?
3. Throughout the essay, Sante introduces French and Walloon words and phrases. How does the author's use of
   code switching (to move back and forth between languages or dialects) contribute to his overall argument? Do
   you find this an effective rhetorical strategy? Focus on
   specific examples from the text to support your answer.
4. Summarize why, according to Sante, the use of Walloon is
   currently in decline. What is the author's reaction toward

this development? Why does the Belgian dialect continue
to affect him emotionally?

5. In the final paragraph of the essay, the author suggests
that he has "had to construct an identity in response to a
double set of demands." What does he mean by this
statement? How has Sante's sense of himself brought
him to an understanding of "human beings of every race
and nationality"?

Should English Be the Law?
ROBERT KING

Given the multilingual landscape of twenty-first century
America, does our government need to pass a law to make
English the official language of the United States? Has language use in our country become a divisive public issue?
Robert King, distinguished professor of linguistics and chair
of Jewish Studies at the University of Texas-Austin, answers
"no" to both questions. Weighing in on the debate using historical and global data, in this excerpt from an article that
originally appeared in the *Atlantic Monthly,* King considers
how cultural differences do and do not threaten our thus far
unofficial national language.

King's research focuses on intersections between language, ethnicity, nationhood, and politics. He is the author of
numerous books and articles, including *Nehru and the Language Politics of India* (1996).

———————— ✦ ————————

We have known race riots, draft riots, labor violence, seces-
sion, anti-war protests, and a whiskey rebellion, but one
kind of trouble we've never had: a language riot. Language
riot? It sounds like a joke. The very idea of language as a political force—as something that might threaten to split a country

wide apart—is alien to our way of thinking and to our cultural traditions.

This may be changing. On August 1 of last year [1996] the U.S. House of Representatives approved a bill that would make English the official language of the United States. The vote was 259 to 169, with 223 Republicans and thirty-six Democrats voting in favor and eight Republicans, 160 Democrats, and one independent voting against. The debate was intense, acrid, and partisan. On March 25 of last year the Supreme Court agreed to review a case involving an Arizona law that would require public employees to conduct government business only in English. Arizona is one of several states that have passed "Official English" or "English Only" laws. The appeal to the Supreme Court followed a 6–to–5–ruling, in October of 1995, by a federal appeals court striking down the Arizona law. These events suggest how divisive a public issue language could become in America—even if it has until now scarcely been taken seriously.

Traditionally, the American way has been to make English the national language—but to do so quietly, locally, without fuss. The Constitution is silent on language: the Founding Fathers had no need to legislate that English be the official language of the country. It has always been taken for granted that English *is* the national language, and that one must learn English in order to make it in America.

To say that language has never been a major force in American history or politics, however, is not to say that politicians have always resisted linguistic jingoism. In 1753 Benjamin Franklin voiced his concern that German immigrants were not learning English: "Those [Germans] who come hither are generally the most ignorant Stupid Sort of their own Nation. . . . [T]hey will soon so out number us, that all the advantages we have will not, in My Opinion, be able to preserve our language, and even our government will become precarious." Theodore Roosevelt articulated the unspoken American linguistic-melting-pot theory when he boomed, "We have room for but one language here, and that is the English language, for we intend to see that the crucible turns our people out as Americans, of American nationality, and not as dwellers in a polyglot boarding house." And: "We must have but one flag. We must also have but one language. That must be the language of the Declaration of Independence, of Washington's Farewell address, of Lincoln's Gettysburg speech and second inaugural."

OFFICIAL ENGLISH

5   TR's linguistic tub-thumping long typified the tradition of American politics. That tradition began to change in the wake of the anything goes attitudes and the celebration of cultural differences arising in the 1960s. A 1975 amendment to the Voting Rights Act of 1965 mandated the "bilingual ballot" under certain circumstances, notably when the voters of selected language groups reached five percent or more in a voting district. Bilingual education became a byword of educational thinking during the 1960s. By the 1970s linguists had demonstrated convincingly—at least to other academics—that black English (today called African-American vernacular English or Ebonics) was not "bad" English but a different kind of authentic English with its own rules. Predictably, there have been scattered demands that black English be included in bilingual-education programs.

It was against this background that the movement to make English the official language of the country arose. In 1981 Senator S. I. Hayakawa, long a leading critic of bilingual education and bilingual ballots, introduced in the U.S. Senate a constitutional amendment that not only would have made English the official language but would have prohibited federal and state laws and regulations requiring the use of other languages. His English Language Amendment died in the Ninety-seventh Congress.

The popular wisdom is that conservatives are pro and liberals con. True, conservatives such as George Will and William F. Buckley Jr. have written columns supporting Official English. But would anyone characterize as conservatives the present and past U.S. English board members Alistair Cooke, Walter Cronkite, and Norman Cousins? One of the strongest opponents of bilingual education is the Mexican-American writer Richard Rodríguez, best known for his eloquent autobiography *Hunger of Memory* (1982). There is a strain of American liberalism that defines itself in nostalgic devotion to the melting pot.

Many issues intersect in the controversy over Official English: immigration (above all), the rights of minorities (Spanish-speaking minorities in particular), the pros and cons of bilingual education, tolerance, how best to educate the children of immigrants, and the place of cultural diversity in school curricula and in American society in general. The question that lies at the root of most of the uneasiness is this: Is America threatened by the preservation of languages other than English? Will America, if it continues on its traditional path of benign linguistic neglect, go the way of Belgium, Canada and Sri Lanka—three countries among many whose unity is gravely imperiled by language and ethnic conflicts?

UNIQUE OTHERNESS

Is there no hope for language tolerance? Some countries manage to maintain their unity in the face of multilingualism. Examples are Finland, with a Swedish minority, and a number of African and Southeast Asian countries. Two others could not be more unlike as countries go: Switzerland and India.

German, French, Italian, and Romansh are the languages   10
of Switzerland. The first three can be and are used for official purposes; all four are designated "national" languages. Switzerland is politically almost hyperstable. It has language problems (Romansh is losing ground), but they are not major, and they are never allowed to threaten national unity.

Contrary to public perception, India gets along pretty well with a host of different languages. The Indian constitution officially recognizes nineteen languages, English among them. Hindi is specified in the constitution as the national language of India, but that is a pious postcolonial fiction: outside the Hindi-speaking northern heartland of India, people don't want to learn it. English functions more nearly than Hindi as India's lingua franca.[2]

History teaches a plain lesson about language and governments: there is almost nothing the government of a free country can do to change language usage and practice significantly, to force its citizens to use certain languages in preference to others, and to discourage people from speaking a language they wish to continue to speak. (The rebirth of Hebrew in Palestine and Israel's successful mandate that Hebrew be spoken and written by Israelis is a unique event in the annals of language history.) Quebec has since the 1970s passed an array of laws giving French a virtual monopoly in the province. One consequence—unintended, one wishes to believe—of these laws is that last year kosher products imported for Passover were kept off the shelves, because the packages were not labeled in French. Wise governments keep their hands off language to the extent that it is politically possible to do so.

We like to believe that to pass a law is to change behavior, but passing laws about language in a free society almost never changes attitudes or behavior. Gaelic (Irish) is living out a slow inexorable decline in Ireland despite enormous government support of every possible kind since Ireland gained its independence from Britain. The Welsh language, in contrast, is alive today in Wales in spite of heavy discrimination during its history. Three out of four people in the northern and western counties of Gwynedd and Dyfed speak Welsh.

I said earlier that language is a convenient surrogate for other national problems. Official English obviously has a lot to do with concern about immigration, perhaps especially Hispanic immigration. America may be threatened by immigration; I don't know. But America is not threatened by language.

15   The usual arguments made by academics against Official English are commonsensical. Who needs a law when, according to the 1990 census, 94 percent of American residents speak English anyway? (Mauro E. Mujica, the chairman of U.S. En-

---

[2]A language or mixture of languages used for communication by people who speak different first languages.

glish, cites a higher figure: 95 percent.) Not many of today's immigrants will see their first language survive into the second generation. This is in fact the common lament of first-generation immigrants: their children are not learning their language and are losing the culture of their parents. Spanish is hardly a threat to English, in spite of isolated (and easily visible) cases such as Miami, New York City, and pockets of the Southwest and southern California. The everyday language of south Texas is Spanish, and yet south Texas is not about to secede from America.

But empirical, calm arguments don't engage the real issue: language is a symbol, an icon. Nobody who favors a constitutional ban against flag burning will ever be persuaded by the argument that the flag is, after all, just a "piece of cloth." A draft card in the 1960s was never merely a piece of paper. Neither is a marriage license.

Language, as one linguist has said, is "not primarily a means of communication but a means of communion." Romanticism exalted language, made it mystical, sublime—a bond of national identity. At the same time, Romanticism created a monster: it made of language a means for destroying a country.

We are not even close to the danger point. I suggest that we relax and luxuriate in our linguistic richness and our traditional tolerance of language differences. Language does not threaten American unity. Benign neglect is a good policy for any country when it comes to language and it's a good policy for America.

Engaging the Text

1. Summarize the central grounds presented in the essay for and against passing legislation to make English the official language of the United States. How does the author arrive at his position in the argument?

2. In his early paragraphs, King summarizes recent legal cases aimed at "Official English" or "English Only" laws, providing context by referencing the Constitution and opinions of famous figures in U.S. political history. Discuss what the author intends to communicate by presenting this background on the issue.

3. According to the author, the rise of bilingual initiatives governing voting and education in the United States coincided with "the celebration of cultural differences" (paragraph 5). Explain the backlash that occurred in the wake of these developments. Who is in favor of bilingual initiatives and who opposes them? What do the detractors envision instead?

4. In the "Unique Otherness" section of the essay, King introduces the notion of "language tolerance." Explain what he means by this concept and discuss the examples used to illustrate it. Next, compare and contrast the circumstances of multilingualism in the United States to that of the other countries discussed in the essay.

5. What is King's reasoning in the final paragraphs of the essay for arguing against the need for "Official English"? What does he ultimately conclude about "language differences" in America?

CHAPTER 6

Workplace

Affirmative Action and the Dilemma of the "Qualified"

ELLIS COSE

What comes to your mind when you hear the words "affirmative action"? The phrase was first used in President Lyndon Johnson's 1965 Executive Order 11246—Equal Employment Opportunity, which requires federal contractors to "not discriminate," but to "take affirmative action to ensure that applicants are employed, and that employees are treated during employment, without regard to their race, creed, color, or national origin." In 1967, Johnson expanded the Executive Order to include requirements benefiting women. Some opponents of affirmative action equate it with unfair advantages afforded "unqualified minorities," a situation distinguished journalist Ellis Cose explores in this excerpt from *The Rage of a Privileged Class* (1994), his best-selling book about race and employment in America. Cose also considers how these same equal-opportunity critics frequently disregard their own advancements obtained through class and race-based "preferential treatment."

The recipient of numerous fellowships, grants, and journalism awards, Cose is the author of several books, most recently *A Man's World* (1995), *Color-Blind: Seeing Beyond Race in a Race-Obsessed World* (1997), and *The Envy of the World: On Being a Black Man in America* (2002). A columnist and contributing editor to *Newsweek* since 1993, he has been chief writer on management and workplace issues for *USA Today,* a member of the editorial board on the *Detroit Free Press,* and a commentator on National Public Radio.

———————————— ✦ ————————————

When the talk turns to affirmative action, I often recall a conversation from years ago. A young white man, a Harvard student and the brother of a close friend, happened to be in Washington when the Supreme Court ruled on an affirmative action question. I have long since forgotten the question and the Court's decision, but I remember the young man's reaction.

He was not only troubled but choleric at the very notion that "unqualified minorities" would dare to demand preferential treatment. Why, he wanted to know, couldn't they compete like everyone else? Why should hardworking whites like himself be pushed aside for second-rate affirmative action hires? Why should he be discriminated against in order to accommodate *them?* His tirade went on for quite a while, and he became more indignant by the second as he conjured up one injustice after another.

When the young man paused to catch his breath, I took the occasion to observe that it seemed more than a bit hypocritical of him to rage on about preferential treatment. A person of modest intellect, he had gotten into Harvard largely on the basis of family connections. His first summer internship, with the White House, had been arranged by a family member. His second, with the World Bank, had been similarly arranged. Thanks to his nice internships and Harvard degree, he had been promised a coveted slot in a major company's executive training program. In short, he was already well on his way to a distinguished career—a career made possible by preferential treatment.

My words seemed not to register, and that did not surprise me. Clearly he had never thought of himself as a beneficiary of special treatment, and no doubt never will. Nor is it likely that either his colleagues or his superiors would be inclined to look down on him as an undeserving incompetent who got ahead on the basis of unfair advantage and was keeping better-qualified people out of work. Yet that assumption is routinely made about black beneficiaries of "affirmative action."

In February 1993, for instance, *Forbes* magazine pub- 5
lished an article purporting to demonstrate "how affirmative
action slows the economy." The authors referred approvingly
to a 1984 poll that "found one in ten white males reporting
they had lost a promotion because of quotas." They went on to
argue that the poll "was quite possibly accurate. Indeed, it
could be an underestimate."

It's impossible from the article to be certain just what poll
Forbes is citing, but it appears to be a never-published tele-
phone survey by Gordon S. Black Corporation for *USA Today*
in which one-tenth of white males answered yes to a much
broader question: "Have you yourself ever lost a job
opportunity or educational *opportunity* at least *partially* as a
result of policies and programs aimed at promoting equal opportunity for minorities?" (Emphasis mine.) That, of course, is
a very different question from the one *Forbes* reported.

In 1993, *Newsweek* magazine commissioned a national
poll that framed the question more narrowly. That poll, interestingly, found even more white males claiming to have been
victimized by affirmative action. When asked, "Have you ever
been a victim of discrimination or reverse discrimination in
getting a promotion?" 15 percent of white males said that they
had—the same percentage reporting such discrimination in
"getting a job."

Let's assume for the sake of discussion that the *Forbes* figure is correct, and that ten percent of white males do indeed
believe that some quota-driven minority person has snatched
a position that would otherwise have gone to them. Let's further assume that the ratio holds across occupational categories, so that one out of ten white men in managerial and
professional jobs (which, after all, is the group *Forbes* caters
to) believes he was unfairly held back by a black or Hispanic
colleague's promotion.

Blacks and Hispanics make up 10 percent of the total employees in such jobs, and white males make up 46 percent. So
if one out of every ten white males has been held back by a
black or Hispanic, that would mean that nearly half of those
blacks and Hispanics received promotions they didn't deserve
at the expense of white men. (If the *Newsweek* numbers are

right, and if we assume that racial and ethnic minorities were the beneficiaries of the "reverse discrimination" suffered by whites, the percentage of minorities who have been unfairly promoted is even higher.) Yet if so many minorities are being promoted ahead of whites, why do black and Hispanic professionals, on average, earn less and hold lower positions than whites? It could be that despite their unfair advantage, minority professionals are so incompetent that whites still manage to get ahead of them on merit. Or it could be that white males who think minorities are zooming ahead of them are way off the mark. *Forbes*, for whatever reason, chose not to consider that possibility. Just as it chose not to consider that the alternative to a system based on "quotas" is not necessarily one based on merit. Or that affirmative action might conceivably result in some competent people getting jobs. Instead, the *Forbes* writers simply assumed such problematic possibilities away. Indeed, like many arguments against affirmative action, their article was not a reasoned analysis at all, but an example of pandering to the anger and anxieties of white males who believe they and their kind are being wronged. And the editors of *Forbes* have plenty of company.

10   In April 1991, for example, a white Georgetown University law student, Timothy Maguire, set off a tempest in Washington's scholarly and legal communities by questioning the academic quality of blacks admitted to the law school. In an article entitled "Admissions Apartheid," written for a student-controlled paper, Maguire charged that the black law students were in general not as qualified as the whites. The blacks, he said, had lower average scores on the Law School Admissions Tests and lower grade point averages—an allegation based on documents he perused, apparently surreptitiously, while working as a file clerk in the student records office.

The article polarized the campus. On one side were those who demanded that Maguire be expelled for unethical behavior in reading and publishing confidential information. They also raised questions about his mastery of statistics, pointing out that the "random sample" on which he based his conclusions was nothing of the sort, since the files he rifled were only a small selection and included the scores of many applicants who had not been admitted. On the other side were those who saw Maguire as a champion of free speech, a courageous young man who—at risk of public censure—had undertaken to disseminate information that deserved to be debated in a public arena. Maguire apparently saw himself as a victim of leftist ideologues, declaring at one point, according to the *Washington Post*, "It's painful not being politically correct."

In the midst of the ruckus, and after a leak focused attention on Maguire's own academic background, he admitted that his own LSAT scores were below the median for Georgetown students. Interestingly, in light of his charges, coverage of the controversy did not highlight the fact that Maguire got into Georgetown through a special screening program for "low testers," people who would not have been admitted on the basis of their scores but were in effect given extra credit for showing other evidence of promise, dedication, or commitment. In Maguire's case, the fact that he had been a Peace Corps volunteer in Africa weighed heavily in his favor. In short, he was every bit as much a beneficiary of special preference as the black students he scorned.

Shortly after it began, the uproar died down. And despite the protests of the black student organization and others, Maguire was permitted to graduate with his class. Though he was formally reprimanded for violating confidentiality, an agreement worked out by attorneys specifically barred the reprimand from becoming part of his official transcript. Maguire, in short, was allowed to resume a normal life and to put both the controversy and his need for special preference behind him.

Unlike the black students he assailed, who will find their careers haunted by the specter of affirmative action, and who will often be greeted by doubts about their competence whatever their real abilities, Maguire is not likely to suffer because he got into law school on grounds other than academic performance. In other words, he will never be seen as an affirmative action man but simply as a lawyer—entitled to all the recognition conferred by his prestigious degree and all the privileges granted to those presumed to be professionally "qualified."

15   Why should the presumption of competence differ for black and white graduates of the same school? One answer may be that blacks should be scrutinized more carefully because they are more likely to have met lower admission standards. While that is true in many cases, it is far from true that every black student admitted to a selective school is academically inferior (in any sense of the word) to every white student admitted. Nor is it true, as Maguire's case illustrates, that whites do not receive special treatment in academia. Just as Maguire benefited from a program for "low testers," others benefit from "diversity" policies in East Coast schools that favor residents of Wyoming over those of Connecticut, or from policies that favor relatives of alumni (or children of faculty members, donors, and other influential figures) over those with no family connections. Sometimes universities wish to attract mature students or veterans, or to nurture relationships with certain high schools by admitting their graduates.

One reason for such policies, as virtually any admissions officer will attest, is that prior academic performance is a far from perfect predictor of who will succeed in any specific school, much less who will succeed in life. And that rationale is apparently accepted even by many fervent opponents of affirmative action, since nonracial preferences never seem to elicit anything like the animosity provoked by so-called racial quotas. And even if we grant that many blacks who gain admission with the help of affirmative action are not objectively "qualified," precisely the same can be said about certain children of alumni or about the student who caught the admissions committee's eye because he spent a year on a mission of mercy in Malaysia.

Moreover, determining what it means to be "qualified" is not as easy as it is often made to seem. Ted Miller, who was associate dean of admissions at Georgetown Law at the time of the Maguire imbroglio, points out that many older white professors there—"if they were being honest"—would admit that they could not have met the standards exceeded by the school's typical black student today. As the number of applicants escalated during the 1940s, notes Miller, law schools turned to the LSAT as "an artificial means" to help them sift through applications. And as the numbers continued to increase, the minimum score needed to get into the more exclusive schools (the "qualified threshold") rose. Yet many of those who met the lower standards of the past nonetheless turned out to be distinguished lawyers. Obviously, they were not "unqualified," even if their test results would not win them admission to a prestigious law school today. By the same token, reasons Miller, as long as black students are capable of doing the work, who is to say they are "unqualified"?

Whatever one thinks of Miller's argument, it is unlikely that hostility to affirmative action programs would suddenly vanish if it could be established that "quota" recruits are in fact "qualified." If that were the only issue, programs favoring the children of alumni, say, would provoke the same animus directed at affirmative action. So the primary cause of the hostility must lie elsewhere. And the most logical place to look for it is in American attitudes about race.

Not surprisingly, people who see blacks as lazier than whites tend to be among those most strongly opposed to affirmative action. To Tom Smith, director of NORC's[1] general social survey, the reason is obvious: "Negative images lead people to conclude these groups don't deserve this special help." Indeed, it's fairly easy to understand why anyone might have a hard time with the idea that lazy, unintelligent, violence-prone people (whom Americans believe to be disproportionately black and Hispanic) deserve any special consideration at all.

Imagine, for a moment, a society in which there are no different races or ethnic groups, in which everyone sounds and looks essentially the same in terms of color, hair texture, etc. But at birth everyone is branded on the forehead with one of two large letters: either U or W, depending on the letters on their parents' heads. In the case of children of mixed parentage, the child is branded with a U—though a smaller U than children of pure lineage. And if in time that child marries someone wearing the W brand, the mark on their offspring will be smaller yet.

Now imagine that though the two groups are officially equal, a gigantic propaganda campaign is mounted, with the full (if unacknowledged) assistance of the government, to convince everyone that "Unworths" (those with the U brand) are

20

---

[1]The University of Chicago's National Opinion Research Center.

congenitally stupid, lazy, ugly, and unpatriotic, that they make poor neighbors and worse leaders, that in just about every way they are inferior to the "Worths."

Assume that more than 60 percent of the population (including a majority of the Unworths themselves) swallows at least part of the propaganda, so that whenever an Unworth walks into a classroom or office, or tries to buy a home, he or she confronts someone who believes Unworths to be—well, unworthy. Now assume that after an outbreak of violent protests, society decides to eliminate discrimination against Unworths.

The republic passes laws not only guaranteeing access to its institutions but in many cases encouraging preferential treatment of the Unworths. The people who believe in the stereotypes created by the propaganda (in other words, the majority of the population) develop ingenious ways to get around the laws. And they feel virtuous in doing so because they consider any law awarding special privileges to the Unworths patently unfair. Many Unworths, fully accepting the stereotypes of inferiority, shrink from competing with Worths in intellectual or business pursuits. And those Unworths who do manage to get prestigious positions find their right to keep them constantly questioned, and discover that although the number of successful Unworths is very small, the Worths still think there are too many.

Some Unworths become so frustrated by the constant doubting of their competence that they blame the special privileges for their plight—and the Worths strongly encourage them to do so. Indeed, the Worths lavishly praise and promote the books of Unworths who advance such a premise; they put them up for tenured professorships and maybe even name one of them to a special Unworth seat on the highest court of the land. From the perspective of the Worths of the world, given the well-known attributes of Unworths, it is much better to require that individual Unworths prove themselves worthy than to continue to reward so many lazy, unintelligent, and generally unmeritorious people with jobs that belong to the more deserving. And what better allies for the Worths in such an enterprise than articulate Unworths who help make the case.

25   Now imagine a different scenario. Envision another society where children are branded at birth. But in this society

there is only one brand, and it only goes to a very select group: the letter B is impressed on the heads of all children who pass a special test. The test is rather mysterious. No one quite knows how it works, but anyone who passes it is certified to be among the best and the brightest in our imaginary world. Let's assume further that the test was cobbled together by a brilliant prankster who died before he could let the world in on his joke, and that it really doesn't measure anything, that the scores it generates are in fact random. Nonetheless, society accepts the test as perfect, and whoever achieves the requisite score gets to wear the B for life.

Since B-kids are special, society develops them with the utmost care. They are sent to special schools and receive advance placement in the nation's top universities. Even if they prove to be incompetent students, they continue as objects of veneration. Their academic inadequacies are made into virtues. Clearly their true potential cannot be unlocked in the dry and irrelevant world of books, but only in the real world of important affairs. Upon completion of schooling, they are assured countless job offers, many leading directly to the top of the corporate pyramid. Indeed, they find it easy to rise to the top of virtually any field they enter, for everywhere they go they are recognized as the best. And everyone takes that as proof of the meritocracy at work.

Whenever B's walk into a building or a store, they are treated with the greatest respect. Whenever they say something stupid, it is assumed that they were misunderstood, or perhaps were using a vernacular only comprehensible to the elite. And whenever they make decisions with catastrophic results, they are shielded from the consequences—in some cases with multimillion dollar settlements. For everyone understands, that whatever mistakes may have been made, these are extremely deserving individuals.

Their entire lives, in short, are played out as a series of special privileges. And they wear the B as a badge of pride. Very few people resent them. Instead, ordinary folks are delighted to travel in their circles. Even if the high court were to rule that no special treatment be given them, people would defer to them anyway. After all, as everyone can see, they deserve it. They are B's.

The point here is obvious. One cannot honestly and intelligently discuss hostility to preferential treatment without examining attitudes toward those who benefit from the treatment. Well before affirmative action came along, a substantial number of people considered blacks deficient—morally, esthetically, and (especially) intellectually. And if survey findings are any indication, that continues to be the case. It does not mean that *nothing* has changed or that race relations have not improved. It does mean that things have not changed quite as much as many people like to think—and that even in the 1990s, even in the most enlightened of places, black people regularly encounter attitudes that make even the most thick-skinned cringe.

Engaging the Text

1. How does the opening anecdote about a Harvard-educated, young, white man's reaction to a Supreme Court decision establish the grounds for Cose's ideas regarding opponents of affirmative action? Later in the essay, what purpose does the story of a white Georgetown University law student serve in furthering Cose's position?

2. How does Cose use logos (logical appeal), ethos (ethical appeal), and pathos (emotional appeal) to define so-called "reverse discrimination"? In particular, how do the author's analyses of polls and statistics (paragraphs 5–9) serve to oppose the concept? What does he pose as a counterpoint to the idea of reverse discrimination?

3. Underline and define key words and phrases in the essay that suggest opposing sides in the affirmative action debate, such as "merit," "quotas," and "preferential treatment." Describe the author's use of and attitude toward this rhetoric. Does it reinforce your previous ideas about equal-opportunity employment or invite you to think about the subject in a new way? Explain your answer using examples from the text to illustrate.

4. Summarize examples throughout the essay that indicate how whites presumably "receive special treatment in academia" or "benefit from 'diversity' policies" exercised by col-

leges and universities (paragraph 15). Cose indicates that, despite these advantages, whites eventually blend into the workplace, forever after deemed "qualified" (paragraph 14). How does this idea support the notion of white-skin privilege, explored by Peggy McIntosh in the visibility chapter?

5. Cose concludes the essay by creating two imaginary societies in which people are branded with letters at birth. Summarize the symbolism of each branding as it correlates to real-life circumstances. How well do these categories delineate opportunities for social advancement in the United States? As a strategy for addressing this issue, do you find Cose's speculative writing more or less effective than concrete information provided earlier in the essay? Explain your answer.

White-Collar Man in a Blue-Collar World
Bob Muldoon

Downsized from his position at an Internet company in 2001, Ivy-League-educated Bob Muldoon accepted a manual-labor job laying hayseed lawn. Struggling to acquire vocational skills in a workplace where book learning is undervalued, Muldoon encountered cultural differences between himself and other employees. He profiles his transition from white-collar to blue-collar worker in this first-person account, which originally appeared in *Newsweek*'s "My Turn" column. In a shrinking job market, should a higher education degree automatically guarantee the right to satisfactory employment? As Muldoon discovered, a college-trained worker just might need to keep some alternative skills in reserve.

◆

Can you drive a forklift?" Those five deflating words instantly alerted me that my prep-school background and advanced degrees would mean nothing on the new job.

Alas, I have two Ivy League master's degrees—and two left thumbs. And neither the degrees nor the digits are serving me well in these times, when many a displaced white-collar worker has gone blue collar. Or, in my case, "green collar"—laying down lush, hydroseeded lawns.

Like thousands last year, I was downsized from one of those sizzling dot-coms, now dot-gone. Faced with a shrinking job market, I turned to manual labor. It's a common trend, now that unemployment is at 5.8 percent. But the transition is seldom seamless.

While the new boss was mildly disgusted when I couldn't drive the forklift ("The guy I just fired could"), he was apoplectic when he tossed me a wrench to open a hydrant and saw me tightening it with all my strength. "Wrong direction!" he exploded. "Lefty loosey; righty tighty."

5   I didn't know that. Indeed, there is a whole tool kit of basic skills that Andover, Bates, Columbia, and Harvard never equipped me with. These include (but are not limited to) any task involving the use of a tool, or any with a small or large gas-powered machine.

But there are moments when I shine. I can read the Latin on every public building we pass. And when the boss once had to leave a note to a customer, he needed help spelling a certain word. "R-e-c-e-i-v-e," I said crisply, reveling in the rare, value-added moment. "I before e, except after c."

When the truckdriver from Quebec arrived with an 18-wheeler of mulch and I began conversing in near-flawless Parisian French about his long journey and breakfast of croissants, my boss's eyes lit up. But when it came time to tell him to "attach the metal chain to the forklift and remove the pallets," all I could muster was a vacuous stare. Evidently I'd been absent from French class the day trucking was covered. I was reduced to grunting and clutching at his sleeve to convey the message.

In hydroseeding, we spread a green slurry of water, seed, fertilizer and mulch. This mixture applies the seed evenly, protects it from wind and rain, and retains water for germination. It's all the rage in suburbia. My main responsibility is to guide 200 feet of heavy, serpentine hose while the boss sprays the slime. But there's more to my job than wrestling the anaconda.

Sometimes the hose gets clogged. Sometimes the chain comes off the mixer. And sometimes I have to use the side mirrors to move the 60,000-pound truck in reverse. All these situations require an all-around mechanical common sense that is as important to the blue-collar worker as the ability to navigate Microsoft Office is to the white-collar one. These are the "value subtracted" moments my background has not prepared me for.

So I'm happy when those occasions arise when I can offer the benefits of my education. Like when a butterfly flutters by in the field and I can identify it—authoritatively—as a great spangled fritillary. Or when I can edit the punctuation in our "How to Care for Your Newly Hydroseeded Lawn" flier.

Of course, it annoys the hell out of my boss how rarely my skill set actually helps us out. And it amazes him how I'm forever dawdling with my coffee and misplacing it at job sites. Or how I'm morbidly preoccupied with safety—like the time, fearing electrocution, when I refused to hold up a low-hanging cable wire to allow our tall truck to pass beneath. ("It carries a signal, not a current!" he hollered, grabbing it for dramatic effect.)

In some ways, ours is a clash of cultures. On days off, the boss changes the oil in his pickup, retiles his kitchen floor or does brickwork; I take my car through the automatic wash, go bird watching or read *Nicholas Nickleby*.[1] This last tickles him—so mighty are my struggles reading maps. ("Turn it in the direction we're traveling," he snaps, spinning it 180 degrees.)

All my life I've been trained in the manipulation of abstractions (words, symbols, figures), so when it now comes to the manipulation of tangibles (nuts, bolts, maps), I'm flummoxed. So much that it's become a running joke with my boss that, whenever there is a choice to push or pull, turn left or

10

---

[1]Novel by British author Charles Dickens, written 1838–1839.

right, I invariably err. At these moments, he signals my mis-judgment in a chortling, sing-song voice: "Fifty-fifty."

But I'm just as strong as he is, and can match him bale for bale, hoisting the 50-pound sacks of seed we fill the truck with. So there is the basis for a bit of grudging respect. And for all of my drawbacks, I am at least reliable—a vestige, per-haps, of the grim "show up at your desk at all costs (if only to sit there)" ethic.

15   But still it caught me off guard when, with the air now cold and the hydroseeding season over, the boss inquired re-cently: "Can you drive a snowplow?"

Engaging the Text

1. Why do you think the author chooses to start the essay with a question directed at his inability to perform a task? What tone does he establish with this opening? How does he sustain the tone throughout the essay and for what purpose?

2. Muldoon compares himself to his boss by distinguishing between "white-collar" and "blue-collar" job skills—"ab-stractions" versus "tangibles" (paragraph 13). Summarize the examples used to illustrate these workplace differ-ences. Of the two kinds of workers represented in the es-say, whom do you most admire and why?

3. Describe how the author incorporates language skills on the job. Can you recall a time when a command of English grammar or knowledge of a second language benefited you at work or might have? Explain the circumstances.

4. Muldoon characterizes the gulf of experience between himself and his boss as "a clash of cultures" (paragraph 12). Discuss what the author means by this claim. Does he see any room for compromise in the workplace? Use ex-amples from the text to explain your answer.

5. How well do you relate to the circumstances described in Muldoon's account? Did you ever experience a time when you lacked the skills necessary to succeed at a task or when you were frustrated by someone else's inexperience? Describe the situation.

The Foreman's Wallet
MARTÍN ESPADA

Martín Espada worked as a bartender, gas station attendant, and factory worker, among other manual-labor jobs, before becoming a tenant lawyer, poet, and currently professor of writing and Latino Poetry at the University of Massachusetts-Amherst. He chronicles many of his former work experiences in *Imagine the Angels of Bread* (1996), a poetry volume in which "The Foreman's Wallet" first appeared. Espada's workplace poems frequently encapsulate sites of cultural difference, including those surrounding race, class, and language use. As a consequence of his Puerto Rican heritage and upbringing, he infuses his verses with social and political history lessons, particularly those affecting the working poor, disenfranchised people, and speakers of languages other than English.

Imagine the Angels of Bread won an American Book Award. Espada's other books of poetry include *Rebellion Is the Circle of a Lover's Hands* (1990), a bilingual collection; *City of Coughing and Dead Radiators* (1993), *A Mayan Astronomer in Hell's Kitchen* (2000), and *Alabanza: New and Selected Poems 1982–2002.* His prose collection, *Zapata's Disciple: Essays,* was published in 1998. The recipient of numerous awards and fellowships, his honors include the PEN/Voelker Award for Poetry, the Paterson Poetry Prize, two fellowships from the National Endowment for the Arts, and a Massachusetts Artists Foundation fellowship.

---------------- ◆ ----------------

At the printing plant,
I operated the machine
that shrink-wrapped paper
in clear plastic.
The bosses were Jehovah's Witnesses,   5
men pale as cheese
who sold Bibles door to door
on Sundays. They were polite,
and assembled the crew one night
to explain politely   10

that all of us were unemployed
by 11 PM.
No government contracts.
The plywood office door
pulled shut.   15

No one knows who set the first
wheel of paper rolling across the floor,
who speared the soda machine
with a two-by-four,
who winged unstapled copies of *Commander's Digest*   20
so they flew, with their diagrams of bombers,
through the room. Towers of legal pads collapsed,
fist-fired paper grenades hissed overhead.
A forklift truck without a driver bumped blindly
down the aisle, and we all saluted.   25
If we knew any songs, we would have sung them.

Saboteurs were unscrewing the punchclock
and rearranging the parts like paleontologists
toying with the backbone of a stegosaurus
when the foreman arrived,   30
his adolescent voice whining authority.
He was my last job.

The conspiracy to shrink-wrap
the foreman's head, turning red
in a wrestling hold, was a failure.   35
His skull was too big
to squeeze through the machine,
and even the radicals among us relented
when his eyes steamed with tears.
So we shrink-wrapped the foreman's wallet,   40
gleaming in the fresh plastic
like a pound of hamburger.

"Here's your wallet," I said. And mine.

Engaging the Text

1. Identify the setting of the poem and summarize the se-
   quence of events that unfold within its narrative frame.
   What is the central source of conflict here?

2. Make a list of all the characters appearing in the poem. What words and images does the narrator use to describe them? How well do these details establish their cultural differences? Explain your answer.
3. Notice the words that Espada uses to relay action in the second stanza of the poem. How and why does this language reflect the narrator's attitude toward the "diagrams of bombers" (line 21) unsettled in the mayhem, or toward the "government contracts" (line 13) of the first stanza?
4. Given the foreman's age and position, how much difference do you detect between him and the assembly-line crew in terms of workplace power? Why do the other printing plant workers conspire to shrink-wrap his head (lines 33–34)? Do you feel sympathy for the foreman? Why or why not?
5. Consider the final lines of stanzas three and five. What do their words imply about the narrator's future job prospects?

Serving in Florida
BARBARA EHRENREICH

Nearly a third of the American workforce earns eight dollars an hour or less. How well do they survive on such low wages? To find out, respected commentator and cultural critic Barbara Ehrenreich embarked on a firsthand investigative study, working her way across the country as a waitress, hotel maid, house cleaner, and superstore salesperson. She documents this experience in her bestseller *Nickled and Dimed: On (Not) Getting By in America* (2001), a searing indictment of social inequality. Her journey into the "low-wage life" begins "Serving in Florida."

Ehrenriech is the author or coauthor of twelve books, including *Fear of Falling: The Inner Life of the Middle Class* (1989) and *Blood Rites: Origins and History of the Passions of War* (1997). Her articles have appeared in dozens of notable magazines, such as *Ms., Harper's,* the *Progressive,* the *New Republic,* and the *Atlantic Monthly.*

———————— ✦ ————————

Mostly out of laziness, I decide to start my low-wage life in the town nearest to where I actually live, Key West, Florida, which with a population of about 25,000 is elbowing its way up to the status of a genuine city. The downside of familiarity, I soon realize, is that it's not easy to go from being a consumer, thoughtlessly throwing money around in exchange for groceries and movies and gas, to being a worker in the very same place. I am terrified, especially at the beginning, of being recognized by some friendly business owner or erstwhile neighbor and having to stammer out some explanation of my project. Happily, though, my fears turn out to be entirely unwarranted: during a month of poverty and toil, no one recognizes my face or my name, which goes unnoticed and for the most part unuttered. In this parallel universe where my father never got out of the mines and I never got through college, I am "baby," "honey," "blondie," and, most commonly, "girl."

My first task is to find a place to live. I figure that if I can earn $7 an hour—which, from the want ads, seems doable—I can afford to spend $500 on rent or maybe, with severe economies, $600 and still have $400 or $500 left over for food and gas. In the Key West area, this pretty much confines me to flophouses and trailer homes—like the one, a pleasing fifteen-minute drive from town, that has no air-conditioning, no screens, no fans, no television, and, by way of diversion, only the challenge of evading the landlord's Doberman pinscher. The big problem with this place, though, is the rent, which at $675 a month is well beyond my reach. All right, Key West is expensive. But so is New York City, or the Bay Area, or Jackson, Wyoming, or Telluride, or Boston, or any other place where tourists and the wealthy compete for living space with the people who clean their toilets and fry their hash browns. Still, it is a shock to realize that "trailer trash" has become, for me, a demographic category to aspire to.

So I decide to make the common trade-off between afford-ability and convenience and go for a $500-a-month "effi-ciency" thirty miles up a two-lane highway from the employ-ment opportunities of Key West, meaning forty-five minutes if there's no road construction and I don't get caught behind some sun-dazed Canadian tourists. I hate the drive, along a roadside studded with white crosses commemorating the more effective head-on collisions, but it's a sweet little place—a cabin, more or less, set in the swampy backyard of the con-verted mobile home where my landlord, an affable TV repair-man, lives with his bartender girlfriend. Anthropologically speaking, the trailer park would be preferable, but here I have a gleaming white floor and a firm mattress, and the few resi-dent bugs are easily vanquished.

The next piece of business is to comb through the want ads and find a job. I rule out various occupations for one rea-son or another: hotel front-desk clerk, for example, which to my surprise is regarded as unskilled and pays only $6 or $7 an hour, gets eliminated because it involves standing in one spot for eight hours a day. Waitressing is also something I'd like to avoid, because I remember it leaving me bone-tired when I was eighteen, and I'm decades of varicosities and back pain beyond that now. Telemarketing, one of the first refuges of the suddenly indigent, can be dismissed on grounds of personal-ity. This leaves certain supermarket jobs, such as deli clerk, or housekeeping in the hotels and guest houses, which pays about $7 and, I imagine, is not too different from what I've been doing part-time, in my own home, all my life.

So I put on what I take to be a respectable-looking outfit 5 of ironed Bermuda shorts and scooped-neck T-shirt and set out for a tour of the local hotels and supermarkets. Best West-ern, Econo Lodge, and HoJo's all let me fill out application forms, and these are, to my relief, mostly interested in whether I am a legal resident of the United States and have committed any felonies. My next stop is Winn-Dixie, the su-permarket, which turns out to have a particularly onerous ap-plication process, featuring a twenty-minute "interview" by computer since, apparently, no human on the premises is deemed capable of representing the corporate point of view. I am conducted to a large room decorated with posters illustrating how to look "professional" (it helps to be white and, if female, permed) and warning of the slick promises that union organizers might try to tempt me with. The interview is multiple-choice: Do I have anything, such as child care problems, that might make it hard for me to get to work on time? Do I think safety on the job is the responsibility of management? Then, popping up cunningly out of the blue: How many dollars' worth of stolen goods have I purchased in the last year? Would I turn in a fellow employee if I caught him stealing? Finally, "Are you an honest person?"

Apparently I ace the interview, because I am told that all I have to do is show up in some doctor's office tomorrow for a urine test. This seems to be a fairly general rule: if you want to stack Cheerios boxes or vacuum hotel rooms in chemically fascist America, you have to be willing to squat down and pee in front of a health worker (who has no doubt had to do the same thing herself.)[1] The wages Winn-Dixie is offering—$6 and a couple of dimes to start with—are not enough, I decide, to compensate for this indignity.

I lunch at Wendy's where $4.99 gets you unlimited refills at the Mexican part of the Super-bar, a comforting surfeit of refried beans and cheese sauce. A teenage employee, seeing me studying the want ads, kindly offers me an application form, which I fill out, though here, too, the pay is just $6 and change an hour. Then it's off for a round of the locally owned inns and guest houses in Key West's Old Town, which is where all the serious sightseeing and guzzling goes on, a couple of miles removed from the functional end of the island, where the discount hotels make their homes. At The Palms, let's call it, a bouncy manager actually takes me around to see the rooms and meet the current housekeepers, who, I note with

---

[1]Eighty-one percent of large employers now require preemployment drug testing, up from 21 percent in 1987. Among all employers, the rate of testing is highest in the South. The drug most likely to be detected—marijuana, which can be detected weeks after use—is also the most innocuous, while heroin and cocaine are generally undetectable three days after use. Alcohol, which clears the body within hours after ingestion, is not tested for.

satisfaction, look pretty much like me—faded ex-hippie types in shorts with long hair pulled back in braids. Mostly, though, no one speaks to me or even looks at me except to proffer an application form. At my last stop, a palatial B & B, I wait twenty minutes to meet "Max," only to be told that there are no jobs now but there should be one soon, since "nobody lasts more than a couple weeks."

Three days go by like this and, to my chagrin, no one from the approximately twenty places at which I've applied calls me for an interview. I had been vain enough to worry about coming across as too educated for the jobs I sought, but no one even seems interested in finding out how overqualified I am. Only later will I realize that the want ads are not a reliable measure of the actual jobs available at any particular time. They are, as I should have guessed from Max's comment, the employers' insurance policy against the relentless turnover of the low-wage workforce. Most of the big hotels run ads almost continually, if only to build a supply of applicants to replace the current workers as they drift away or are fired, so finding a job is just a matter of being in the right place at the right time and flexible enough to take whatever is being offered that day. This finally happens to me at one of the big discount chain hotels where I go, as usual, for housekeeping and am sent instead to try out as a waitress at the attached "family restaurant," a dismal spot looking out on a parking garage, which is featuring "Pollish [sic] sausage and BBQ sauce" on this 95-degree day. Phillip, the dapper young West Indian who introduces himself as the manager, interviews me with about as much enthusiasm as if he were a clerk processing me for Medicare, the principal questions being what shifts I can work and when I can start. I mutter about being woefully out of practice as a waitress, but he's already on to the uniform: I'm to show up tomorrow wearing black slacks and black shoes; he'll provide the rust-colored polo shirt with "Hearthside," as we'll call the place, embroidered on it, though I might want to wear my own shirt to get to work, ha ha. At the word *tomorrow*, something between fear and indignation rises in my chest. I want to say, "Thank you for your time, sir, but this is just an experiment, you know, not my actual life."

So begins my career at the Hearthside, where for two weeks I work from 2:00 till 10:00 P.M. for $2.43 an hour plus tips.[2] Employees are barred from using the front door, so I enter the first day through the kitchen, where a red-faced man with shoulder-length blond hair is throwing frozen steaks against the wall and yelling. . . . "That's just Billy," explains Gail, the wiry middle-aged waitress who is assigned to train me. "He's on the rag again"—a condition occasioned, in this instance, by the fact that the cook on the morning shift had forgotten to thaw out the steaks. For the next eight hours, I run after the agile Gail, absorbing bits of instruction along with fragments of personal tragedy. All food must be trayed, and the reason she's so tired today is that she woke up in a cold sweat thinking of her boyfriend, who was killed a few months ago in a scuffle in an upstate prison. No refills on lemonade. And the reason he was in prison is that a few DUIs caught up with him, that's all, could have happened to anyone. Carry the creamers to the table in a "monkey bowl," never in your hand. And after he was gone she spent several months living in her truck, peeing in a plastic pee bottle and reading by candlelight at night, but you can't live in a truck in the summer, since you need to have the windows down, which means anything can get in, from mosquitoes on up.

10   At least Gail puts to rest any fears I had of appearing overqualified. From the first day on, I find that of all the things that I have left behind, such as home and identity, what I miss the most is competence. Not that I have ever felt 100 percent competent in the writing business, where one day's success augurs nothing at all for the next. But in my writing life, I at least have some notion of *procedure*: do the research, make the outline, rough out a draft, etc. As a server, though, I am beset by requests as if by bees: more iced tea here, catsup

---

[2]According to the Fair Labor Standards Act, employers are not required to pay "tipped employees," such as restaurant servers, more than $2.13 an hour in direct wages. However, if the sum of tips plus $2.13 an hour falls below the minimum wage, or $5.15 an hour, the employer is required to make up the difference. This fact was not mentioned by managers or otherwise publicized at either of the restaurants where [Ehrenreich] worked.

over there, a to-go box for table 14, and where are the high chairs, anyway? Of the twenty-seven tables, up to six are usually mine at any time, though on slow afternoons or if Gail is off, I sometimes have the whole place to myself. There is the touch-screen computer-ordering system to master, which I suppose is meant to minimize server-cook contacts but in practice requires constant verbal fine-tuning: "That's gravy on the mashed, OK? None on the meatloaf," and so forth. Plus, something I had forgotten in the years since I was eighteen: about a third of a server's job is "side work" invisible to customers—sweeping, scrubbing, slicing, refilling, and restocking. If it isn't all done, every little bit of it, you're going to face the 6:00 P.M. dinner rush defenseless and probably go down in flames. I screw up dozens of times at the beginning, sustained in my shame entirely by Gail's support—"It's OK, baby, everyone does that sometime"—because, to my total surprise and despite the scientific detachment I am doing my best to maintain, I *care*.

The seductive thing about waitressing is that you don't have to wait for payday to feel a few bills in your pocket, and my tips usually cover meals and gas, plus something left over to stuff into the kitchen drawer I use as a bank. But as the tourist business slows in the summer heat, I sometimes leave work with only $20 in tips (the gross is higher, but servers share about 15 percent of their tips with the busboys and bartenders). With wages included, this amounts to about the minimum wage of $5.15 an hour. The sum in the drawer is piling up but at the present rate of accumulation will be more than $100 short of my rent when the end of the month comes around. Nor can I see any expenses to cut. True, I haven't gone the lentil stew route yet, but that's because I don't have a large cooking pot, potholders, or a ladle to stir with (which would cost a total of about $30 at Kmart, somewhat less at a thrift store), not to mention onions, carrots, and the indispensable bay leaf. I do make my lunch almost every day—usually some slow-burning, high-protein combo like frozen chicken patties with melted cheese on top and canned pinto beans on the side. Dinner is at the Hearthside, which offers its employees a choice of BLT, fish sandwich, or hamburger for only $2. The burger lasts longest, especially if it's heaped with gut-puckering jalapeños, but by midnight my stomach is growling again.

So unless I want to start using my car as a residence, I have to find a second or an alternative job. I call all the hotels I'd filled out housekeeping applications at weeks ago—the Hyatt, Holiday Inn, Econo Lodge, HoJo's, Best Western, plus a half dozen locally run guest houses. Nothing. Then I start making the rounds again, wasting whole mornings waiting for some assistant manager to show up, even dipping into places so creepy that the front-desk clerk greets you from behind bullet-proof glass and sells pints of liquor over the counter. But either someone has exposed my real-life housekeeping habits—which are, shall we say, mellow—or I am at the wrong end of some infallible ethnic equation: most, but by no means all, of the working housekeepers I see on my job searches are African Americans, Spanish-speaking, or refugees from the Central European post-Communist world, while servers are almost invariably white and monolingually English-speaking. When I finally get a positive response, I have been identified once again as server material. Jerry's—again, not the real name—which is part of a well-known national chain and physically attached here to another budget hotel, is ready to use me at once. The prospect is both exciting and terrifying because, with about the same number of tables and counter seats, Jerry's attracts three or four times the volume of customers as the gloomy old Hearthside.

I start out with the beautiful, heroic idea of handling the two jobs at once, and for two days I almost do it: working the breakfast/lunch shift at Jerry's from 8:00 till 2:00, arriving at the Hearthside a few minutes late, at 2:10, and attempting to hold out until 10:00. In the few minutes I have between jobs, I pick up a spicy chicken sandwich at the Wendy's drive-through window, gobble it down in the car, and change from khaki slacks to black, from Hawaiian to rust-colored polo. There is a problem, though. When, during the 3:00–4:00 o'clock dead time, I finally sit down to wrap silver, my flesh seems to bond to the seat. I try to refuel with a purloined cup of clam chowder, as I've seen Gail and Joan do dozens of time, but Stu catches me and hisses "No *eating!*" although there's not a customer around to be offended by the sight of food making contact with a server's lips. So I tell Gail I'm going to quit, and she hugs me and says she might just follow me to Jerry's herself.

But the chances of this are minuscule. She has left the flophouse and her annoying roommate and is back to living in her truck. But, guess what, she reports to me excitedly later that evening, Phillip has given her permission to park overnight in the hotel parking lot, as long as she keeps out of sight, and the parking lot should be totally safe since it's patrolled by a hotel security guard! With the Hearthside offering benefits like that, how could anyone think of leaving? This must be Phillip's theory, anyway. He accepts my resignation with a shrug, his main concern being that I return my two polo shirts and aprons.

Management at Jerry's is generally calmer and more "professional" than at the Hearthside, with two exceptions. One is Joy, a plump, blowsy woman in her early thirties who once kindly devoted several minutes of her time to instructing me in the correct one-handed method of tray carrying but whose moods change disconcertingly from shift to shift and even within one. The other is B.J., aka B.J. the Bitch, whose contribution is to stand by the kitchen counter and yell, "Nita, your order's up, move it!" or "Barbara, didn't you see you've got another table out there? Come *on,* girl!" Among other things, she is hated for having replaced the whipped cream squirt cans with big plastic whipped-cream-filled baggies that have to be squeezed with both hands—because, reportedly, she saw or thought she saw employees trying to inhale the propellant gas from the squirt cans, in the hope that it might be nitrous oxide. On my third night, she pulls me aside abruptly and brings her face so close that it looks like she's planning to butt me with her forehead. But instead of saying "You're fired," she says, "You're doing fine."

Then it comes, the perfect storm. Four of my tables fill up at once. Four tables is nothing for me now, but only so long as they are obligingly staggered. As I bev table 27, tables 25, 28,

15

and 24 are watching enviously. As I bev 25, 24 glowers because their bevs haven't even been ordered. Twenty-eight is four yuppyish types, meaning everything on the side and agonizing instructions as to the chicken Caesars. Twenty-five is a middle-aged black couple who complain, with some justice, that the iced tea isn't fresh and the tabletop is sticky. But table 24 is the meteorological event of the century: ten British tourists who seem to have made the decision to absorb the American experience entirely by mouth. Here everyone has at least two drinks—iced tea *and* milk shake. Michelob *and* water (with lemon slice in the water, please)—and a huge, promiscuous orgy of breakfast specials, mozz sticks, chicken strips, quesadillas, burgers with cheese and without, sides of hash browns with cheddar, with onions, with gravy, seasoned fries, plain fries, banana splits. Poor Jesus! Poor me! Because when I arrive with their first tray of food—after three prior trips just to refill bevs—Princess Di refuses to eat her chicken strips with her pancake and sausage special since, as she now reveals, the strips were meant to be an appetizer. Maybe the others would have accepted their meals, but Di, who is deep into her third Michelob, insists that everything else go back while they work on their starters. Meanwhile, the yuppies are waving me down for more decaf and the black couple looks ready to summon the NAACP.

Much of what happens next is lost in the fog of war.

I leave. I don't walk out, I just leave. I don't finish my side work or pick up my credit card tips, if any, at the cash register or, of course, ask Joy's permission to go. And the surprising thing is that you *can* walk out without permission, that the door opens, that the thick tropical night air parts to let me pass, that my car is still parked where I left it. There is no vindication in this exit, no . . . surge of relief, just an overwhelming dank sense of failure pressing down on me and the entire parking lot. I had gone into this venture in the spirit of science, to test a mathematical proposition, but somewhere along the line, in the tunnel vision imposed by long shifts and relentless concentration, it became a test of myself, and clearly I have failed.

Engaging the Text

1. Why does Ehrenreich elect to begin her investigation into "low-wage life" (paragraph 1) in Key West, Florida? What does she perceive are the advantages and disadvantages of her chosen location?

2. Throughout the essay, Ehrenreich makes a point of noting hourly wages offered for service-industry jobs as well as cataloguing basic cost-of-living expenses in dollar amounts. Make a list of the dollar figures mentioned in the essay, identifying the items to which they correspond. What does the author attempt to demonstrate in supplying these numbers?

3. Paragraphs 5–6 describe job application questions, processes, and procedures at various restaurants, hotels, and grocery stores. What does this information suggest about the respective employers' attitudes toward potential job seekers?

4. Notice the language and stylistic devices that the author uses in paragraphs 1–3 of the second section of the essay. Why does she juxtapose details about specific characters in the narrative with descriptions of setting and process analysis (step-by-step instructions explaining how to complete specific tasks)? How does this technique serve Ehrenreich in critiquing socioeconomic realities of the workplace? Do you find it an effective rhetorical strategy? Explain why or why not.

5. Throughout the narrative, the author repeatedly expresses her frustrations with, and failures at, "serving in Florida." What lessons does Ehrenreich imply we might learn from those who eek out a living for low or minimum wages?

The Insiders

Marc Peyser

The image of the successful, corporate billionaire was called into question in the opening years of the new millennium as so-called Wall Street scandals erupted. Enron, WorldCom, Global Crossing, and other companies made headlines, accused of bilking investors of close to two trillion dollars while CEOs and other industry insiders walked away with millions. Among those supposedly profiting from "insider trading" (the illegal use of information in the world of finance) was celebrity Martha Stewart, a personal friend of Sam Waksal, the CEO of a biotechnology company called ImClone. In this exposé, a team of *Newsweek* reporters led by Marc Peyser investigates the now infamous case.

A 1986 graduate of Stanford University, Peyser earned a master's degree from Columbia University in 1989 and then worked for the *Red Bank Register* in New Jersey before landing a job at *Newsweek*, where he serves as a senior editor for the Arts & Entertainment section. "The Insiders" (written with Keith Naughton, Peg Tyre, Tamara Lipper, T. Trent Gegax, and Lisa Bergtaum) appeared in *Best Business Crime Writing of the Year* (2002), edited by James Surowiecki.

———————— ✦ ————————

It was two days after Christmas, and Martha Stewart—magazine editor, TV host, syndicated columnist and high priestess of domesticity—wanted to get away from it all. She was flying with two friends from Connecticut to Mexico's ultratony Las Ventanas resort (a junior suite starts at $585) when her private jet stopped in San Antonio, Texas, to refuel. Just like the rest of us hardworking folks, she called her office to check her messages. The most important one was from her broker, Peter Bacanovic, and Stewart had her assistant patch him into her cell. Bacanovic's news: one of her stocks, a high-flying biotech company called ImClone, had dropped below $60, the price at which she says they had previously agreed to sell. Stewart told Bacanovic to dump her 3,928 shares. Then she did something that only the Martha Stewarts of this world can do. She dialed Sam Waksal, who just happened to be the CEO of ImClone, not to mention one of Martha's closest friends. "Something's going on with ImClone," Martha said in her message, "and I want to know what it is."

And thus sprouted a very big weed in Martha Stewart's well-manicured life. In the past few weeks, Stewart has found herself drawn deeper and deeper into another one of those Wall Street scandals that turn the rich and powerful into losers. Martha isn't accused of setting up phony off-balance-sheet companies like the Enron boys, or of borrowing an obscene amount of money from her own corporation like the guy at WorldCom. Nor did she pretend to ship art works out of state to avoid sales taxes, as Tyco's CEO allegedly did. She's being questioned on the more mundane issue of insider trading, for selling her ImClone shares (and banking $228,000) just a day before the FDA announced it wouldn't review the company's cancer drug called Erbitux. (If she'd sold after the FDA announcement, it would have cost her $43,000.)

Stewart denies any wrongdoing, but the heat keeps rising. Just days after the congressional committee investigating ImClone seemed to be backing away from Martha, Merrill Lynch last week abruptly put her broker on leave. Investigators, who hope to interview Bacanovic on Thursday or Friday, now say they are specifically targeting the nature of his conversation with Martha on Dec. 27 for evidence that she knew more about ImClone's fate than she's saying. For politicians eager to make a show of frying high-profile CEOs, they may be closer to reeling in a very big fish.

But *l'affaire* Martha isn't just about ImClone. It has also pulled back the crushed-velvet curtain on the clubby world of New York's social elite, a place where the rich and powerful pass around insider business gossip as readily as the help passes out smoked-salmon canapes. With post-Enron investors already questioning the fairness of the marketplace, Stewart's case is the most visible reminder yet that folks on the inside get richer while the rest of us watch our 401(k)s shrivel. And that's put Martha smack in the middle of the one thing in the world she hates the most—a mess.

The irony is that, for a brief, shining moment, it seemed   5
like people were getting tired of bashing Martha Stewart. The latest tell-all book, *Martha Inc.*, got lousy reviews and faded after a few weeks. *Saturday Night Live* parodied her only twice this season. One skit made her look downright heroic, with

the *SNL* Martha stitching a needlepoint napkin that read SUCK IT, OSAMA. Even the bankruptcy of Kmart, where Stewart has been selling her housewares since 1997, didn't bruise her for long. We'd finally come to accept her. She was tough. She was a survivor. Time and time again, Martha had been given lemons, and she'd always found a way to make sparkling ginger-plum lemonade.

This time, she may need a heavy-duty juicer. The case against Martha will come down to what she knew about Im-Clone, when she knew it and, most important, how she got the information. Just before Stewart dumped her stock in December, ImClone was a very hot company. Erbitux, a miracle cancer drug that was its primary product, had already appeared on the cover of *Business Week*, and the FDA had accelerated its process for approving it. But suddenly, something went wrong. On Dec. 26, Waksal learned that the government found the Erbitux clinical trials to be inadequate, and it wouldn't be approved after all. According to congressional investigators, the next day Waksal attempted to sell 72,000 shares before news of the FDA's decision broke. When ImClone's lawyers stopped him, he allegedly attempted to give his shares to his daughter Aliza, but was again blocked. (Aliza has refused to comment.) Nonetheless, she unloaded her own 39,472 shares on the morning of Dec. 27 for $2.5 million. Not coincidentally, Aliza's broker was also Bacanovic. Just hours after he is believed to have executed her sales, he spoke to Stewart. If the daughter of the CEO was bailing out, surely Bacanovic knew there was trouble, right? And wouldn't he have wanted to pass along that information to Stewart? "He's the one that's either going to blow this thing wide open or put it to bed in terms of Martha Stewart," says Ken Johnson, a spokesman for the House committee. Bacanovic could not be reached, and Merrill Lynch has refused to comment.

It's often said that New York is actually a very small town, and nowhere is that more true than at the tippy-top of the social ladder. In the world of black-tie parties and nonstop charity events, executive musings are what make for idle cocktail chatter, at least after the guests finish gossiping about who just had another face-lift. "A lot of information is being passed amongst each other just for reasons of talking," says David Patrick Columbia, editor in chief of NewYorkSocialDiary.com. "They don't even think of it as insider information." In fact, while stockbrokers usually require the little people to fill out a written order to automatically sell a stock when it reaches a predetermined price, that's not always the case with the Park Avenue crowd. "Sometimes verbally he would say, 'We should sell this when it gets to a certain point,' and I don't remember any paperwork," says Patrick McMullan, who is something of the official photographer to New York society, as well as a client of Bacanovic's. "Sometimes there would be an order written, but sometimes he'd say, 'Look, I'll call.'"

And Stewart, Waksal and Bacanovic travel in an especially small social circle. Waksal actually came to know Martha through her daughter, Alexis, whom he once dated, even though Alexis is now 36 and Waksal is 54. Martha and Waksal often talk on the phone as early as 6 a.m. She designed the kitchen in his palatial Manhattan loft. He treats her like the royalty she sometimes appears to think she is. Two years ago Waksal asked Martha to be the guest of honor at the annual gala at the New York Council for the Humanities, which he chairs. The guest of honor traditionally has made a significant contribution to the humanities, which, despite her tireless efforts to promote the importance of handmade paper, does not really apply to Martha. "The response by people invited to the benefit," says someone affiliated with the organization, "was close to incredulity."

Then again, Waksal is famous for over-the-top gestures. His 5,000-square-foot apartment is littered with paintings by Picasso, de Kooning, Rothko and Bacon—$20 million in art. He hosts a monthly salon, inviting dozens of people to hear an artist or writer discuss his work. And his Christmas parties are lavish and legendary. The guests (Mick Jagger showed up last year) are always A list. So A list that two years ago, some high-priced call girls managed to slip through the front door. This year Waksal had someone checking names, though, presumably, they didn't bother with Martha. When she breezed through the door, the buzz from the roomful of politicos and power brokers grew noticeably quieter. Waksal abruptly stopped his conversation and walked over to her. For a brief moment, his head touched Martha's softly.

10   Even though he is more of an employee than a peer, Bacanovic, 40, was a full-fledged member of the Waksal-Stewart universe. He's accompanied Martha on photo shoots for her magazine (though it's Waksal whose picture turned up in a spread last year about her backyard birthday party). Bacanovic has been friends with Alexis Stewart for more than 20 years and was the person who helped introduce her to Waksal, when Bacanovic was the director of business development at ImClone in the early '90s. Perhaps just as important, he shares with Stewart (born Martha Kostyra, to a working-class Polish family in New Jersey) and Waksal (the child of two Holocaust survivors who got a Ph.D. in immunology from Ohio State) the tireless desire to climb the social ladder. Bacanovic delights in telling people that he lives in the town house used to shoot the exteriors for *Breakfast at Tiffany's*. Bacanovic has also made a name for himself as a "walker," a single man who often escorts well-heeled older women to social functions. Even rarer in that rare breed, he actually insists on paying his own way. "Peter Bacanovic is one of my dearest friends," says Nan Kempner, widely considered to be the grande dame of New York high society. "He is probably the most honest, conscientious, generous, kind, sweet, wonderful, intelligent person I know. I just can't believe that he has done anything scandalous." Though he can be a tad shallow. When he was interviewed for an interior-design book called *Bright Young Things*, he was asked, "What to your mind would be the greatest of misfortunes?" His answer: "For one's child to predecease you and male-pattern baldness."

For Martha, the greatest misfortune may be that the scandal comes when her own company is thriving. Martha Stewart Living Omnimedia is performing so well, Martha's just brought out her own line of linoleum. (Who knew Martha even approved of linoleum?) The question is whether Stewart's company can keep up that steam in the middle of a PR storm. The stock is down 16 percent since news broke of her involvement with ImClone (Martha's personal hit on her 31 million shares: $94 million). More than most corporations, Stewart's is unusually sensitive to criticism because her image and the business are so closely entwined. But not everyone thinks that bad Martha publicity will hurt—after all, it's hardly new. "There's a love-hate thing with Martha. You always hear negative stories," says Laura Richardson, an analyst for Adams, Harkness & Hill. In Bedford, New York, where Stewart is building yet another home, folks are still talking about how she brought homemade chocolate-chip cookies to win over the zoning board, only to insult her neighbors by saying she wanted to enlarge her barn to block the view of the ugly property across the street. Still, says Richardson, "most readers don't care about that. They accept her for what she is." What about stockholders? "If this turns out to be a temporary problem, the stock will weather it," she says. "If it means Martha can't be on TV anymore—well, that would be a crippling blow."

At the moment, the chances of Martha's going to prison are unlikely, though cartoonists are already having a field day imaging how she'd spruce up her jail cell. To be convicted of insider trading, Stewart would have to know both that she was acting on insider information when she sold the ImClone stock and that the person who gave her the information was trying to illegally tip her off. Considering that Waksal said he didn't talk to her on Dec. 27, he's probably not a source of trouble. It's more likely that Bacanovic deduced that ImClone was sinking and acted accordingly. "If Martha Stewart was tipped off, we always thought it was from her broker," says a congressional investigator. "If Bacanovic was tipped by Aliza, he probably called his A-list clients. That's the way this jet-set crowd works." But Martha—who worked as a stockbroker in the '70s—would still have had to know she was acting on insider information, and no one has asserted that she did. "I haven't heard anything more than fairly weak, circumstantial evidence against Martha Stewart," says Jack Coffee, a professor at Columbia Law School.

But this is Martha Stewart, the woman who insists that visitors outside her house walk in a prescribed direction so the grass will wear evenly. She is not leaving anything to chance. Last week, just as the Energy and Commerce Committee was poring over her records, *Martha Stewart Living* broadcast an episode featuring Billy Tauzin, the congressman leading the ImClone investigation. Talk about amazing timing—or was it? In fact, the Tauzin segment, in which the congressman cooks gumbo with Martha, first ran a year ago. Oh, and by the way, Tauzin's segment also featured him promoting his own book. Its title: *Cook and Tell.*

Engaging the Text

1. In the opening paragraph of the essay, the authors call Martha Stewart a "high priestess of domesticity." How does figurative language used in the remaining paragraphs help extend this metaphor and for what purpose? In considering these turns of phrase, is it possible to establish the authors' attitude toward their subject? Use specific examples to support your answer.

2. Is Martha Stewart guilty of insider trading? Summarize the case for and against Stewart as presented by Peyser and his coauthors. Do they deliver information objectively, or is it possible to determine their point of view from the facts presented or overall tone of the essay? Support your answer with specific examples from the text.

3. What role does Peter Bacanovic play in the ImClone drama? According to the authors, what workplace dilemmas do stockbrokers such as Bacanovic face in the world of high-stakes finance? Do they make his occupation sound like a promising career choice? Explain your answer.

4. How does the portrayal of the business dealings and lifestyles of "the rich and powerful" (paragraph 4) found in the essay differ from that of "the little people" (paragraph 7)? What does this contrast imply about social class in relation to equal opportunity in the United States?

5. Do you feel better informed about the activities and business practices governing Wall Street as a result of reading "The Insiders"? If so, indicate what you have learned. Given the opportunity, do you think that you would invest in the stock market? Explain why or why not, using the text to support your speculation.

Responding in Writing

1. Research a recent or pending state, federal, or U.S. Supreme Court decision on "Official English," "English Only," or bilingual education as recorded in government documents or reported in the mass media. Determine the central parties in the case as well as the specific linguistic rights that they are seeking or refuting. Summarize positions on both sides of the debate, considering your own knowledge and experience in the process. Use this information to write an essay in which you argue for or against the decision. To further your thinking on the subject, refer to Robert King's essay, "Should English Be the Law?"

2. In the CCCC statement on "Students' Right to Their Own Language," the authors "affirm the students' right to their own patterns and varieties of language—the dialects of their nature or whatever dialects in which they find their own identity and style" (paragraph 7). In the same paragraph they likewise assert: "The claim that any one dialect is unacceptable amounts to an attempt of one social group to exert its dominance over another." Look for evidence of these assertions elsewhere in the language chapter, such as in Amy Tan's "Mother Tongue" and Luc Sante's "Living in Tongues." Then write a paper in which you illustrate the CCCC edicts using examples from the texts as well as your own knowledge to illustrate. You may wish to showcase your own idiolect (a term mentioned in the CCCC statement referring to speech habits and patterns of an individual at a certain point in life) or the dialect of a specific culture group in the process. Or, taking a cue from Tan or Sante, write a narrative essay about how you acquired your own dialect, writing or code switching in that dialect to affirm the right to your own language.

3. Judith Ortiz Cofer in "The Paterson Library" and Barbara Ehrenreich in "Serving in Florida" write first-person accounts of their struggles for the right to learn or to work in the face of hostile environments due to cultural differences. To a lesser degree, Bob Muldoon's "White-Collar Man in a Blue-Collar World" portrays similar circumstances. Additionally, notice the extent to which all three essays concern language as well as work. Modeling one of these selections, write a narrative essay in which you document your own struggles to achieve mastery in a language or success in a work environment when some aspect of your cultural identity (for example, race, class, gender, or aptitude in a specific language) proved a hindrance.

4. Near the end of "Affirmative Action and the Dilemma of the 'Qualified,'" Ellis Cose creates fictional circumstances in order to compare and contrast "affirmative action" and what the author calls "preferential treatment." Using information provided in Cose's essay overall as a starting point, use imaginative writing to express your own understanding of affirmative action versus preferential treatment. In the course of the essay, assert your viewpoint on whether or not affirmative action should be the law.

5. The selection by Ehrenreich and Martín Espada's poem "The Foreman's Wallet" implicate socioeconomic class as a factor in determining the hiring, firing, and pay scales of employees in the low-wage workforce. Should workers in the United States have the right to work for an equitable living wage? Use evidence gathered from your readings of these two texts as grounds for a claim and then write an essay in which you argue for or against the proposition.

6. In describing talk between family members, Tan refers to "the language of intimacy" (paragraph 4) and Sante to "a family dialect" (paragraph 14). Write a paper in which you summarize, compare, and contrast what each author means by her or his respective phrase. You also may wish to augment your discussion by describing and illustrating the language developed and used within your own family.

7. Both "Serving in Florida" by Ehrenreich and "The Insiders" by Marc Peyser and his *Newsweek* coauthors qualify as workplace exposés. Ehrenreich reveals the struggles of low-wage earners while Peyser and company document the excesses of some of the wealthiest executives in the United States. Both pieces of investigative journalism likewise include profiles of individual workers. Using the two selections as models, investigate a recent controversy in the news about the workplace, paying attention to key figures in the texts that you are studying. Then write a paper in which you report on your findings. As an alternative to the assignment, write an exposé about a workplace with which you are familiar or know well.

8. Look at the selections in Part III that describe work and consider how the authors depict the socioeconomic circumstances of the workplace, including locations and settings, the application process, people employed, tasks performed, and wages earned. Next, think about a job that you have held and reflect on it in a similar manner. Then write a paper in which you chronicle your own experience on the job. To appeal to your readers, you may wish to include setting (time and place), process-analysis (a step-by-step explanation of a procedure, activity, or task), profiles of workers (including their specific job titles and personalities), and numerical data (such as salaries and scheduled hours).

CREDITS